Marriage,
Faith and Love

MARRIAGE, FAITH AND LOVE

JACK DOMINIAN

CROSSROAD · NEW YORK

1982
The Crossroad Publishing Company
575 Lexington Avenue, New York, NY 10022

Printed in the United States of America

Library of Congress Catalog Card Number: 81-70879

ISBN: 0-8245-0425-9

The author is grateful to Darton, Longman and Todd Ltd.,
and Doubleday and Co. Inc., for permission to reproduce
material from the Jerusalem Bible published and copyright
1966, 1967, and 1968.

To my wife

Contents

Introduction

A previous book,[1] written in the early sixties, discussed the problem
that was challenging the Roman Catholic thought on marriage,
namely its essential nature. At that time a juridical approach still
held sway in Roman Catholic circles. Marriage was seen as a
contract and successive documents had used a language which was
suitable to express its contractual nature.

Perhaps one of the shortest ways of summarizing this approach
is to quote briefly from a declaration of the judges of the Roman
Rota in January 1944. 'There are several ends of marriage and one
of these is primary and the others are secondary. As Canon 1013
states, the primary end is the procreation and upbringing of
children, the secondary is mutual help and the remedy of
concupiscence.'

In the book *Christian Marriage* it was argued that describing marriage in such nomenclature as primary and secondary and using the
term 'end' was not the most satisfactory way of attempting to
describe the nature of marriage.

At the conclusion of that book, the following definition was given:
'Christian marriage seen in this way is a God-given, life-long community, created to ensure the most appropriate conditions for the
promotion of life, the life of the children and that of the spouses. It
is based on a series of relationships of love which in a chronological
order are those of spouses, the spouses and the children and the
children among themselves. It is upon the physical, psychological
and social integrity of these relationships, participating in the sacramental life of grace, that the essence of marriage ultimately
rests.'[2]

In this present book I intend to pursue a further detailed analysis
of this definition. One addition to it is its enlargement to include
the relationship of parents and the children outside the family group

to relations, friends and others, so that marriage is expanded into a family open to the whole community.

The above definition of marriage was written before the Vatican II Council gave its own view on marriage and the family. This it did in the most unequivocal terms. The conciliar statement brought to a conclusion the terminology of 'ends' with their primary and secondary purposes. Instead it placed marriage and the family at the centre of what is called a community of love.[3] The intimate partnership of married life and love is 'rooted in the conjugal covenant of irrevocable personal consent. Hence, by that human act whereby spouses mutually bestow and accept each other, a relationship arises which by divine will and in the eyes of society is a lasting one.'[4]

The Council now links together the concepts of community, covenant and relationship and in doing so places marriage in a scriptural setting in which the key note is the relationships of love between the various members of the family. 'Authentic married love is caught up into divine love.'[5] Thus the daily social, physical, psychological realities of the married state become the constituent parts of the presence of the divine.

The Church of England was also faced with the need to clarify its doctrine of marriage and published two reports on the subject in 1971 and in 1978 called *Marriage, Divorce and the Church*[6] and *Marriage and the Church's Task*[7] respectively. In both these reports there was an emphasis on marriage as a relationship. In a remarkable congruence of conceptualization the second report summarizes the basis of marriage by saying, 'It is their (husband–wife) relationships with each other which is the basis of marriage.'[8]

By placing the focus of marriage on the relationship between the couple, the other members of the family and the family with the world, there are clearly social and personal dimensions which have to be considered. In so far as society is in a phase of marked transition, so marriage within it reflects the various elements of change. These elements impinge on the working life of the partners, their economic standing, housing, resources, childbearing, size of family, their own physical, emotional and sexual bond, and their relationship with the wider community. There is a delicate interaction between marriage, family and society, and in a pluralistic society different forces influence the resultant composition of behaviour.

Whatever the structure of the forces which influence the make-up of marriage and the family the fact is that the saving mystery of marriage reflects its human reality, and as the latter alters it is vital to appreciate in detail its changing character. There is no eternal and unchanging nature in the social and psychological aspects of marriage for, as is suggested by the subtitle of Edward Schillebeeckx's book on marriage, 'Human Reality and Saving Mystery',[9] the saving grace is implicitly situated in the human reality. The two are inextricably united and, in order to comprehend the way that Christian marriage is unfolding, its social and psychological character is essential to its understanding.

This unfolding is occurring at different rates and in different ways throughout the world. In western societies and in urban centres of developing countries a pattern is observed which can be described with confidence as a move from traditional role to companionship marriage.[10] In the traditional role the husband's responsibility was to be the principal income earner and to be the head of the family, whilst that of his wife was to look after the home and the children. This pattern is slowly evolving into one in which the partners seek an equality of worth, a much greater flexibility in their complementary tasks, and emphasis on communication, demonstration of affection, sexual fulfilment and mutual realization of potential. The last aim has a disturbing note of apparent self-indulgence. At its best it achieves the opposite. The greater the self-fulfilment the stronger are the resources for availability to others.

Love will be described in this book in terms of availability. This is availability of oneself in so far as a person feels and knows that their mind, body, feelings and will are truly possessed by themselves and on balance that their capacity to feel and to be good is greater than it is to be bad. Under these circumstances we feel lovable, can register other people's love and at the same time reciprocate as richly as our positively possessed resources permit.

Self-realization within marriage is a mutual process between the spouses and requires patience, effort and sacrifice. The pace and rate of growth will differ for the partners and it will be an expression of love to have the ability to wait for one's partner to advance to the same level as oneself. So much marital breakdown is due to unilateral growth which leaves the other spouse behind and consequently produces alienation between the two. A loving commitment attempts to appreciate in depth the level of development of one's partner and requires a sincere attempt to respond to it. Then the feeling expressed so often in marital breakdown that 'he/she doesn't understand nor care about me' will be heard less often.

The biblical text which approaches most clearly the notion of availability is to be found in Paul's letter to the Philippians.

> In your minds you must be the same as Christ Jesus:
> His state was divine,
> yet he did not cling
> to his equality with God
> but emptied himself
> to assume the condition of a slave,
> and became as men are. (Phil. 2:5-7)

All of us have to empty ourselves as Christ does out of love for God and others. But we cannot empty ourselves if we have little or nothing to donate. The greater our loving resources the more we can give. Indeed ultimately we give our all as Christ did out of love for our neighbour.

The most precious neighbour in marriage is our spouse followed by our children, and within the family spouses share the depths of availability which in turn is given to others outside the family circle.

It is well known that there is a constant gap between how much we want to offer of ourselves and how much we actually achieve. This psychological truth is once again captured clearly by Paul. 'I cannot understand my own behaviour. I fail to carry out the things I want to do, and I find myself doing the very things I hate.' (Rom. 7:15-16)

In the course of this book which, as its title suggests, will be inquiring about the relationship of marital love and faith we will have occasion to penetrate a little into Paul's paradox. Marital love, like all love, has endless possibilities of fulfilment which we only approximate, as Paul noticed two thousand years ago. But in so far as we have to undertake the call to perfection there is a constant invitation to discover the possibilities of loving as marriage unfolds.

In the two thousand years since Paul, Christianity has developed its understanding of love and marriage basing its development on the truths expressed in the Bible and developed during the Christian era. The first chapter gives a brief account of this historical development.

References (Introduction)

1. Dominian, J., *Christian Marriage*. Darton, Longman and Todd, 1967.

2. ibid., p.244.

3. *Pastoral Constitution on the Church in the Modern World*, Part II, Chap. 1. Chapman, 1967.

4. ibid., p.250.

5. ibid., p.251.

6. *Marriage, Divorce and the Church*. SPCK, 1971.

7. *Marriage and the Church's Task*. Church Information Office, 1978.

8. ibid., p.33.

9. Schillebeeckx, E., *Marriage: Human Reality and Saving Mystery*. Sheed and Ward, 1965.

10. Hicks, M.W. and Platt, M., 'Marital Stability and Happiness' in *A Decade of Family Research and Action*, p.59. National Council on Family Relations, 1970.

PART I

The Nature of Contemporary Marriage

CHAPTER 1

The Judaeo-Christian Background

Old Testament

CREATION

God's revelation to his people in the Old Testament about sexuality and marriage comes at the very beginning of Genesis with the description of creation. There are two accounts; the second or Yahwistic account is the older of the two and dates from about the tenth century B.C.

> Yahweh God said, 'It is not good that man should be alone. I will make him a helpmate.' So from the soil Yahweh God fashioned all the wild beasts and all the birds of heaven. These he brought to the man to see what he would call them; each one was to bear the name the man would give it. The man gave names to all the cattle, all the birds of heaven and all the wild beasts. But no helpmate suitable for man was found for him. So Yahweh God made the man fall into a deep sleep. And while he slept, he took one of his ribs and enclosed it in flesh. Yahweh God built the rib he had taken from the man into a woman, and brought her to the man. The man exclaimed: 'This at last is bone from my bones, and flesh from my flesh! This is to be called woman, for this was taken from man.' This is why a man leaves his father and mother and joins himself to his wife, and they become one body. Now both of them were naked, the man and his wife, but they felt no shame in front of each other. (Gen. 2:18-25)

Thus at the very beginning of the scriptures is found first of all the principle of relationship. Clearly it is not human to be alone, the man–woman relationship is the right order for humanity. This relationship has a quality of equivalency. The woman is derived from the man and has an equal value as a person. The man recognizes her appropriateness for him and rejoices at this equality of worth. Furthermore the destiny of the relationship is towards oneness. They are capable of being one body and there is no other way to experience total togetherness and intimacy. Indeed such are the requirements of this new state that the couple have to leave their home and establish a new social and psychological unit. They establish now a new bond which can only be adequately formed when they separate from the closest bond hitherto, the parental one.

It is remarkable how at the very beginning of Genesis a truth is found which has not diminished after three thousand years. Today, as much as ever, the western tradition has required that the newly wed have to form their own independent married life free from parental constraints. This ideal has not always been achieved, but in contemporary society the shift of focus from parents as the principal figures of significance to spouses is one of the desiderata of modern matrimony. It is well known that when parents interfere they store up problems for their child's marriage.

The second account, given in the first chapter of Genesis, the priestly narrative, was written some five hundred years later.

> God said, 'Let us make man in our own image, in the likeness of ourselves and let them be masters of the fish of the sea, the birds of heaven, the cattle, all the wild beasts and all the reptiles that crawl upon the earth.'
> God created man in the image of himself,
> in the image of God he created him,
> male and female he created them.
> God blessed them, saying to them, 'Be fruitful, multiply, fill the earth and conquer it'. (Gen. 1:26-8)

These words show the momentous truth that both male and female were created in the image of God and therefore both bear an intrinsic goodness in so far as they reflect the divine image in themselves. Here is more evidence of the equality of worth of the sexes. Much later Paul was to insist on the same principle of equality in Christ in his epistle to the Galatians. 'All baptised in Christ, you have all clothed yourselves in Christ, and there are no more distinctions between Jew and Greek, slave and free, male and female, but all of you are one in Christ Jesus' (Gal 3:27-8).

These declarations of divinely derived principles needed time to become social realities. For thousands of years women have been in a subordinate role to man. It is only in our day and time that these perennial truths are being slowly realized. The current drive for equality of worth by woman is perfectly consistent with revelation and indeed Christian women may come to realize that at a profound level St Paul is their champion and pioneer of the modern emancipation movement. Despite all his social strictures on women which were the accepted social norms of the day, his Christian insights led him to ultimate truths and one of these was the equality of male and female persons despite their biological differences.

Another feature of the second account is the establishment of one of the purposes of marriage. In the first narrative Yahweh enjoins them to become one body, i.e. to have sexual intercourse, and the anticipatory state of erotic nakedness caused no embarrassment. Sexual intercourse is now linked with procreation, but it is important to note that having children was a blessing, not a command or a demand. In creation God gave life and this life was a gift which could be perpetuated by the two sexes.

In these two passages sexual intercourse and procreation are both linked and also stand separate. In the second account intercourse is associated with a gift and the blessing of children. These realities are separate and between them contain the appropriate possibilities of the man–woman relationship in marriage.

After the fall, 'Then the eyes of both of them were opened and they realised that they were naked' (Gen. 3:7). In this brief sentence the entry of disorder in sexuality is made clear. It is still part of what 'God saw all he had made and indeed it was very good' (Gen. 1:31), but now the ideal, the perfect, has become harder to realize. All the familiar problems of sexual difficulties in behaviour and function become obstacles to be overcome. But the basic goodness of the gift of sex remains and it is realizable. The Song of Songs, an astonishing part of the scriptures, shows in an extensive form the joy and beauty of the erotic, vividly protrayed in a man–woman relationship.

PROCREATION

These two accounts combine to advocate a monogamous relationship which is orientated towards procreation. The Old Testament is full of statements praising children. Children are described as stars in the sky (Gen. 15:5), as the crown of man (Prov 17:6) and like arrows in the hand of a warrior whose quiver is full (Ps. 127:3-5).

Infertility was a form of disgrace illustrated by the heart-rending cry of Rachel to Jacob. 'Give me children or I shall die' (Gen. 30:2). Such was the imperative need for children, particularly boys, that the husband was permitted to sleep with slave girls and in this instance two boys were conceived.

Having a family, and a stable family at that, was highly important to Israel. Monogamy was not fully preserved and polygamy was allowed, particularly in cases of infertility and of the kings who could sometimes afford a large harem. Nevertheless these are the exceptions and monogamy remained the ideal.

DIVORCE

The same applies to divorce. Divorce was permitted and was described thus: 'Supposing a man has taken a wife and consummated the marriage; but she has not pleased him and he has found some impropriety of which to accuse her; so he has made out a writ of divorce for her and handed it to her and then dismissed her from his house; she leaves his home and goes away to become the wife of another man' (Deut. 24:1-2). The grounds for divorce were disputed. The school of Hillel would accept minor reasons, indeed any reasons, whereas that of Shammai, which also allowed divorce, needed more grevious reasons such as adultery and misconduct. (Later on, Christ was asked his views on the matter and his audience were amazed at his defiant, absolute answer that no grounds exist for divorce). The formality of divorce was straightforward and simple; the husband declared, 'She is no longer my wife and I am no longer her husband' (Ho. 2:4). But despite these provisions the ideal of indissolubility remains and we find Malachi declaring, 'I hate divorce, says the Yahweh the God of Israel' (Mal. 2:16).

PROPHETIC COVENANT TRADITION

Marriage, children and the family were held in high esteem in Israel. But with the prophet Hosea a new dimension was reached in the significance of marriage. The secular reality of marriage was used as a symbol for the covenant of grace existing between Yahweh and Israel.

First of all Yahweh instructed Hosea to marry a prostitute,

Gomer. Hosea did as he was told. Here we have a symbol of Israel's tendency to veer away from the true religion and prostitute herself with the worship of Baal.

'In the Baal cult the myth of the marriage between the land, the goddess, and the heavenly god prevailed, and it was believed that the people were a result of this marriage between the goddess and the god. Religious prostitution was practised in the worship of the temple.'[1] Hosea is aware of this dilution of faith and Yahweh uses his marriage to portray a personal marriage problem which in turn reflects the wider problem of the People of God losing their way into the surrounding religions and being unfaithful to Yahweh. This alienation between God and his people is further indicated in the names of the two children conceived; they are called 'Unloved' and 'No-people-of-mine'. Gomer returns to her sexual infidelity and her behaviour is shown to resemble the unfaithfulness of Israel. There follows a passage full of this double meaning of God being angry with Israel as Hosea is angry with his wife.

Denounce your mother, denounce her,
for she is not my wife
nor am I her husband.
Let her rid her face of her whoring,
and her breasts of her adultery,
or else I will strip her naked,
expose her as on the day she was born;
I will make a wilderness of her,
turn her into an arid land,
and leave her to die of thirst.
I will not love her children,
since they are the children of whoring.
Yes, their mother has played the whore,
she who conceived them has disgraced herself,
'I am going to court my lovers' she said
'who give me my bread and water,
my wool, flax, my oil and my drink.'
She would not acknowledge, not she,
that I was the one who was giving her
the corn, the wine, the oil,
and who freely gave her that silver and gold
of which they have made Baals. (Hos. 2:4-10)

Gomer in fact leaves her husband and commits adultery. She is divorced from him and comes into the possession of another man. By the tenets of the law Hosea is forbidden to take her back, but Yahweh commands Hosea to do just this and to love her tenderly. Hosea plans to woo her afresh as indeed Yahweh loved his People when they came out of Egypt into the wilderness and commenced the special relationship of the covenant of grace.

> That is why I am going to lure her
> and lead her out into the wilderness
> and speak to her heart . . .
> When that day comes . . .
> I will betroth you to myself for ever,
> betroth you with integrity and justice,
> with tenderness and love. (Hos. 2:16, 18, 21)

Hosea takes his wife back, forgives her and establishes afresh the marital bond which she broke. Thus marriage, a secular reality, becomes a symbol of the relationship between God and his people and it expresses the fact that however often the People of God are unfaithful God will forgive and repair the damage of the relationship. In this sense his prophetic approach to marriage anticipates the high standards of permanency set up later by Christ who allows no ground for divorce. Furthermore the special relationship of love between husband and wife enunciated by the prophets is completed later on by Paul's insight in Ephesians on marriage and the relationship between Christ and the Church.

This vision of Hosea on marriage is repeated by Jeremiah (3:13), Ezekiel; (16:8) and Isaiah (54). Thus faithful married love was one of the fundamental ways of revealing and confirming the covenant of grace between God and his people.

The daily experience of marriage is not ignored, and in the Wisdom literature the wife is in turn praised and warned severely against loose behaviour. As the social climate of the day perceived most misdemeanours coming from the wife, so the warnings are specially designed to protect the husband from the wiles of women.

The essential need of a man for a wife is repeatedly proclaimed:

> The man who takes a wife has the makings of a fortune,
> a helper that suits him, and a pillar to lean on.
> If a property has no fence, it will be plundered.
> When a man has no wife, he is aimless and querulous. (Ecclus. 36:24-5)

Beauty within marriage is safe but there is a warning: 'Woman's beauty has led many astray' (Ecclus. 9:9). Rather than beauty the emphasis is on the prudent and wise woman, and Proverbs offers the apotheosis of the Old Testament view of the good wife. She is trustworthy, industrious, a good manager, and housekeeper, capable of producing for the needs of the house, speaks wisely. The citation finishes with this comment:

Charm is deceitful, and beauty empty;
the woman who is wise is the one to praise. (Prov. 31:30)

New Testament

JESUS CHRIST

In the New Testament there are both continuities with the Old and some startling new requirements. The teaching of Christ emphasizes throughout the importance of love — love of God and neighbour. Since marriage is a community of love it is the direct recipient of this proclamation of the supreme good. This good consists of fidelity and permanence.

Fidelity is not merely a question of avoiding sexual intercourse before marriage and extramaritally after marriage; it is an ideal which permeates the whole man — woman relationship. All encounters between the sexes require a high degree of sexual integrity. External behaviour has to be matched with internal intention.

'You have learned how it was said, You must not commit adultery. But I say this to you: if a man looks at a woman lustfully, he has already committed adultery with her in his heart' (Mat. 5:27-8). This teaching does not mean that it is forbidden to enjoy physical beauty in either sex. It means that the integrity of the person must be preserved. What is forbidden is twofold, first to treat a person as a sexual object only and secondly to use a person sexually in the absence of a relationship of love. Sexual intercourse rightly belongs in a setting of love whose fullness is to be found within a permanent relationship we call marriage.

This permanency was in fact questioned in the Old Testament where, as indicated, divorce was not desirable but permissible.

Christ was asked about divorce and his reply astonished his audience and his own disciples.

> Some Pharisees approached him, and to test him they said, 'Is it against the law for a man to divorce his wife on any pretext whatever?' He answered, 'Have you not read that the creator from the beginning made them male and female and that he said: This is why a man must leave father and mother and cling to his wife, and the two become one body? They are no longer two, therefore, but one body. So then, what God has united, man must not divide.'
>
> They said to him, 'Then why did Moses command that a writ of dismissal should be given in cases of divorce?' 'It was because you were so unteachable,' he said, 'that Moses allowed you to divorce your wives, but it was not like this from the beginning. Now I say this to you: the man who divorces his wife – I am not speaking of fornication – and marries another, is guilty of adultery'.
>
> The disciples said to him, 'If that is how things are between husband and wife, it is not advisable to marry.' But he replied, 'It is not everyone who can accept what I have said, but only those to whom it is granted. There are eunuchs born that way from their mother's womb, there are eunuchs made so by men and there are eunuchs who have made themselves that way for the sake of the kingdom of heaven. Let anyone accept this who can.' (Mat. 19:3-12)

There are three points which are of crucial significance in this passage. Firstly, Christ abolishes divorce and reverts to the original intention of the creator that once a husband–wife unity has been established in a genuine marriage then its nature is that of permanency. The bodily unity encompasses the whole being of the two persons.

Secondly, Matthew is the only evangelist who appears to offer an escape clause, that of fornication, which would permit divorce. These words have been examined exhaustively throughout the Christian era and have been variously interpreted.[2] In brief, some traditions find here the basis for exemptions and others, like the Roman Catholic Church, interpret this sentence strictly as not offering any exemption to the general statement made by Christ. There is certainly unanimity about the clear intention of Jesus to abolish divorce, but various churches differ on the absoluteness of the command.

Thirdly, Jesus takes into his confidence the apostles, who were very confused about his adamant declaration, and reveals to them that continence for the sake of the Kingdom was possible and desirable for those who could accept that sacrifice. Thus Christ was introducing here a new concept which was going to feature specifically in the Christian tradition. Such continence was in no way an attack on the gift of sex but love was extended to anticipate a state beyond marriage. 'For at the resurrection men and women do not marry: no they are like the angels in heaven.' (Mat. 22:30)

PAUL

Unlike Jesus, Paul said many things about sex and marriage. As far as marriage is concerned Paul's position is contradictory. He is totally realistic about human exigencies and the need for marriage and indeed gives us an unprecedented vision of its meaning. But as far as he personally is concerned he prefers the single state. Whatever he has to teach, Paul, like Christ, emphasizes the supremacy of love and it is in that context that his words have to be interpreted. Writing to the Corinthians he says:

> Now for the questions about which you wrote. Yes, it is a good thing for a man not to touch a woman; but since sex is always a danger, let each man have his own wife and each woman her own husband . . . Do not refuse each other except by mutual consent, and then only for an agreed time, to leave yourselves free for prayer; then come together again in case Satan should take advantage of your weakness to tempt you . . . I should like every one to be like me, but everybody has his own particular gifts from God . . . (1 Cor. 7:1-2, 5-7)

Paul's ambivalence towards the single state and marriage in no way hinders his appreciation of the meaning of the covenant of marriage. He takes the prophetic theme of the Old Testament which saw marriage as a covenant symbol and shows its basic similarity to the relationship between Christ and the Church. Here he describes the unity, love, fidelity and permanence of marriage as it mirrors the same characteristics which unite Christ and the Church. In other words Christ's redemptive love is made actual and present in the personal relationship of marriage.[3]

Give way to one another in obedience to Christ. Wives should regard their husbands as they regard the Lord, since as Christ is the head of the Church and saves the whole body, so is a husband the head of his wife; and as the Church submits to Christ, so should wives to their husbands, in everything. Husbands should love their wives just as Christ loved the Church and sacrificed himself for her to make her holy . . . In the same way, husbands must love their wives as they love their own bodies; for a man to love his wife is for him to love himself. A man never hates his own body, but he feeds it and looks after it; and that is the way Christ treats the Church, because it is his body and we are living parts. For this reason, a man must leave his father and mother and be joined to his wife and the two will become one body. This mystery has many implications; but I am saying it applies to Christ and the Church. (Eph. 5:21-5, 28-32)

Modern ears may not receive sympathetically the submission of the wife to the husband in all matters. There has been much discussion whether this submission is a permanent feature of appropriate behaviour for all time. Modern exegesis offers the alternative explanation that, whilst Paul is expressing a supreme unity between the total oneness of spouses and the relationship of Christ to the Church, nevertheless he is using the social conventions and ordering of the day.[4]

Although the social subordination of the wife to the husband was the norm of the times, there is a remarkable silence in the New Testament about children. In view of the emphasis that Christianity has placed on the link between coitus and procreation, the absence of any definitive teaching on this matter is startling.

Paul exhorts children to be obedient to their parents in the Lord, and parents are advised in terms which have a most modern ring, to avoid driving their offspring to frustration and resentment (Eph. 6:1-4). In the first epistle to Timothy the wife is promised salvation through childbearing (2:15), but there are no direct references to procreation. The reasons for this omission are subject to speculation. The Jewish emphasis on childbearing remained deeply embedded in the social climate of the times. But the time was short and a Second Coming was expected.

Brothers, this is what I mean: our time is growing short. Those who have wives should live as though they had none, and those who mourn should live as though they had nothing to mourn for;

those who are enjoying life should live as though there were
nothing to laugh about; those whose life is buying things should
live as though they had nothing of their own; and those who
have to deal with the world should not become engrossed in it.
I say this because the world as we know it is passing away. (1
Cor. 7:29-31)

In fact the expected did not happen. The world did not pass
away and the patristic period had to develop further ideas about
marriage. As things stood there were a number of influences which
exerted pressure. Christianity had to put virginity in the service of
the Lord on the map. It was influenced by Stoic thought which
sought an inner composure and peace with which instinctual drives
would interfere. Early Christianity was surrounded by Gnostic and
Manichean philosophies which saw the body as a trap for the soul
and procreation as the means of extending the imprisonment of the
spiritual principle in man. Although some Church fathers took a
fairly negative view of marriage[5] the Church preserved the basic
goodness of marriage and sex for the purpose of procreation. Sex
was seen somehow to be tainted with sin, but this view did not
stand the test of time and was in due course corrected in the
medieval period.

Patristic period

Perhaps the single most important figure in the patristic period is
Augustine. His pronouncement on marriage had an impact on
Christianity which remains to this very day. Augustine formulated
the blessings or 'goods' of marriage as being threefold, namely
children, mutual fidelity of the spouses and the sacrament which in
his day meant indissolubility, a consequence of the sacred symbolism of the union of Christ and the Church.

Fidelity signifies that, outside the matrimonial bond, there shall
be no sexual intercourse; offspring, that children shall be lovingly
welcomed, tenderly reared and religiously educated; sacrament,
that the bond of wedlock shall never be broken and that neither
party, if separated, shall form a union with another, even for the
sake of offspring. Such is the law of marriage which gives lustre

to the fruitfulness of nature and sets a curb upon shameful incontinence.[6]

These principles remain the guiding spirit of Christian marriage and were taken up in the medieval period when Aquinas converted 'the goods' to 'primary and secondary ends'. The principal end of marriage was procreation and upbringing of children and the secondary ends were mutual fidelity and the sacrament. The terminology 'primary and secondary ends' has been a source of confusion[7] and in fact disappeared from current usage with the declaration on marriage and the family at the Vatican II Council.[8]

Middle Ages to the present day

The single most important advance in the theology of marriage in the Middle Ages was its incorporation in the sacramental content of grace. The discussion lasted several centuries but an infallible declaration was finally made at the Council of Trent, which, in opposition to the denial by Luther and Calvin that marriage was a sacrament and conferred grace, proclaimed, 'If anyone says that matrimony is not truly and properly one of the seven sacraments of the gospel law instituted by Christ, our Lord, but was introduced into the Church by men or that it does not confer grace, let him be anathema.' The grace of marriage completes the natural mutual love of the partners, a teaching that forms the background of this book.

The debate on the sacramental nature of marriage lasted some five centuries from about the eleventh century to the infallible declaration of Trent. As the Church moved increasingly in the direction of the sacramental nature of marriage, the crucial question that emerged was the characteristic which defined the beginning of the sacrament. There were extensive arguments in favour of the moments either of mutual consent between the spouses or of sexual consummation. The controversy was solved in favour of lawful mutual consent which was necessary for marriage, but it was coitus which rendered the full significance of the indissoluble unity of Christ and the Church. Hence to this day the Church has the power to dissolve an unconsummated marriage by papal dispensation.

One of the unfortunate consequences of this decision was that marriage matters slowly moved into the hands of canon lawyers who became concerned with the legal requirements for the validity of the wedding. Thus the emphasis on marriage matters was narrowly restricted to the events that surrounded the wedding and the wedding day. Canon law became concerned with the freedom of the spouses to give their consent, the presence and absence of relational and other impediments and the carrying out of the ceremony in the correct way in a Catholic church before the parish priest and two witnesses. This ruling further developed with the Decree *Ne Temere* in 1908 which was meant primarily to prevent clandestine marriages. These marriages, although illegal, were accepted as valid in circumstances where the spouses gave initial consent in private. Unfortunately, human nature being what it is, men in particular offered themselves to more than one woman causing confusion as to who was the legitimate wife. The new form of marriage was first operated in those countries in which it was officially promulgated but soon it was required of all Catholics even those intending to form a mixed marriage, and this produced real difficulties for other Churches.

Apart from this problem a much more serious one for all Christians is the fact that for these historical reasons the wedding day became the focus of the Christian community's concern. But in fact the marriage relationship *begins* on the wedding day and the whole pastoral concern and care which the couple need during the married life-cycle has been seriously neglected.

The emphasis remained with procreation and education of children, whilst the secondary ends of mutual help and the remedy of concupiscence which were the contents of Canon 1013 received little attention. This is not to say that there was no continuing strand of the personal side in the major encyclicals of the nineteenth and twentieth centuries. Leo XIII writing in his encyclical *Arcanum Divinae* in 1880 says:

> Not only, in strict truth, was marriage instituted for the propagation of the human race, but also that the lives of husbands and wives might be better and happier. This comes about in many ways: by their lightening each other's burdens through mutual help; by constant and faithful love; by having all their possessions in common and by the heavenly grace which flows from the sacrament.[9]

In the major encyclical of Pius XI, *Casti Connubii*, the language of
primary and secondary ends continues but the feature of relationship is also present.

> This mutual interior formation of husband and wife, this persev-
> ering endeavour to bring each other to the state of perfection,
> may, in a true sense, be called as the Roman Catechism calls it,
> the primary cause and reason for matrimony, so long as marriage
> is considered not in its stricter sense, as the institution destined
> for the procreation and education of children, but in the wider
> sense as a complete and intimate life-partnership and
> association.[10]

During the thirties, forties and fifties a debate continued within
the Catholic Church led by Doms[11] as to the meaning of marriage
with strong arguments being put forward that marriage was 'something in itself' before it was 'something for'. 'It is rather the fulfilment of love in the community of life of two persons who make one
person,' says Doms. He continues by asking for the abolition of the
language of primary and secondary ends. Doms was criticized for
his views, but this is precisely what happened in the short statement
on marriage and the family in the Second Vatican Council.[12] Marriage and the family are now called a 'community of love'.

> The intimate partnership of married life and love has been es-
> tablished by the Creator and qualified by His laws. It is rooted
> in the conjugal covenant of irrevocable personal consent. Hence,
> by that human act whereby spouses mutually bestow and accept
> each other, a relationship arises which by divine will and in the
> eyes of society too is a lasting one.[13]

Thus the cycle is completed and the covenant relationship first
enunciated fully by the prophets in the Old Testament is reinstated
as a major theological character of marriage. All the other features
– of procreation, mutual fidelity and permanence in a monogamous
bond – are present but, as Atkinson [14] quotes in his book, 'Karl
Barth is surely right in expounding covenant fidelity as the inner
meaning and purpose of our creation as human beings in the divine
image, and the whole of the created order as the external framework
for and condition of the possibility of keeping covenant.'

The teaching on marriage of the Roman Catholic Church was
one of a number of pronouncements by Christian Churches. The
Church of England has been primarily concerned with the discipline

of divorce in its own ranks. Two reports have emanated between 1970 and 1978. The first[15] allocated the whole of its second chapter to the subject of marriage as relationship. The second report [16] describes marriage as 'a relationship of shared commitment and love. It is a commitment in which nothing is deliberately withheld. As such it is a profound sharing of present experience. As such it also anticipates the sharing of future experience. It is a commitment through time. It embraces the future as well as the present. It intends and promises permanence.' This is the language of covenant and the whole report emphasizes relationship in love.

The report presented to the Methodist Conference of 1979 refers to marriage thus:

> Christians believe that marriage is contracted by the free consent of two adults to live permanently together as husband and wife. This consent should be validated by the State as a sign that marriage is upheld by society as a whole. Whilst such marriage is only fulfilled if it is characterised by the fullest love between the partners, its basis exists in the mutual commitment. Its marks are mutuality, intimacy and permanence. Its fruits are a mutual growth in maturity, creativity and interdependence and often in the gift of children.[17]

Thus, all the Churches quoted and others have moved significantly in the last few years to describe marriage in terms of covenant, commitment, relationship, and thus have reached the central core of the human experience and the divine mystery of this partnership. The Augustine tenets of children, fidelity and permanence remain within a framework of a love signified by a faithful mutuality between spouses, spouses and their children and the whole family with the community. This mutuality depends on a relationship which is constantly unfolding and is being shaped by social and psychological factors. In the next two chapters the social and psychological reality will be examined.

References (Chapter 1)

1. Schillebeeckx, E., *Marriage: Human Reality and Saving Mystery*. Sheed and Ward, 1965.

2. ibid., ch. 5.

3. ibid., ch. 4.

4. ibid., ch. 5.

5. Bailey, D.S., *The Man–Woman Relationship in Christian Thought.* Longmans, 1959.

6. Augustine, *De Gen ad litt*, IX, 7, n12.

7. Dominian J., *Christian Marriage*, ch. 10. Darton, Longman and Todd, 1967.

8. *Gaudium et Spes*, Part II, ch. 1.

9. 'Arcanum Divinae' in *The Pope and the People*. Catholic Truth Society, 1939

10. *Casti Connubii*. Catholic Truth Society, 1930.

11. Doms, H.,*The Meaning of Marriage*. Sheed and Ward, 1939.

12. *Gaudium et Spes*.

13. ibid.

14. Atkinson, D., *To Have and to Hold*, Collins 1979.

15. *Marriage, Divorce and the Church*. SPCK, 1971.

16. *Marriage and the Church's Task*, p.33. Church Information Office 1978.

17. Methodist Conference, *Statement on the Christian Understanding of Human Sexuality*, 1979.

CHAPTER 2

Social Reality

There is no detailed social history of marriage and the family. In general it can be said that for the first thousand years of Christianity an attempt was made to bring the various versions of matchmaking, engagement and wedding into a semblance of similar order as the Catholic Church reached into territories beyond its original influence. Basically the conventions of the day required that parents and the community made the match arrangements to which the young people had little chance of objecting. In some instances the husband compensated the father and/or offered some material provisions for his bride, and her family in turn produced a dowry. These financial arrangements were crucial for all those who had the means and property to dispense.

There were a variety of betrothal ceremonies in various parts of Europe depending on local custom, and ultimately the future wife left the parental home and moved to her future husband's abode. For her this was a straight transfer from one male authority to another. She now began a life of helping her husband, managing the house, having children and looking after them. The authority of the husband remained unchallenged except that one suspects that, even within a social structure that allocated so much authority to the husband, there were a number of dominant patterns in which the wife assumed an ascendancy over a husband who remained dependent and incompetent. Nevertheless the significant social entity was the authority given to the husband over wife and children.

At the beginning of the Christian era the wedding ceremony was a strictly household affair, celebration and religious enactment. As the authority of the Church spread and gathered momentum, marriage and weddings came increasingly under its jurisdiction and during the first five centuries of the second millenium the wedding ceremony became a stricter religious affair organized and blessed by the Church. Ultimately after the Council of Trent, weddings

were valid if held in a church in the presence of the parish priest
and two witnesses. But as can be seen the emphasis was totally
directed to the wedding ceremony.

Modern family

According to L. Stone[1] and E. Shorter[2] the beginnings of the modern
family can be traced from the sixteenth century onwards. At that
time three of the modern objectives for marriage did not exist.

1550-1700
The moral premises of the period 1550-1700 need a fundamental
conceptual rearrangement from contemporary thinking. Thus it is
necessary to remove three current ideologies to get at the background of marriage and family at the beginning of the modern era.
This is how Stone describes it.

> The first [to be removed] is that there is a clear dichotomy
> between marriage for interest, meaning money, status or power,
> and marriage for affect, meaning love, friendship or sexual at-
> traction; and that the first is morally reprehensible. In practice
> in the sixteenth century, no such distinction existed; and if it did,
> affect was of secondary importance to interest, while romantic
> love and lust were strongly condemned as ephemeral and irra-
> tional grounds for marriage. The second modern preconception
> is that sexual intercourse unaccompanied by an emotional rela-
> tionship is immoral, and that marriage for interest is therefore
> a form of prostitution. The third is that personal autonomy, the
> pursuit by the individual of his or her own happiness, is para-
> mount, a claim justified by the theory that it in fact contributes
> to the well-being of the group. To an Elizabethan audience the
> tragedy of Romeo and Juliet, like that of Othello, lay not so
> much in their ill-starred romance as in the way they brought
> destruction upon themselves by violating the norms of the society
> in which they lived.[3]

These norms meant filial obedience and the inception of marriage
being left to the collective decision of the family and kin. In those

changing religious times when social order was under great strain, the family assumed a strict authoritarian character. There was a marked tendency to patriarchy with a subordination of children to parents and wife to husband. The father took the place of the priest within the home and he expected unquestioning obedience from the children, whose will had to be bent by flogging, and also from the wife who could also be corrected physically if needs be. The household was ruled by the father who acted as the pastoral head of the family.

1640-1800

The next phase overlaps with the previous one and it shows an emergence of some of the contemporary features of the family. Thus the pursuit of happiness or affective individualism began to emerge. During this phase young people had gained the right to choose their future spouse with the parents having only a veto. Stone summarizes these changes thus: 'It is obvious that at the root of both these changes in the power to make decisions about marriage and in the [affective] motive that guided these decisions, there lies a deep shift of consciousness, a new recognition of the need for personal autonomy and a new respect for the individual pursuit of happiness.'[4]

Romantic love began to become a respectable motive, particularly for those belonging to the upper socio-economic groups. However, although choice and affective pursuit became more common during this period, the wife and children remained subordinate to the husband and father. The obedience of both however was no longer obtained by coercive means and in particular physical punishment abated. But, as Blackstone puts it succinctly, 'The husband and wife are one and the husband is that one.'

The discrimination against women remained strong. The wife could not buy anything that did not then belong to her husband. All rights and property as well as all freedom of action were in the husband's hands. By law too the children belonged to the husband. Even after the death of the husband the mother had no automatic rights over her children unless she was made their guardian in his will. In this atmosphere marital breakdown was not uncommon, and Stone comments that the rise in separations in the eighteenth century, like the rise in divorce in the twentieth, was an indication of rising emotional expectations.[5]

Thus the second half of the seventeenth century and the whole of the eighteenth century saw an amelioration of strictness within the family and a rise in individual pursuit of happiness within marriage.

1800-1914

The change in the family atmosphere of the seventeenth and eighteenth centuries would normally be expected to have proceeded uninterruptedly. But this did not prove the case. There was a return to patriarchy with the already existing authority of the husband reinforced. Children came once again under the discipline of the rod and there was intense repression of sexual activity at least in the upper socio-economic group.

A well-known medical authority, Dr William Acton,[6] maintained that the majority of women were happy not to be troubled by sexual feelings. Mrs Ellis' advice in 1845 was 'suffer and be still'.[7]

Just as in the first period of the modern era of the family the tension in society tended to make the home the place of safety and order so, in the wake of the industrial revolution with its marked social change, the family became once again a citadel of entrenched hierarchical order. The industrial revolution had a differential effect on the social scene with the poorer families in the community tending to be split from each other as children, husband and wife moved to different industries. For the poor, life became hard, insensitive and its whole focus narrowed down to survival. In the upper socio-economic group the wife tended to preoccupy herself with children and home in a subordinate role to her husband who remained in social and psychological ascendancy.

1914 ONWARD

From the time of the First World War the pendulum began to swing yet again. The indubitable contribution of women to the war effort and the widening of horizons as the upper socio-economic group went out to work meant that after the war there was a new cry for an increase in the status of women, and the fight to gain the vote dominated the militant wing of the women's movement in the immediate post-war period.

At the same time educational facilities for women began to increase and the relationship between spouses began to resume a quality of affective individualization. This did not fully emerge until after the Second World War, but from then on the independence and assertiveness of women in choosing a spouse and a career became marked.

There was a further wave of militancy by the women's emancipation movement in the sixties and seventies. A number of powerful books written by women signalled another upsurge in their social, psychological, economic and legal emancipation.[8,9,10,11] Their claims are gradually being met through greater equality of opportunity for work, the obtaining of higher posts, and more justice in property distribution particularly when the marriage breaks down. The widespread employment of women means that few women are now forced by economic necessity to stay in a marriage which has become unbearable.

The pursuit of equity at work is being aided by the widespread presence and use of contraceptives which have reduced considerably the time when women are involved with pregnancy and child-rearing. This equity is also extending in personal relationships whereby there is an ever increasing movement towards an equality of worth.

In addition to limiting the number of children and controlling the time of their arrival, there has also been an extensive campaign to make abortion easier. It has become the aim of some women to take possession of their bodies, to control with the aid of contraception their reproductive destiny and to terminate with abortion the unwanted child. Such freedom of action is the cherished wish of a number of women but not all. The majority of women have accepted contraception but draw back from abortion which they feel instinctively is an attack on life. In addition to these intimate feelings there are also strong religious beliefs against both contraception and abortion and, whilst the taboo on the former is becoming less, opposition to abortion remains high among committed Christians.

Thus in contemporary society the situation is such that couples choose each other with or without parental consent, may live together prior to marriage, marry, pursue a relationship whose emphasis is affective companionship, with a sexual life that attempts mutual fulfilment and is fruitful in a small family whose timing is achieved by the use of contraceptives.

This is the ultimate withdrawal of the family from the influence of kith and kin in what has come to be known as the nuclear family made up primarily of parents and children.

The relationship of the spouses reveals a movement away from the patriarchal style in which the husband was head of the household, its natural leader to whom obedience and respect were owed and who took charge of all the economic needs of the family and the conduct of its external affairs. Similarly the wife is losing her exclusive responsibility for looking after children and home and for providing affective nurturing for all. There is a much greater equity of responsibility, fluidity in roles and expectancy of complementarity. Thus the modern companionship marriage reduces the social space of reverence and hierarchy between spouses, and between spouses and children. This means inevitably an intimacy which engages the deeper layers of the personality and it will be one of the tasks of this book to focus on the nature of a companionate, intimate relationship between spouses which is no longer governed by the traditional roles and functions but has a marked social and psychological intimacy as its principal characteristic. This is what is happening to marriage today and it has consequences of enormous importance which will be taken up in subsequent chapters.

Demography

In order to assess the significance of the companionship marriage it is pertinent to see how the structure of marriage has been influenced by demographic factors such as age at marriage, its duration, pregnancy and children.

AGE AT MARRIAGE
Women tended to marry on the average at about the age of 20 in the late sixteenth century, rising to 22 in the late seventeenth and eighteenth centuries. Rising still further in the nineteenth century and at the beginning of the twentieth century, the mean age stood at 25 where it remained until the Second World War and thereafter began to drop so that the mean age of marriage for spinsters was 24 in 1954, 22.5 in 1969 with a slight increase in 1977 to 22.9

The figures for men are on average higher. They remained high during the nineteenth and early twentieth century and then began to drop after the Second World War so that the mean age in 1951 was 26.7 and in 1969 24.53, rising again in the last decade to 25.1 in 1977.

DURATION OF MARRIAGE

The duration of marriage depends on three variables. These are age at marriage, age at death and the dissolution of the marriage for any reason apart from death. Thus expectation of life is a crucial criterion for length of marriage. The expectation of life for a thirty-year-old male in the seventeenth and early eighteenth century was about twenty-two to twenty-six years. Thus the duration of marriage was short, and in one study it is suggested that the median duration of first marriages among the poor was about seventeen to nineteen years rising to twenty-two years in the late nineteenth century. Mortality of both sexes, and in particular of women during pregnancy and childbirth and in the postpuerperal period, was the principal reason for this short duration.

By 1971 the average expectation of life at birth was 68.6 years for men and 74.9 for women, and thus average durations of marriages of fifty years are not unusual in contemporary society, and the combination of high expectation from marriage with such longevity provides one of the principal challenges to permanency.

CHILDREN

The high mortality of adults meant that children in the sixteenth, seventeenth, and early eighteenth centuries were likely to have lost one parent before they reached adulthood. The high rate of adult mortality was matched by that of children. In the late seventeenth and early eighteenth centuries about half of the recorded children of French peasantry were dead by the age of ten and between a half and two-thirds by the age of twenty. In London in 1764, 49 per cent of all recorded children were dead by the age of two and 60 per cent by the age of five. It was not until after 1750 that the level of infant and child mortality began to fall.[12]

At the opening of the twentieth century a working-class mother would have experienced ten pregnancies and spent about fifteen years in a state of pregnancy and in nursing a child for the first year of its life. In the period after the Second World War the time would be in the order of four to five years.

One of the dramatic reasons for this change of affairs is the current safety of pregnancy and the life of the newborn child. But both the drop in infant mortality (deaths under one year) and stillbirths are relatively recent events. Thus the total infant mortality in 1911 was calculated to be 129.4 per 1000 live births while in 1977 it was 14.[13] Stillbirths were calculated at 40.1 per 1000 actual births in 1928 dropping to 9.3 in 1977. The greater curative and preventive advances in medicine, coupled with birth regulation, which allows women to have the number of children they want when they want them, has been called 'nothing less than a revolutionary enlargement of freedom.'[14]

This freedom has led to a reduction of the family size to an average of about two children per family and the resources thus freed have been taken up largely by women going to work. Married women with young children cease to work and after several years of marriage gradually return to paid employment reaching a figure of nearly 60 per cent after twenty years of marriage.[15]

Summary

The social reality of contemporary marriage is the nuclear family of parents and children, with three phases in the married-life cycle. The early years prior to the advent of children, the arrival and growth of children and, after the departure of adolescents, a return to a one-to-one relationship of the parents – a third stage which may last twenty years or more. Throughout marriage there is a mixture of traditional role activity, with the spouses accepting parts of the assigned roles of the past, and a much greater degree of fluidity of roles, social and psychological intimacy with distinctly higher expectations for exhibition of affection and sexual fulfilment as well as the engagement of the personality at a deeper layer of being. All this, coupled with a smaller family size and a much higher rate of divorce, are the ingredients of contemporary marriage.

The social characteristics which have led to a personal choice of partner, an emphasis on equity of relationship and the presence of a marked intimacy have pyschological repercussions because fixed roles no longer hide the world of feelings and emotions which consequently govern the exchange between spouses. It is this topic that will be examined in the next chapter.

References (Chapter 2)

1. Stone, L., *The Family, Sex and Marriage in England 1500-1800*. Weidenfeld and Nicolson, 1971.

2. Shorter, E., *The Making of the Modern Family*. Collins, 1976.

3. Stone, p.86.

4. ibid., p.273.

5. ibid., p.233.

6. Acton, W., *Functions and Disorders of the Reproductive System*. London (4th edn), 1865.

7. Ellis, F., *The Daughters of England*. London, 1845.

8. de Beauvoir, S., *The Second Sex*. Penguin, 1972.

9. Greer, G., *The Female Eunuch*. MacGibbon and Kee, 1970.

10. Millett, K., *Sexual Politics*. Rupert Hart-Davis, 1971.

11. Tweedie, J., *In the Name of Love*. Jonathan Cape, 1979.

12. Stone, pp.68, 72.

13. *Population Trends*, No.15. Office of Population Censuses and Surveys, HMSO, 1979.

14. Titmuss, R.M., *Essays on the Welfare State*. Allen and Unwin (2nd edn), 1963.

15. *Population Trends*, No.2. Office of Population Censuses and Surveys, HMSO, 1975.

CHAPTER 3

Psychological Reality

In the previous chapter the social framework of contemporary marriage was outlined and the point was made that the various changes had brought about a greater intimacy in the husband – wife relation to an extent that a deeper layer of being is often engaged between spouses in their relationship with each other. What is meant by 'a deeper layer of being'?

At the centre of contemporary western marriage lies a covenant relationship between husband and wife in which feelings, emotions and instincts provide a central framework of basic reference and expectations. It is no longer enough for the husband to be provider and head of the family, nor for the wife to be childbearer and keeper of the household, with affectionate feelings entering as a secondary phenomenon with the passage of time. From the very beginning, or soon afterwards, there is an affective and sexual interaction which is often expressed through the repertoire of previously learned behaviour between the spouses and their own family, in particular the parents. The child–parent relationship with any significant contribution from relatives forms the first intimate relationship which equips the person to relate in every subsequent intimate relationship, and marriage is the second intimate relationship in the life of husband or wife.

For the 90 to 95 per cent of people who marry, life is a two-act drama. Act One is the experience between the child and significant members in its family, and the second act is a repetition and further development of this experience in the marital relationship. The reason for this is that whenever we encounter an intimate affective relationship in life we use ultimately all the emotional experiences learned in the first two decades of life. In the past these affective responses were kept strictly subordinate to the social roles, nowadays they play a crucial role in the relationship from its beginning. In this reality lies one of the major dangers of contemporary marriage, and lack of psychological knowledge and suitable preparation for this aspect of matrimony is one of the principal reasons for the failure and cynicism surrounding marriage. The social and psychological interaction has advanced imperceptibly to a level where both preparation and society's support for marriage are woefully inadequate.

Psychological contribution – biological

Two major factors contribute to the growth of our personality. The first is broadly the biological. At the moment of fertilization genes from both parents fuse and determine the emergence of a boy or girl. But the genes are not the only defining contribution. In the course of the intra-uterine life the baby may be subjected to toxic factors such as infection in the mother, for example german measles, or the tragic consequences associated with such drugs as the hypnotic, Thalidomide.

Genetic research is showing that traits such as anxiety,[1] mood swings, or cyclothymic temperament[2] and withdrawn solitary, schizoid features[3] are partially determined by genetic influences inherited from the parents. This means that people who are the inheritors of such traits may show them in their youth, particularly at adolescence or later on in life. Since these traits affect considerably the interaction between spouses, their presence can have a decisive impact on the relationship. This biological contribution is called nature as opposed to nurture, or the experiences of the child in its family environment.

The controversy over the exact contribution of nature and nurture to the adult personality is a continuous one, with biologically orientated pyschiatrists and psychologists favouring a much greater physical contribution and the dynamically orientated emphasizing the human environment and influences of the family as being the significant events. There is no agreed answer to this question except the certainty that both make major contributions.

Psychological contribution – dynamic

FIRST YEAR

From the moment of birth the child is subjected to interaction processes with its principal caretakers. This interaction is dynamic, that is to say it is carried out with feelings which are in a constant state of change. These feelings determine the quality of intimacy between child and parents and other significant figures such as siblings, relatives, teachers and prominent friends.

These feelings become translated into specific emotional patterns which the child acquires in the process of its growth. As Erikson says,[4] what is acquired is the 'sense of' which is then built in or eroded in subsequent years.

In the first year of life the baby is held a great deal, played with, fed frequently from the breast, and is often encircled in the arms of its mother, father or parental substitute. One of the earliest experiences is the acquisition of a basic sense[5] of trust in absolute physical closeness. The oneness of this closeness makes it a symbiotic union whereby the child feels one with mother. In the course of life physical proximity will either be associated with a basic sense of trust or its opposite, mistrust. This is of particular importance in sexual activity which is carried out in a bodily union where trust and security are paramount. When things go wrong men and women will say that they have reached a point where they cannot stand any proximity or even being touched, let alone made love to. The physical sense of trustworthy security which is the normal accompaniment of a loving encounter can become a tense, frightening nightmare where no proximity can be tolerated.

At the same time that trust is developing, the baby is either breast-feeding, bottle-feeding or is being weaned in the first year. This activity focuses on the mouth and is the 'oral phase' of Freud. The mouth, lips, tongue – all become associated with the vital activity of swallowing and gradually masticating. The smooth character of the lips, and the inside of the mouth arouse a distinct pleasure, which for Freud was the first erotic zone in the evolution of the libido.[6] Feeding gives repeated oral satisfaction but the mouth is the site of kissing and other sexual activity. Once again there has to be a sense of trust to allow two people to reach one another and communicate through the mouth.

Freud, Erikson and Bowlby are all main-line dynamic theorists.

Bowlby's work is recent, in the last fifteen years, but of fundamental importance in understanding human relationships. For Freud, the bond between mother and child was at this stage, of the first year, an oral one. The baby focused on the mother because the mother regularly met its food needs. The bond of attachment between mother and child was postulated to rely heavily on this exchange. Bowlby questioned this explanation and proposed instead that the attachment of the baby to its mother was based on a wider contact through the instinctual channels of touch, vision and sound. The baby recognizes and gets attached to its mother by the fourth month of life because it recognizes her visually, is accustomed to her voice and above all to the feel of her touch. Bowlby has written three volumes on this topic[7] and a smaller volume which summarizes his main ideas.[8] The affectionate bond or the attachment of love thus begins in the first six months and continues throughout childhood. At first the attachment is very intimate and close. The young child who has learnt how to crawl and walk does not separate itself too far from mother. Mother is the physical and emotional centre of its life and there is a constant return to her when there is anything frightening or anxiety-making in the immediate vicinity. Strangers, animals, noise, water are some of the disturbing elements that bring the youngster scurrying back to the safety of mother. This attachment is a bond of love in which anxiety and safety play major roles. The beginning of love is security in physical proximity and, as Erikson pointed out, this security carries a quality of trust.

All this which is beginning during the first year will continue throughout life. Our friendships and intimate relationships are bonds of affective attachment. Whenever a bond is particularly strong or unique, as in marriage, then the spouse carries a significance of security and trust and we move towards them for safety and support.

SECOND AND THIRD YEAR

The first year is a time of great physical intimacy during which the foundations of trust, security and attachment are laid. But as the child grows it is slowly differentiating itself from mother. Erikson calls this phase the 'sense of self-control without the loss of self-esteem'.[9]

During these two years the child goes through the first phase of autonomy. Now is the time and urge for the acquisition of self-mastery. The young child wants to feed itself, to learn how to dress, to run about, and to do things. All this is achieved by trial and error and with the active assistance of mother. There are ample opportunities for praise when something of value has been achieved and there are also many occasions when mother gets impatient, scolds her child for its incompetence and takes over, humiliating the child who feels unable to do anything successfully.

Perhaps the most particular experience of autonomy is the ability to control defecation. A great deal of emotional display occurs in this aspect of toilet training. Mother naturally wants to have a toilet-trained child as soon as possible. It is important however for the child to feel that it controls its own body, not out of fear or simply to please mother but with a degree of personal freedom. With an understanding parent this is precisely what is allowed and toilet training becomes part of a successful phase of autonomy.

Freud focused on the process of defecation. He called this phase, the anal one. The child learns to retain or release what feels like its inner world. This gives immense power into its hands and often these are years which echo with turbulence. They are the years of the most manifest emergence of aggression. The withholding of faeces can be an act of rage but disobeying mother in general can be the first signs of independence. If this independence is punished, then the child experiences for the first time ambivalence, that is to say it loves and hates the same person. One moment mother is the source of all goodness, the next she is angry, shouts and may smack. The ability to move from love to anger and hatred, guilt, forgiveness and back to love is a familiar cycle which is observed in this phase, even though some psychoanalysts like Melanie Klein put it at an earlier stage. With autonomy and the anal phase enters ambivalence. Freud also stressed that the anus, like the lips and the mouth, is lined with smooth skin which has a pleasurable surface. Defecation can be pleasurable and, as is well known, the rectum is used for sexual purposes as well. So this infantile sexuality also has adult repercussions.

Part of autonomy is the gradual phase of the child's physical separation from its mother. This separation is a delicate matter and needs to take place at a graduated pace. Gradually the child can cope with physical aloneness without feeling the panic of isolation and loneliness. By the third year it can leave mother for a few hours and go to a nursery school or playgroup. It is ready now to miss her physical presence because it carries safely the memory of her presence within, which gives the first secure period of being distant from her. This period of separation from mother will gradually lengthen throughout childhood, and children will begin to develop a balance between closeness and distance. This balance between closeness and distance permeates all relationships but is of particular importance in marriage. Too much closeness shows an infantile dependence, i.e. the separation of the early years has not occurred, and too little closeness suggests that intimacy does not feel either safe or secure.

The ability to become partially autonomous, to separate from mother and feel secure in her absence are all important steps in acquiring self-esteem and a sense of possessing oneself. The opposite features, according to Erikson, are the sense of doubt and shame. In adult life many are plagued with lack of self-esteem which makes them feel incapable of doing things by themselves and they rapidly dissolve into self-doubt and the shame of inadequacy when they fail. In marriage, spouses who are laden with these emotional difficulties are easy prey to criticism from each other and the relationship can become one of continuous mutual recrimination.

FOURTH AND FIFTH YEAR

During the fourth and fifth years there is, according to Erikson, the development of a sense of initiative. This sense of initiative is expressed by intrusion. The intrusion can be into space by vigorous locomotion, into the unknown by conquering curiosity, intrusion into other people by an aggressive voice, intrusion by physical attacks and the fear of the phallus entering into the female body.[10]

This phase of initiative can cause pandemonium in a household as the youngsters shout, leap about, climb trees, interrupt conversations. In a few people it may continue into adult life, and they go on treating others as if they were objects for exploration and intrusion, seeing them as existing only to be played with without any regard for their wishes. When such people realize their insensitivity they feel guilty, but they do not develop any insight and are soon back in a state of shallow frivolity. This is of course very different from the child. Allowances are made for the child, but the adult who behaves in this way is considered immature.

The opposite characteristics of this robust exploration is a sense of passivity, and marriages between passive, active and dominant people do occur. The passivity can be tolerated for a while but after

a few years it is resented and the spouse attempts in vain to mobilize
some interest or activity in their partner.

The intrusive mode also involves penetration by the penis, and
here Erikson, the Freudian, reiterates the classical Freudian theme.
This theme is the triangular Oedipal complex whereby the young
boy is sexually attracted to mother, wishes to possess her, is frightened of the father, gives up the desire and becomes identified with
the father. When Freud introduced his third and phallic phase in
the theory of libido development with the resolution of the Oedipus
complex, there were few who could accept such emotional proceedings in a young child. Nowadays we are far more aware of infantile
sexuality and its complex unconscious links. The boy, who remains
attached to his mother as he grows up, may find a sexual attraction
to women difficult and may marry in order to continue a maternal
relationship, and similarly the girl, who idealizes her father or on
the contrary never had any closeness with her father, may want a
father figure for her husband.

The unresolved Oedipal complex and Erikson's sense of intrusion
are said to be accompanied by a deep sense of guilt but, as we have
seen, guilt enters the life of a child at an earlier phase when it feels
it is attacking and possibly damaging or destroying mother with its
anger. Jealousy, essentially a triangular situation in which a third
person is threatening to take away the affection received from a
significant person, may also enter at this phase. Envy is a twosome
experience in which there is a competition between two persons,
and this feeling may enter at any stage in childhood when the child
feels envious of the parent and/or sibling.

DISTANT AFFECTIVE ATTACHMENT
By the time the child goes to school between five and six it has
negotiated the ability to remain away from mother for the whole of
the day and increasingly as it gets older it will progressively be able
to stay alone without fear or anxiety for a longer period. Its attachment to mother and father feels safe. The sense of being recognized,
wanted and appreciated is an experience which is communicated
by looks and words, with touch playing a reduced role as a means
of conveying love. The young person knows that he/she is in a safe
affective attachment, which may be interrupted by small incidents
of dissonance but the loving relationship is rapidly re-established.
They carry within them a sense of recognition, acceptance and

feeling wanted which needs continuous affirmation but does not require to be constantly built afresh.

But what happens when the attachment is not safe? And what factors contribute to an unsafe attachment, which undoubtedly is one of the prominent reasons for marital difficulties, that is to say when one or both spouses feel no recognition, no sense of being wanted or appreciated and live with the dread of being abandoned at any time?

Bowlby describes anxious attachment in this way.

Research shows that to have been exposed to at least one, and usually more than one, of certain typical patterns of pathogenic parenting (leads to anxious attachment). These include:
(i) one or both parents being persistently unresponsive to the child's care-eliciting behaviour and/or actively disparaging and rejecting him;
(ii) discontinuities of parenting, occurring more or less frequently, including periods in hospital or institutions;
(iii) persistent threats by parents not to love a child, used as a means of controlling him;
(iv) threats by parents to abandon the family, used either as a method of disciplining the child or as a way of coercing a spouse;
(v) threats by one parent either to desert or even to kill the other or else to commit suicide;
(vi) inducing a child to feel guilty by claiming that his behaviour is or will be responsible for the parent's illness or death.
Any of these experiences can lead a child, an adolescent or an adult to live in constant anxiety lest he lose his attachment figure and, as a result, to have a low threshold for manifesting attachment behaviour.[11]

The married adult who lives with an anxious attachment is constantly frightened that their spouse will go. This may lead them to behave as if they were supremely independent and do not care whether their spouse went or stayed. If in fact they decide to go, the so-called independent spouse breaks down. The person with an insecure attachment is anxious, possessive, jealous and attempts to circumscribe the life of their partner in order to keep a hold over them. Many partners complain that they feel suffocated or imprisoned by such an attitude. The roots of such anxious attachment are often to be found in childhood, and the pattern continues in the marital relationship where often the fear of losing their partner makes them hesitant to show their anger and they often seethe underneath their dependent, frightened relationship.

DEFENCES AND ANXIETY

Anxiety plays a prominent part in human attachment. In the process of growth, anxiety is experienced when we are young and fear abandonment. This fear continues in adult life and is the basis of anxious attachment. Anxiety grows when the child is afraid that its anger will destroy or damage the beloved parent. Anxiety is also experienced when the child feels threatened with rejection or is made to feel unlovable, insignificant or treated as an object. These anxieties repeat themselves in adult intimate relationships where fear of abandonment or rejection, of feeling insignificant, feelings of badness and guilt or of aggression are all repeated.

Such anxieties are so painful that we all produce counter-measures or what are technically known as defences. We can deny our responsibility, we can project it on our partner who becomes responsible for whatever goes wrong, we can displace our bad feelings for someone we are afraid of, such as our boss, and take it out on our spouse or children, we can rationalize our behaviour and drive our spouse to distraction as we refuse to see the feeling consequences of our actions or omissions. These and other defences have been described in detail by Anna Freud.[12]

Thus as the child grows it learns how to cope with its anxiety by insulating itself psychologically from the consequences through defence mechanisms. When these defences are used in adult intimate relationships, like marriage, the most common defences are denial, projection, rationalization, repression and suppression, whereby each spouse denies responsibility for what goes wrong

Other forms of defences arising out of anxious attachment may lead a person to trust so little that they will not form any close attachment at all. Or if they form an attachment they insist they do not need the presence of their partner in any way, and so they create a pseudo-independence which puts them beyond the point of being hurt by any let-down. Alternatively they remain so dependent that they spend their life ingratiating themselves in the hope that if they please sufficiently they will reduce the danger of being rejected. These patterns will be examined afresh but their roots are to be found in excessive anxiety, the origins of which are to be found in childhood.

THE SCHOOL YEARS

By the end of the first decade the fundamental relationship experiences are laid down. Persistent upheaval in the second decade can of course distort growth but in general the experiences of the first decade are further developed and reinforced. In Freud's schema the period from about six to puberty is a quiescent period in which no libidinal development is occurring.

Erikson sees in these years the entry of the child into a world of social activity, with the development of a sense of industry along with the opposite feeling of inferiority. Certainly in western society the emphasis placed on intelligence and the intellect often means that the less-gifted child acquires a sense of intellectual inferiority. But, as already indicated in this chapter, the child's worth is cultivated in earlier years when it receives unconditional acceptance, appreciation for its own worth intrinsically before it is valued for what it can achieve. The secure person who has been loved in this way continues to feel worthy and has a high self-esteem whatever their physical and intellectual achievements. The person who lacks a sense of personal self-esteem seeks compensation in achievement. This incongruity of successful achievers who lack emotional self-esteem is one of the recurrent problems in the wounded personality and in marriage. People who are visibly successful may exhibit, to their spouse's surprise, a whole variety of feelings and emotional problems with an inability to love or register love.

PUBERTY AND ADOLESCENCE

Puberty is the period when the secondary sexual characteristics manifest themselves. The identity of the person has to absorb and integrate this new dimension and the adolescent is heading for a gradual complete separation from parents with the capacity to know and possess themselves sufficiently in order to relate to other adults.

A number of adolescents find themselves on the threshold of adult life without any clarification of their own identity. They still do not know who they are, where they are going, what is their worth or the type of work they want to do. With time these issues will be gradually resolved. The most unsuitable response is to marry at eighteen or earlier in the hope that marriage will resolve the difficulties by giving a role and an identity. These are short-term gains and the basic personality problems will have to be negotiated sooner or later, possibly at the expense of the marriage.

SECOND INTIMATE RELATIONSHIP – MARRIAGE

Most men and women arrive at their second intimate relationship with a complexity of mature growth, unresolved conflicts and occasionally severe emotional wounds. The entry into the second intimate relationship will bring the spouses into a social and psychological relationship which is currently designed to bring their inner worlds, the next layer of being, which is largely psychological, into intimate contact with each other. The psychological interaction will start from the very beginning of marriage and, depending on the state of growth and temperament, an alliance will be established which has the resources to form a satisfactory social and psychological relationship. If the wounds or difficulties which the couple bring to each other are extensive and deep, their negotiation will be a challenge to them. The manifestation of difficulties will develop from the very beginning of the marriage in most cases and in some will develop later on. But whenever they appear they will be central to the happiness and stability of the marriage.

In the process of negotiating the emotional aspects of the second relationship, difficulties will emerge which may either overcome the couple or provide opportunities for sustaining, healing and growth;[13] these will become the basis for transforming the phase of falling in love to loving each other.

Summary

The current intimate relationship of marriage is one in which feelings, emotions and instincts play a major part. The spouses relate at a deeper level of engagement of their being. This sense of being, of being a person who experiences love and returns it in intimate relationships, is acquired in childhood. Marriage becomes the second act of a two-act play, the first act being childhood. Partners come to marriage with a mixture of good and bad experiences of love. Marital stability depends on whether the good experiences outweigh the bad ones.

References (Chapter 3)

1. Slater, E. and Shields, J., 'Genetical Aspects of Anxiety' in *Studies of Anxiety* (ed. M.H. Lader). RMPA, 1969.

2. Price, J., *British Journal of Psychiatry*, Special Publication (1968) No. 2, 37.

3. Shields, J., *Psychological Medicine*, 1977, 7, 1, 7.

4. Erikson, E.H., *Identity*. Faber and Faber, 1968.

5. ibid., p.96.

6. Freud, S., *Three Essays on Sexuality*. Hogarth Press, 1968.

7. Bowlby, J., *Attachment and Loss*, vol.1: Attachment (1969) vol.2: Separation: Anxiety and Anger (1973); vol.3: Loss, Sadness and Depression (1980). Hogarth Press.

8. Bowlby, J., *The Making and Breaking of Affectional Bonds*.Tavistock Publications, 1979.

9. Erikson, p.109.

10. ibid., p.116.

11. Bowlby, *Affectional Bonds*, p.137.

12. Freud, A., *The Ego and the Mechanisms of Defence*. Hogarth Press, 1966.

13. Dominian, J, *Cycles of Affirmation*. Darton, Longman and Todd, 1975.

PART II

The Personal Encounter

CHAPTER 4

Sustaining

The childhood years, during which emotional growth takes place against a background of physical, social and intellectual growth, need the facilitating environment supplied by the parents. This environment consists of a material, social, intellectual and emotional sustenance. In the second intimate relationship of marriage spouses expect not only material but also emotional support.

Material sustenance

The economic support of the wife and children by the husband is part of the traditional pattern of marriage. This is one of the responsibilities which society allocated to the husband. Nowadays, as marriages are gradually transformed from traditional fixed-role entities to companionship ones, the material sustenance is becoming a shared responsibility. Wives work before children arrive and often return to work when their children grow up sufficiently not to need their immediate and constant attention. This increasing economic independence on the part of the wife changes the financial atmosphere of the home. The wife is accustomed to economic independence and does not see herself as a subservient receiver of the husband's bounty. Her maintenance and that of her children is seen as a right and duty which entitles her to receive financial support regularly and without strings.

Increasingly this means that there is a change of values. The wife feels it is her right to know what her husband is earning and expects him to handle his income efficiently, pay the bills and act responsibly in handling the financial affairs of the family provided the wife remains responsible for the housekeeping. In practice difficulties

emerge when the husband does not remain in continuous employment, is in steady work but cannot handle the bills of the household
or remains irresponsible with money which is spent impulsively on
non-essentials. There are particular difficulties when the money is
spent on drink or is gambled away. The wife may also show financial
incompetence and multiply the strains of the household.

Particular problems arise when the husband finds it difficult to
be generous with money. An attitude develops in which what is
given is constantly short of what is required to cope with the demands of the family. In this way she is made to feel incapable,
having constantly to make further requests which are met with,
'What again? What do you do with the money?' If the wife enters
marriage with innate doubts about her housekeeping efficiency,
such an approach gradually erodes her confidence in herself. Gradually such treatment evokes a counter-response on the part of the
wife. She begins to feel the injustice of the situation and rebels.
Money becomes the recurrent source of dispute, but behind the
arguments over actual sums there is a contentious exchange regarding the way the wife feels treated. It gradually dawns on her
that her husband's approach is reprehensible. It is mean, unjust,
unfair, demeaning and there comes the point where she is no longer
prepared to put up with it. In extreme circumstances she may refuse
to carry on the housekeeping and ask her husband to take over,
which he may do. Very soon he finds out the truth and a new reality
is established about the sums involved. Occasionally the husband
may in fact be more competent and in these circumstances a caring
approach is to help the wife rather than to reduce her confidence
further.

Thus money is often much more than an economic reality. The
way it is given to the wife is symbolic of trust, care and affection.
Trust means that in the companionship marriage there are no
secrets about the family's resources, all that is available is known
and shared according to need. Care means that flexibility in financial matters allows for individual variations and special circumstances in which the budgeting falls short. Money is often seen as
a vital part of self and it is not the amount but the way the exchange
takes place that matters. Spouses feel cared for financially when
money is exchanged on a basis of reality and generosity. Affection
is demonstrated by hard work which raises the financial status of
the family, generous housekeeping money, extraordinary allocations
in the form of gifts, not so much for their worth, but as a reminder

that the spouse remains a person of significance who is appreciated. Giving and receiving are the earliest experiences of love between child and mother, and they continue throughout life to signify concerned awareness and love. This concerned awareness is very far from buying, coercing or trying to influence a person by money. It is rather a spontaneous extension of oneself through a material object which carries the affection of the donor.

So far reference has been made to giving. The art of receiving is just as important. The ability to receive and feel the loving intentions of the donor is a vital part of the exchange. Most people receive with joy and gratitude, but not all. There are those who feel they have not deserved or earned any reward, who find it difficult to receive unconditionally, who feel unlovable enough to receive only what is strictly justified by their responsibilities and achievements and not an iota more. These are men and women who can give but cannot receive or spend anything on themselves. If they don't receive gifts, they feel their deprivation acutely, but if they are given gifts, they often ask, 'What for? What did you do that for? Wasting money again.' These are people who grew up without a sufficient sense of self-esteem, worth, or unconditional love, who find it very difficult to receive love and can only be given what they think they have earned or merited in some way.

Very often such people are also plagued by insecurity. Money or resources need to be accumulated, not to be used or spent, but in order for them to feel secure and safe. Little is spent on themselves but an acquisitive temperament is developed as a means of fighting off the imagined catastrophe of the ultimate deprivation. Goods and money are collected but not spent, and a style of poverty is pursued out of fear. If one spouse feels like this and the other differently, there are constant angry exchanges about the spendthrift habits of the unconcerned partner.

Bringing together all these patterns, it can be seen that in the companionship marriage there is increasingly financial independence of the spouses who at the same time agree to pool their resources for the running of their married life. This is a further extension of the equity between the spouses. The wife becomes temporarily economically dependent when the children are young but expects to be treated no differently from the periods when she is earning her own livelihood. The husband's support is not only a duty but a part of the co-responsibility between adults who retain their worth and dignity even if they are not earning. Granted this equity of exchange which respects economic independence and contributes to the common pool of household costs, there is in the depths of giving and receiving emotional overtones which make money one of the most sensitive areas for marital life.

Emotional sustaining

(i) PHYSICAL

The enlargement of mutual responsibility extends now to an emotional sustaining, one of the new values or expectations of contemporary marriage.

Emotional sustaining is a recapitulation of the child's experience of being made to feel physically safe, recognized, wanted and appreciated. Spouses need from time to time to be held. Holding is usually a preliminary to a sexual encounter but before touching received its characteristic sexual connotation it was the means through which safety and reassurance were communicated, and this remains so in adult life. This can be expressed by holding the partner in whatever manner feels safe. This holding for security needs to be distinguished from the erotic touch. Security is conveyed in an encompassing, enfolding, holding encounter in which one spouse conveys safety to the other. These moments can vary from waking up in the middle of the night with a nightmare to all occasions when crippling fear enters a spouse's life. Sometimes the holding is a mutual defence against a common fear.

There are men and women, but particularly the former, who find it very difficult to touch and hold. Physical encounter is frightening to them, and these are the spouses who are considered to be indifferent. They may be so, but often a combination of tension and an absence of childhood cuddling makes it very difficult for them to show their affection physically. If the husband is the undemonstrative one, the wife begins to feel that the only time he wants to get near her is at times of sexual intercourse. There is an incongruity between frequent sex and the absence of affectionate demonstration at all other times. The wife may gradually feel used instead of loved and may withdraw sexual availability. If one examines the personality of such a husband a little more closely, it will be found that there is a deep-seated inability to show physical affection, not because of indifference, but because of difficulty in physical demonstration. Sex which appears to the wife as a selfish, self-centred satisfaction on the part of the husband is in fact his only way of getting physically close. The frequency of intercourse is a way of avoiding isolation and is pursued as much for the legitimate means of achieving physical proximity as for the sexual pleasure. Rarely it is the wife who cannot demonstrate physical affection even though she appears warm and caring.

Sometimes the man or woman who cannot show overt affection physically or verbalize it will, instead, do things for their partner. They will buy things e.g. flowers, household goods, jewellery and convey their loving feelings through these bought goods. Alternatively they will become busy round the house, improving it and particularly trying to meet the specific requirements of the wife. But a wife who needs physical demonstration finds the indirect display of affection deficient and unacceptable. 'If you love me, hold me, talk to me; tell me that you love me.' The more desperate for reassurance she becomes, the further the husband withdraws and a cycle of alienation is initiated.

Sometimes the difficulties begin early in marriage after a courtship which was full of demonstrative affection. After marriage the man, or more rarely the woman, begins to change abruptly to the consternation of their spouse. 'Now that we are married we don't need such things.' This transformation is difficult to comprehend. What may happen is that during courtship the undemonstrative partner makes a determined effort to conquer their difficulty with a demonstration of care and affection. As soon as the marriage starts such a person reverts to their usual undemonstrative self.

Sometimes the undemonstrative spouse is chosen because their future partner finds expressed affection difficult to register or retain. They chose someone who is shy because this minimizes the effort they have to make to respond. But the need for reassurance is present, and gradually within marriage one of the spouses becomes desperate for emotional reassurance and resents the silence of their partner. This is another common pattern of marital conflict.

(ii) RECOGNITION

The baby and young child first feel recognized by seeing mother's face smiling approvingly; this is before language is established. A bodily language is developed through which the child feels recognized. In the presence of parents children feel they exist and have significance for them. This recognition is not because of merit; it exists simply because of the relationship between parent and child and it is intrinsic to it.

This recognition remains a vital part of any close relationship and particularly of marriage. A look, a smile, a touch can all convey recognition. When this exchange does not take place a feeling overcomes the spouses in which they gradually come to feel impermanent or absent. Acute loneliness in the presence of a non-recognizing partner is a constant reiteration of a major problem in troubled marriages.

Recognition without words is soon followed in childhood by a verbal exchange of affirmation. This does not eliminate the non-verbal communication, which is simply enriched by words. The silent spouse is acceptable to a partner who needs very little reassurance but, if recognition is constantly needed, then the absence of verbal and non-verbal acknowledgement can make the partner feel they do not exist. Absence of recognition leads to existential annihilation. Such annihilation was of no concern in a relationship where recognition was not expected. Now it is required as part of the relationship and its absence is a modern phenomenon of deprivation.

(iii) FEELING WANTED

We recognize all sorts of people in transient or permanent relationships. This is a social requirement of everyday life but we are under no obligation to make our casual or work associates feel wanted. Out of kindness we may make sure we do not reject them, because every person has a natural God-given dignity but we confine our acceptance to those close to us. Our spouse is a key person to elicit the feeling that, beyond recognition, we actually need and want them. The need we express is not a utilitarian one. We need all sorts of people who serve and meet our needs in a utilitarian fashion. The acceptance of a spouse is the reception of a person. It is an acceptance which goes beyond the meeting of needs although these are important. We make another person feel wanted by appreciating their talents but much more important by accepting unconditionally their presence as a reality of love.

Similarly part of our own need is to feel wanted. This is not a need to be justified by productive results. We want to feel unconditionally wanted for what we are as a person, over and above the fact that we meet the needs of our spouse.

This feeling of being wanted is an emotional security that we matter simply because we exist and prior to proving our worth. Life is punctuated by deficiency, failure, shortcomings. In the midst of these fluctuating fortunes of achievement, spouses need to feel recognized and wanted. Many marriage problems are focused on a feeling of uselessness in the presence of their partner, who succeeds in conveying a message which makes the spouse feel redundant, an insignificant object in their partner's life.

(iv) APPRECIATION

Feeling recognized and wanted is completed by the emotional reassurance of appreciation. In the course of growth the child constantly receives signals of being recognized, wanted and appreciated. Its presence is valued and its achievements praised. Similarly in the second intimate relationship spouses need to feel appreciated as subjects of love. This may be conveyed, once again, through a touch, a look, a word. This is not an appreciation of reflected glory. It is a genuine conveying of loving regard.

Regard means confirmation of worth, the worth of being a person. It is an acknowledgement which comes before and after that deserved by achievement. It is a mutual gift of unconditional justification in the eyes of the beholding spouse. This appreciation is expressed in a myriad of ways through gratitude, thanksgiving, verbal affirmation and physical love. But all the time there is rejoicing in a personal presence.

Feelings of being recognized, wanted and appreciated can become blunted in the course of ordinary contact. They can be resurrected naturally if a spouse is absent, ill or goes through a crisis. The steady everyday appreciation requires sustained and renewed effort.

(v) CORRECTION

Many parents ignore their children until the moment when they feel they must correct them. The child learns that it comes to life only when it has done wrong or omitted to do something. It grows up with the feeling that it really exists only when it is subject to reprimand and correction. Its internal world leaps to attention when fault is found with its way of life.

Spouses may continue this behaviour. They remain uncommunicative until they can draw the attention of their partner to a fault. Then they correct it, and it is all done 'for your good'. Such a relationship can live only on the compilation of how many faults the partners can find in each other. The correction and degradation of one becomes the self-esteem of the other. There is no affirmation but a competition of self-righteousness. Partners may not go to such extremes but there is no doubt that one major aspect of intimacy can be the mutual exploration in depth of each other's limitations. Such a relationship is a far cry from the approach of recognition, acceptance and appreciation. For recognition, neglectful omission is substituted. For acceptance, rejection is offered and for appreciation, correction. This does not mean that criticism has no place in marriage. It means that it needs to be positive rather than negative and destructive.

There was a time when such a negative emotional exchange was tolerated without a murmur. It is no longer so. Human dignity has deepened its requirements and spouses feel that they have a right to escape from such a personal annihilation. Thousands upon thousands of marriages have foundered on the rocks of absent emotional sustaining which truly engages the very deepest layers of being.

Sustaining and God's love

In the covenant relationship between God and man, we experience God's presence by the sense of feeling recognized, wanted and appreciated as unique persons. God's love is powerfully expressed through these channels of experience. We return this love by recognizing and reaching out towards God, appreciating his presence, particularly the incarnate presence of Christ in the world. The mystery of God's covenant is partially expressed in marital love, where in the depth of the exchange couples experience a glimpse of unconditional recognition, acceptance and appreciation, in brief of mutual love. Similarly the hell of vacuum, emptiness and non-being is felt by the spouse who feels ignored, rejected and taken for granted. In brief they feel invalidated as persons. Emotional support is one of the main meeting points between human and divine love and is a channel through which marriage directs the spouses to God.

Summary

As we grow up we feel recognized, wanted and appreciated, firstly for our intrinsic worth as children for parents and secondly for our achievements. In contemporary marriage this deepest layer of emotional engagement has become a new value and partners expect to feel significant to each other prior to and simultaneously with earning approval for achievement. The absence of such an acknowledgement is generally considered a basic omission in the marriage relationship.

CHAPTER 5

Healing

Reference has already been made to the fact that by the time a couple get married they bring with them several wounds which they have accumulated in the course of their first two decades. At the centre of the marital relationship is love, which operates in different ways. Material and emotional sustaining are the basic framework within which another dimension of love is realized, namely healing.

The concept of healing is an intimate part of the sense of holiness which in turn is a seeking of wholeness. Grace, God's life, is especially present in the marital relationship to effect an inward transformation of the couple, moving them to respond to God's call and seek holiness through wholeness. These concepts are clearly enunciated in all the theological treatises on the sacramental nature of marriage. Matrimony is a special channel for God's pouring of strength to animate the couple. In the declaration of Vatican II on marriage and the family the Council, referring to married love, says, 'This love the Lord has judged worthy of spiritual gifts, healing, perfecting and exalting gifts of grace and of charity.'[1] The idea of healing is clear but the method remains something of a mystery. How does God's grace alter human behaviour? There is a certain reluctance to subject mysteries to analysis, but this is precisely what needs to be done if the work of healing is to be consciously maximized. To understand healing we have to turn to the psychological sciences which have made personal therapy a special concern of theirs. In this chapter I shall describe four forms of healing – the dynamic, the behaviouristic, the spontaneous and the miraculous.

Dynamic therapy

The dynamic approach is as old as mankind but it has taken a specific form in the hands of Freud[2] and his successors. Freud, like many other doctors, was faced with people complaining of physical and emotional symptoms. Anxiety, depression, physical complaints, guilt feelings, a sense of shame and self-rejection were common features of his patients' complaints. Hitherto patients of this kind were subjected to physical treatments such as rest, change of location, baths and various medicines. The results were patchy and unsatisfactory. Freud adopted instead a revolutionary approach.

He placed the patients on a couch, sat behind them and allowed them to speak, listening in an uninterrupting, non-judgemental, non-advisory manner. No judgement was passed on the utterances of the patient or advice given. In this way the patient began to reach feelings which were buried in the unconscious. Feelings and emotions which were repressed (removed from consciousness by the defence of repression) now emerged and these feelings were transferred (transference) to the analyst. Freud did not discover the unconscious;[3] it was well recognized from the time of the ancient Greeks. What he did was to develop a method which was reliable enough to examine the contents of the unconscious. The patients began to treat the neutral but concerned analyst as a significant figure of their past life. By identifying the analyst with a person with whom there was an incomplete or traumatic emotional experience, the possibility arises of resolving the conflict by reliving the experience which hitherto was too painful to be faced.

The interpretation of events is based on the particular theory of the analyst, and in the case of Freud the underlying basis of distorted behaviour, excessive guilt, fear, and other emotions were all linked to the sexual and aggressive development of the personality. However it cannot be stressed too strongly that the technique of psychoanalysis, whereby a patient relives past experiences and has a second chance to order, integrate and reconcile the past with the present, does not depend on the theoretical dynamic stance of the analyst. Increasingly it is realized that what matters is the ability to become conscious of the unconscious, to unlearn previous patterns of experience and to acquire a more wholesome sense of self. Where guilt is rampant, peace is to be found. Where anger is overwhelming, tolerance and patience emerge. Where sex was laden with taboos, there is a freeing of the instinctual life. Where jealousy and envy predominate, they are replaced by a growth of self-esteem which is far less threatening. Where doubt and indecision prevail, they are replaced by a sense of certainty and self-acceptance. Where childhood dependence dominates behaviour, there is a development of autonomy.

Now the remarkable aspect of psychoanalysis is the fact that it has revealed a method of healing which has much wider implications than the strict analytical situation. Thus whenever two people reach the degree of mutual trust similar to that which the analyst establishes with the patient, the possibility arises for healing to occur by the same technique as in psychoanalysis. This healing possibility is uniquely present in marriage.

In the presence of a sound sustaining atmosphere, the conditions are unfolded for the spouses to act as therapists to each other. What happens in psychoanalysis or psychotherapy is that the patient feels secure enough to divulge moments and experiences of the past which are painful. This distress can be linked with sexual episodes or with experiences that are laden with anxiety, guilt, shame, un-controlled anger and/or embarrassment. These disclosures are usually not made unless there is some certainty that they will not be occasions of repeating the same original feeling of hurt. Thus these revelations need a safe relationship which allow recall and revelation with some assurance that the exchange will receive a different treatment on this second occasion. This is achieved by the therapist remaining non-judgemental and non-advisory. He or she is there to receive these feelings, interpret them to the point where they make sense and allow their repetition until they begin to change and lose their affective pain as they are replaced by reality or appropriate growth. Normally they will not be revealed if there is some fear that the original wound of rejection, devaluation, se-duction, excessive dependence or ostracism will simply be repeated. There has to be sufficient guarantee that the repetition of the orig-inal experience will be treated differently on this occasion; disclosure then becomes a process in which the person feels safe enough to reveal their wounds and, is prepared to remove the defences which held the anxiety and pain in check.

Spouses can and do act therapeutically in this way. Having gained the trust of their partner they can begin to disclose parts of themselves which are wounded and painful. The spouse listens and ensures that he/she does not behave like the original parent. They listen and neither judge nor advise. Instead they offer themselves as an alternative model to the original person who was the source of the wound. The couple can thus re-experience the original pain and find an alternative solution now. Furthermore as they get to know each other the couple can help each other with the penetration of parts of the unconscious which hitherto contained the most painful and unavailable experiences.

Thus a woman may see in her husband the distant, aloof, undemonstrative father and will expect him to behave likewise. She acts as if her husband does behave in this way and all he does is interpreted in this matter. Alternatively the husband may insist on treating his wife as a mother with all the unresolved feelings of infantile sexuality, resentful dependence and fear of being smothered. Each one of these symptoms can be understood and interpreted and steadfastly repudiated by the wife. Gradually the projected parental figure diminishes in significance and the reality of the spouse emerges. But the wife needs to be patient and clear about her identity so that she can offer her husband the model which he needs and to which he has to relate as an adult.

The gradual disclosure of wounds may take years to reach its finality. The atmosphere has to feel reliable and safe, and one of the reasons for the need of permanency in marriage is that only within reliable continuity can the depths of the self emerge and be subjected to change. It is not possible to reveal the whole of oneself at once because further confiding of the incomplete and wounded self may depend on the triggering mechanisms of various events, such as the advent of the first child or middle age. Marriage allows a gradual process of disclosure which emerges in appropriate circumstances. After all, the healing of a full analysis may take five years of intense and regular therapeutic meetings of between three to five times a week. Spouses meet each other daily but they are not consciously in analysis with each other. They have to await the appropriate circumstances, often a crisis, and thus healing for them may take a life-time of openness, careful listening and non-judgemental availability.

In this model of healing it has been presumed that both partners have a reservoir of maturity in order to act as therapists to each other. Marriages can founder from their outset when two people marry who are so deprived, dependent and self-negating that neither has the resources to offer any healing to the other. These are the marriages that need a counselling support which allows the couple to grow internally to a point at which they can act as therapists to each other. This is the hoped-for outcome. But the frequent disappointing result is that the needs of both are so enormous that the marriage breaks down because of the sheer weight of emotional requirements which cannot be met. These are some of the marriages which disintegrate in their early phase.

Healing is not confined to the wounds brought into marriage. New wounds and hurts arise within the marriage itself and these have to be dealt with as well.

Behaviour therapy

Behaviour therapy is a relatively recent phenomenon in clinical psychiatric work.[4] As with psychoanalysis the underlying theory has been practised for a very long time, as human behaviour has been influenced and shaped through fear, punishment and reward but the detailed techniques arrived with the introductory book of Wolpe.[5]

What are the origins of this therapy and what are the principles which dictate its approach? The father of this therapy is Pavlov.[6] He was working with dogs in his laboratory where he carried out his famous salivation experiments. Dogs, like human beings, salivate when hungry and in anticipation of food. Pavlov noticed that certain signals such as sounds or lights, when presented to the dog just before food was offered, continued to produce salivation without the actual introduction of food. In other words the dog learns a new association, or is subject to conditioned reflexes through association. The dog for example can salivate when a gong is sounded or a light shows. If however the food is not offered repeatedly, i.e. there is an absence of reinforcement, the signal will lose its effectiveness; in other words the reflex will be gradually extinguished. A great deal of human behaviour is an amalgam of conditioned reflexes. The child learns how to feel recognized, wanted and appreciated. Equally it can learn to feel ignored, rejected and disregarded.

Behaviour therapy has advanced sufficiently to be confident in claiming that a good deal of maladaptive or neurotic behaviour can be eliminated by associating the noxious feeling, thought or act with an opposite experience of relaxed, pleasant, welcoming sensation.

In the relationship of spouses conditioning techniques abound. On the negative side, a spouse can be presented repeatedly with signals of disapproval, rejection or indifference, and, if there is no strong and differentiated identity to oppose this systematic invalidation, these signals are accepted as an appropriate assessment of the self. Even if the spouse has some positive feelings for themselves, they can be systematically stripped of their self-esteem if their successful actions are not recognized (no reinforcement) and their unsuccessful ones are underlined. In this way new learning can be acquired which makes the spouse feel empty and impotent. Brainwashing is carried out in this way. The desired ideology is praised when learned and the previous beliefs ignored, ridiculed or dismissed. Many a spouse will complain bitterly of systematic diminution in the hands of their spouse, and this becomes a new multiplication of wounds.

On the positive side the behaviour therapy principles of extinction, reinforcement, new learning can all play a healing part. Excessive and repeated angry outbursts which are the result of a pattern of behaviour established in childhood and adolescence can be eliminated. Anger can be met with anger or alternatively an attempt can be made to understand its origin dynamically and ignore it behaviourally. Having understood the reason behind repetitive anger and met the underlying needs, repetitive anger can be extinguished by not reinforcing it with attention or even associating it with disapproval. This applies to other symptoms as well.

Anxiety in all its forms can be countered with relaxed security. Anxiety is present when a person is afraid of something, such as going out into open spaces (agoraphobia), staying in enclosed spaces (claustrophobia), meeting people in crowds (social phobia) or speaking up in company. These and many other examples can be gradually extinguished. The spouse who is not afraid gives their partner a sense of relaxed security by their presence during the dreaded situation of activity which is now undertaken for progressively longer periods. The spouse withdraws by stages and leaves the partner with their newly discovered freedom.

The withdrawn, frightened, undemonstrative person can be made to feel increasingly secure. Their spouse creates an atmosphere of relaxed proximity within which the partner can slowly lose their fear and acquire a new sense of courage to encounter people.

Guilt and shame associated with some past trauma can be replaced by self-forgiveness and acceptance as the spouse acts as an agent of forgiveness and acceptance. Here of course the activity of the forgiving spouse reminds us of God's unceasing forgiveness and recurrently fresh acceptance.

Spouses can also give each other the opportunity to promote self-esteem and self-acceptance. Negative feelings in this area are continously associated with positive ones and little by little the rejection of self is eradicated and replaced by acceptance.

Jealousy is a canker in the centre of self. It is to be found in triangular situations where, as already discussed, the predominant fear is that of loss, of losing the person we love or losing their love for us to somebody else. The insecure person is constantly threatened by the fear of loss. The spouse can gradually ensure, through reliable behaviour, that this fear is without foundation. They can teach their partner to trust without fearing that they will lose their loved one in the process. They can be reassured that they need not live in the grips of terror and competition to ensure that they keep their spouse. Every expression of doubt is ignored, gradually eliminating fear, and every intimation of trust reinforced. The same principles apply to envy, where one spouse compares themselves unfavourably to the other and is constantly struggling to equalize and if possible overtake their value. The partner can reassure their spouse that they are lovable as they are, however welcome their increase in stature may be. Repeated intimations of self-criticisms are ignored and any sign of worthiness reinforced vigorously.

The passive, frightened spouse who is scared to take any or special initiatives can be helped by being encouraged to do things he/she is frightened of. Inept activity is played down; success, however partial, is praised.

Recently a good deal of behaviour therapy has been applied to sexual problems. The work of Masters and Johnson[7] and Kaplan[8] show how difficulties such as premature ejaculation and impotence in the male, vaginismus, anorgasm, loss of libido in the female can be overcome. The spouses play a significant role in helping each other to relax, unlearn faulty habits and learn new approaches which restore sexual success. These techniques have made profound differences to sexual problems and have given hope to many.

Differences between dynamic and behaviour therapy

What is the difference between dynamic and behaviour therapy? Dynamic psychology requires that the patient uncovers the unconscious past whereas behaviour therapy is concerned with the removal of the presenting symptoms. According to behaviour therapy there is no need to trace the symptom to its roots, it simply needs eradicating. However sometimes the symptom cannot be eradicated unless its origin is recognized, hence what is usually used is a mixture of dynamic and behaviour therapy. Couples can take heart from the fact that psychotherapies are concerned increasingly with the transformation of the here and now situation, so they need not fear that skills beyond their capacity are required.

What is required is a sensitive awareness of the painful experiences of the spouse, the presence and absence of something that hurts. The hurtful presence can be gradually eliminated and replaced by something more acceptable and the omission can also be gradually filled with what is missing. The intimacy of contemporary marriage means that there exists between spouses the opportunity for a degree of trust and closeness for the application of both systems.

Spontaneous healing

Many people will claim experiences of healing when on their own, with others, during prayer, meditating or by being suddenly emotionally aroused. This can be the result of ecstasy, or what Maslow[9] calls a peak experience, when the whole being is aroused in a unity of heightened awareness of the reality of the surroundings, life and something beyond, the spiritual. These are moments of blinding revelation, penetrating insights, conversions. These are all apparently sudden awarenesses which have a profound effect on the individual. I use the word 'apparently' because it is possible that a great deal of thought and preparation has been going on unconsciously which reaches fruition suddenly. These kinds of experience have been described for a long time,[10,11,12] and they may transform

people like St Paul whose life took a totally new direction as a result
of such an experience.

There is no doubt that such sudden, though generally smaller,
insights are also experienced within marriage. Their exact nature
is poorly understood, but the quest for clarification, with or without
prayer, can be rewarded with instinctive flashes of truth, truth
about each other and about God who reigns over the whole family.

Miraculous healing

Apart from the miraculous, all the forms of healing described here
are the common experience of mankind, and all marriages share
these possibilities. The religious man goes beyond and enters the
dimension of conscious and deliberate communication with God.
This does not mean that all the previous forms of healing exist in
a God-vacuum. For the believer, all life is subject to God's everlasting presence and active sustenance. But there are some specific
channels for man's communication with God. Prayer is the supreme
example of this genre of interaction. In all ages there have been
special shrines where God's miraculous intervention is sought and
sometimes found. Seeking to understand the miraculous is an
attempt to reach the centre of God's person and find out his mysterious ways. Apart from the fact that these ways are steeped in
love, and wherever love exists God is present, our understanding
closes before the infinite.

For many people whose sense of God is fleeting, marital love and
its qualities of healing are one of the strongest signs of God's presence. It is not an accident that love is associated with superlative
and divine characteristics, or that, in the presence of its married
manifestation, husbands and wives approach the nature of God.
Healing in all its forms provides a powerful proof of the existence
of something which eclipses human effort.

The pentecostal movement is perhaps the most recent religious
development to remind Christians that God, prayer and healing are
a triad which forms the infrastructure of Christian life, illuminated
and perfused with the Holy Spirit. Marital healing in the form
described in this book is perhaps the commonest source of healing
in the community and once the principles outlined here are grasped

and promoted we have in contemporary marriage one of the most powerful sources of healing, where man, woman, God and love meet.

Summary

In the presence of a reliable and trusting relationship, couples disclose their wounds to one another, wounds which are often psychological in nature. These wounds are open to healing by dynamic, behaviouristic, spontaneous and miraculous means. This healing, which is probably the commonest in modern society, is a meeting between human and divine love and is a forceful factor of wholeness and holiness. It is a particular expression of love and the meeting ground of man and God within the family.

References (Chapter 5)

1. *Gaudium et Spes*, Part II, ch. 1. Chapman, 1967.
2. Freud, S., *Psychoanalytic Procedure*, vol.VII. Hogarth Press, 1968.
3. Ellenberger, H.F., *The Discovery of the Unconscious*. Allen Lane, 1970.
4. Beech, H.R., *Changing Man's Behaviour*. Penguin, 1969.
5. Wolpe, J., *Psychotherapy by Reciprocal Inhibition*. Stamford University Press (USA), 1958.
6. Pavlov, I.P., *Conditioned Reflexes*. Oxford University Press, 1927.
7. Masters, W.H. and Johnson, V.E., *Human Sexual Inadequacy*. Little Brown, Boston, 1970.
8. Kaplan, H.S., *The New Sex Therapy*. Penguin, 1974.
9. Maslow, A., *Religions, Values and Peak Experience*. Viking Press, New York, 1964.
10. James, W., *The Varieties of Religious Experience*. Longmans, New York, 1902.
11. Hardy, A., *The Biology of God*. Jonathan Cape, 1975.
12. Hardy, A., *The Spiritual Nature of Man*. Clarendon Press, 1979.

CHAPTER 6

Growth

One of the most recurrent criticisms of contemporary marriage is its current duration. In previous ages the life cycle for marriage was much shorter and parents usually died about the time their offspring reached marriageable age. Thus the cycle of life was marriage, rearing of the children, marriage of the children, death of parents. The main purpose of marriage and sexuality was to safeguard the wellbeing of the next generation, who in turn became parents.

Nowadays the life cycle of marriage is much longer. A duration of forty to fifty years of married life is no longer the exception. The critics of traditional marriage insist that it is not possible for two people to remain together for all these years without getting bored with each other. Children still unite the parents, but the modern couple postpone their childbearing for a few years and have some twenty years, after the children have left, during which they return to a one-to-one relationship. The critics say that this is not a formula for happiness but a prison sentence. These are advocates for serial marriages, short-term contracts renewable by both partners every five years. The length of modern marriage has introduced anxiety that a couple's ability to sustain and heal each other is limited and cannot extend over four to five decades. Religions which support the permanent commitment of marriage are being challenged to show how couples can remain married for so long and still realize their potential as fully as possible. On the whole the Judaeo-Christian tradition has faltered over the answer to this challenge. It proclaims permanency but says very little about how this is to be achieved. Clearly spouses are more likely to stay together if their human and spiritual needs are matched by opportunities of self-realization.[1,2]

When self-realization or actualization is mentioned, voices are raised that these are selfish, self-centred quests which should be circumscribed rather than encouraged. There is a different form of criticism which sees the primary task of spouses as parents and does not accept marriage as the institution for the realization of human potential. This view claims that too much is asked of modern marriage and the right answer is to curtail these ambitions and subordinate the self for the sake of the child.

It is perfectly true that children are demanding creatures and parents have to make sacrifices on their behalf. But ultimately the success of parenting depends on the quality of the personality and the more complete the wholeness of parents, the more likely it is that their children will derive the benefit of parental maturity. Thus self-realization is not a selfish pursuit; the children gain by the richness of the parents' potential. This self-realization or actualization is achieved through physical, intellectual, emotional, affective and spiritual growth.

Physical growth

The peak of physical growth occurs towards the end of the second decade[3] or the beginning of the third, when the body achieves its final physical configuration. From then onwards degeneration begins to set in, but this is not visible and when it occurs, as in the case of hardening of arteries (atheroma), the changes are minute and microscopic.

Thus people find themselves in their late teens and twenties at the peak of their physical potential. This potential can be converted into the physique of the athlete or the skill of the sportsman who achieves extraordinary feats e.g. visio-spatially as in golf. Such transformation needs hard work and discipline and often the spouse has to make sacrifices to make time available to the partner to reach and maintain these standards. This physical growth is not a matter of adding physical ingredients to the body but of realizing its potential in its functioning capacity. The crude and undifferentiated energy is converted into athletic prowess.

The body however is not only capable of developing in its absolute physical resources. The hand, eye and ear can combine with aesthetic resources to develop artistic skills of painting, drawing and music as well as knitting, dressmaking, modelling and other feats.

Finally the body is a sexually embodied reality. This sexual embodiment differentiates humanity and the couple. The sexual body is a central means by which the couple complement each other, and the way it is dressed, used and cared for remains important for the sexual communication of the couple.

Thus physical growth encompasses changes from the mere functional to the athletic, the descriptive to the artistic and the gender to the living sexual communication. Growth in all these aspects requires the motivation of the spouse and the affirmative support of the partner. The body grows, remains stable for long periods and then declines. Its growth is an increased awareness of its potential which remains part of the image of self even when overtaken by age. Old age is a time when the growth of the person should have reached a degree of maturity to give back little by little the gifts of the body to the creator. The gradual diminution is not a loss but a preparation for an awareness of self in relation to God in eternity. Old age is not a chain of destruction but a gradual surrender of experienced self which has become a permanent part of the inner world, so that the outward part of the self surrenders, leaving intact the inward awareness. It is this awareness which spans several decades and remains part of the relationship between spouses in old age and between the individual and God in the mystery of eternity prior to the general resurrection.

Intellectual growth

Just as physical growth reaches its acme towards the end of the second decade, so intellectual growth as measured by intelligence quotient reaches its peak at about the same time, with abstract or formal thinking predominating.[4]

Intelligence allows us to tackle concrete measurements of height, weight, size, shape, colour, distance, numerical values, visio-spatial arrangements, focus of part and whole, language and communication, thinking, both concrete and abstract, to reason and discern, to evaluate and integrate. We are constantly bombarded by sensory and abstract messages and, through the mediation of the brain which is responsible for our consciousness, we need to make sense of all that impinges from outside and inside ourselves and to act.

The translation of all this knowledge into wisdom is the continuous seeking of every person and becomes the collective wisdom of the community. Wisdom is not to be equated with absolute intelligence. Western tradition has hallowed intelligence and rationality, other cultures have taken other criteria, such as intuition, mysticism, feeling states, for their outstanding values. Reason and feeling the objective and the subjective, the concrete and the abstract, the immanent and the transcendent have vied for prominence as expression of the pinnacle of wisdom. Jung's psychology, which was an expression of his familiarity with western and eastern thought, has attempted to combine representative elements of both in the process he calls individuation.[5] 'To achieve wholeness in man as in the deity, the opposites are cancelled out; good and evil, conscious and unconscious, masculine and feminine, dark and light are raised to a synthesis symbolically expressed by the *coniunctio oppositorum.*' So that for Jung, wisdom is reached in a synthesis of the self's separate parts.

In the ordinary sense of the word 'wisdom' proclaims the evaluation of what is presented by intelligence, refined by culture and feelings. The collective wisdom of a culture is a standard by which individual predicaments are judged. Part of wisdom is to assess the received, from family, culture and religion and constantly reassess it in the light of personal experience. Movement of thought takes place when the received does not elicit a blind obedience but is judged according to the contemporary exigencies. Thus tension between the received and the innovatory exists not only in society but in every marriage.

Spouses are the inheritors of the collective wisdom of their society, culture and family upbringing. They bring to each other their intelligence and their unchallenged beliefs and myths. It is possible that one may try to impose their point of view on the other because no alternative tenets are tolerable. Such rigid and even paranoid persons can make an assault on the beliefs of their spouses and undermine their most sincerely held convictions. These convictions may be repeatedly derided, dismissed or ridiculed, the only ones tolerated being the views of the dominant spouse. This subjection to the spouse's view of life can go on for a long time until the suppressed spouse gains enough confidence to challenge and rebel against the mental stranglehold.

Such coercive biases are unusual. Usually spouses agree to disagree on some issue they cannot reconcile. Often they act as midwives to each other. A thought, idea, view is puzzled over inwardly without being elucidated. It is offered to the partner in a confused, unclarified state and their spouse can help them to bring order to the confusion. The ability of spouses to bring out of each other depths that were not recognized before depends on a growing awareness of each other's inner world, empathy with its contents and the ability to draw out of each other latent resources. This is the exact opposite of systematic diminution of each other whereby every fresh thought however minute is stamped upon as ridiculous or when the exchange is between two very bright people, who pull each other to pieces as they point out all the possible deficiencies in the other's arguments. This does not mean that constructive criticism is not needed. What is really required is a welcoming, affirmative reception.

The danger in the mutuality of intellectual growth is that one partner will operate principally via reason and the other intuitively and through feelings. One speaks with the mind and the other with the heart. This course can be one of collision; it can also be a complementary journey of mutual growth. The feeling person rounds off ideas predominated by reason, and the rational mind puts order into the feeling world and draws out the logical consequences. The combination of reason and feelings is a vital journey of maturation in which the couple can assist each other if their gifts are complementary.

Wisdom is slowly developed by trial and error. Knowledge of how things and people work often develops from the results of repeated alternative approaches. Spouses can help each other to minimize their errors as they share their gifts and give to each other the fruits of their experiences. This of course requires an attitude of mutual regard and respect and an avoidance of envy and competition whereby the acquisition of wisdom is used to show up the deficiency of the other.

Wisdom is also an expression of increasingly correct anticipation and interpretation of situations and people. Taking risks, saying things at the right moment, judging responses accurately, evaluating correctly what can be expected from life and other people without exaggeration (too much optimism) or cynicism (too much pessimism) and above all having an increasing trust in one's resources realistically appraised – these are all ingredients of wisdom. This wisdom is repeatedly tested within the confines of the home where mistakes can be made with confidence that the consequences will not be disastrous.

Thus the way the self and others are experienced, the way knowledge is used, the expectations from actions, the speed with which lessons are learned, the courage to try the new and accurate self-reflection, all aid the process of mutual illumination. This mutual illumination is not of course confined to the home, but it can receive its most constant and powerful reinforcement there.

The description so far refers to growth in the use of available resources. Increasingly it is recognized that new knowledge can be acquired at a later stage than the traditional learning years. Both men and women can take courses for the first time in their thirties or forties, particularly with the assistance of their spouse. This applies particularly to wives who go to college for the first time after their children have grown up. These mature students approach their subject with a considerable practical wisdom and they combine their academic learning with a practical knowledge of life which may make them particularly successful students.

Finally, as with healing, wisdom can be the product of sudden insights which can come in a flash in any situation, during sleep, in a dream or at the conclusion of some penetrating meditation. This insight is not confined to the married, but the married have the advantage of immediate sharing and testing the contents with their spouse.

Emotional growth

Some of the major changes in the personality which impinge seriously on the marital relationship are changes from dependence to independence, identity confusion to differentiation, and self-rejection to self-esteem.

Dependence

The growing child, adolescent and young person have realized a sufficiency of physical and intellectual growth to establish themselves in the world of adults. But their emotional development is often much less than complete. Dependence is one of the principal features of childhood. Dependence then is physical, social, intellectual, emotional and spiritual. Physical and intellectual dependence recede as the adult's physical and intellectual resources are now sufficient to negotiate life. Social and emotional resources are not always in tune with the other areas of growth. Young people have to leave home and establish themselves in a new social milieu and become acclimatized. After experiencing several new social settings, sufficient social skills are developed at work, with friends and in recreation to handle these requirements.

Emotional growth occurs at a variable pace but is often far behind the other developments. The growth from dependence to independence often occurs in the first decade of marriage with marked implications for the relationship of the couple. Basically one or both spouses continue to experience the other as a parental figure. The husband looks upon the wife as a mother or the wife looks upon the husband as a father. Sometimes the actual parent was not particularly endearing or close and the spouse is treated with substitute idealization. They are made to be the missing loving parent.

Dependence means that the spouse concerned uses their partner as a prop or crutch. Decisions are referred to the spouse, initiatives are not taken without permission, approval is sought on thoughts, acts, ideas, and these are shaped according to the dominant partner's ideology. Most of the life of the dependent person takes its cues from the partner who conducts the essentials for both. Such dependence often means that the couple are very close to each other. There is what is known technically as a symbiotic relationship. Two people live as if they were one and that one is often the predominant personality.

But with the passage of time the dependence lessens. Maturation begins to occur and the dependent person gradually starts to become less dependent on their spouse. They are now prepared to think, feel, see, act, take risks, on their own account. The important step is that they are no longer afraid to feel in the wrong and are able to learn from their mistakes. The anxiety of being mistaken is no longer overwhelming. A gradual sense of freedom begins to percolate throughout the personality and the consequences are that the dependent person ceases to idealize and follow the partner and begins to establish their own boundaries, develop the courage and strength to stand on their own two feet and utilize their own available resources. Such changes will affect the marital relationship and can make or break it. The partner who has acted as the parental figure will need to adjust to a relationship of equality of worth. Most spouses can do that but some find it difficult to give up their headship and power structure, and severe conflict may follow.

Identity confusion

Part of the reason why emotional dependence is maintained is that the husband or wife are not clear about their identity. They are not clear about their resources and work potential, about their femininity or masculinity, their priorities in terms of earning an income or experiencing life, their spiritual values, their commitments to their parents, friends, colleagues, and, above all, about the meaning of life. Many a young person will confront and challenge one about the meaning of life. 'Tell me why I should go on living?'[6] 'What's the point of it all?' One of the dangers is that in this undifferentiated state of identity confusion, men and women get married in the hope that a ring on their finger will give them the social identity of the married which will at least allow them a standing in the community.

Gradually this confusion begins to clarify itself. After several trials of different types of work something begins to make sense and fits in with the attributes of the person. Little by little they can accept their sexuality and rejoice in its presence. They may have married on the basis that they were fortunate to find anyone who wanted them, now they realize some of their worth and feel that they deserve a richer personality as their partner. Their spiritual values in terms of material versus aesthetic pursuits, their ability to remain constant in friendship, to appreciate others, to be interested in their welfare, all this begins to become far more clear. Little by little the meaning and value of life begins to assume some order with a sense of the immanent, the here and now, and the transcendent beginning to play an important part in the life of the individual.

Such differentiation within the self which orders and accepts the meaning of the body and its sexual gender, intelligence with its potential, the various relationships with different degrees of commitment and an emergence of the meaning of life as something which is possessed by the self is growth from identity confusion to self-possession. This differentiation inevitably means that marriage can be rejected as the sole source of meaning. It is a development which taxes a great deal the abilities of spouses to adapt to each other for, in the course of this development, the personality changes to a considerable degree and in some instances it can be truly said that the person who married changes completely in the next few years. Spouses have to adapt to each other's gradual transformations but it is not surprising that such major alterations in identity may be incompatible with the continuation of a marriage.

Self-esteem

Dependence on another person, coupled with uncertainty regarding the meaning of life, combine to give a sense of inferiority. Such people feel empty and confused and their inner world is constantly transmitting messages of uncertainty. As a person gradually withdraws from the influence of dependence and begins to possess themselves, their self-esteem rises. They feel now a sense of clear boundaries between themselves and others and are no longer afraid of being absorbed within the orbit of parents, spouse or dominant friend. This esteem means that they are increasingly aware of their resources and can begin the process of donating parts of themselves, in and through love to others. Equally they can begin to receive messages of love from others.

The processes of change from dependence to independence, confusion to clarity of identity, from self-rejection to self-acceptance can go on from the twenties, right through to the forties and sometimes the fifties. These are changes which profoundly affect marriage, for the relationship between spouses must change if it is to accommodate the emergent self of the partner. Such changes are accepted and adapted to in the course of a marriage which becomes enhanced in quality by the encounter of equals who can dialogue with each other on a basis of loving equity. As might be expected and as will be developed in Chapter 11, these changes which are able to transform marriages can also destroy them, if one spouse finds it impossible to change or accept the change in their partner.

Affective growth

The fact that an essential part of the affective or feeling life is the ability of the spouses to recognize, want and appreciate each other has been mentioned. This is one of the deepest layers of love and requires discipline, effort and sacrifice to achieve. But how is this deepening of love to occur? There are certain aspects of affective communication which increase the capacity to love. These are the processes of listening, responding, reducing criticism, increasing affirmation, and forgiving with appropriate reparation.

Listening

Listening with care is an art which can go on being developed until the end of life. Essentially the listening has to go beyond words to the feeling meaning behind them. The intellectual, factual, concrete meanings of words are not usually difficult to grasp. What is more demanding is the multiple layers of meaning which are conveyed. Thus it is vital to listen with care, without interruption, judgement and advice until the message is completed. It is of paramount importance that the teller feels that he/she has been received comprehensively. Throughout this book references are made repeatedly to the danger of listening only in a reasoning way and omitting to receive the affective or feeling communication.

Part of the growth of love is to listen to the whole person and receive their message with as much depth as possible. This is where sometimes the listener becomes a midwife, who delivers the meaning of what is being said, even though their partner is not fully clear what they are trying to say. It is important of course that such delivery brings forth the inner world of the speaker and does not simply reflect the approach of the listener who interprets all that is heard through their own feelings. The ability to listen and do justice to the originality of the message, neither ignoring nor misinterpreting it, is an important element of receiving another person.

Sometimes a hurt individual is afraid to express their views or needs in case they are rejected as they were in childhood. Such a person expects their spouse to read them accurately in silence and anticipate the contents of their inner world. Such expectation is part of the spouse's hope that if they are really loved then their message will be read accurately before it is pronounced. It is one of the hardest tasks of love to care with penetrating anticipation just as the good mother seems always to know what her child needs without having to be told. 'If you loved me you would really know me,' meaning that the spouse should know what is going on in the inner world of their partner and respond appropriately.

Sometimes conversation is no dialogue at all because the listener is not attending to the details manifested by speech and feeling but is simply waiting for the other person to cease so that he/she can start. The only good part about this exchange is that the spouse does not interrupt. But in practice there is no listening here. An interval is created to be followed by showing the partner where they have gone wrong with judgement and advice.

Such a dialogue is one of mutual deafness. Neither party is listening in depth, or indeed listening at all. Such people will swear that they love their spouse but over the crucial exchange of listening, they cannot receive the inner world of their partner. They may be afraid that new demands will be made of them or that they may have to change their way of life.

Of course not all listening is a matter of grave exchange. Spontaneous reflection, answers and advice are given at frequent intervals, and so they should be. But these spontaneous exchanges are not to be confused with the more significant ones when something vital is at stake. Listening in these circumstances is trying to recognize the depths of the partner and assist them to reach their own conclusions. Careful listening which is intent on facilitating the emergence of the spouse is a very special form of love. Married people in distress often complain that they cannot talk to one another, and this makes them feel exceedingly lonely in the midst of apparent plenitude of receptivity.

Responding

Response is not primarily concerned with a rational answer. The right answer, however welcome, is secondary to the feeling which needs to be conveyed that at that moment in time the speaker has the undivided attention of the listener. Cultivating this ability of listening with care is a development which may challenge couples over a long time, but feeling that one has been listened to carefully is equivalent to the experience of being received as a person. So in listening to others we have to receive them as whole persons. Married couples learn, little by little, the art of concentrated listening on those occasions when it is necessary, distinguishing them from the daily routine exchanges.

Whenever careful listening is carried out, there emerges one powerful anxiety, that it may not be possible to give the correct answer. The response of the loving partner however is not judged by the giving of accurate advice. Rather the listening spouse acts as a mirror and the speaker sees himself/herself in a different light. The very act of speaking gives the partner access to a new insight. These new insights are not found in every dialogue. What is often achieved by the careful responder is a deeper awareness of their partner's inner world which breaks down isolation and loneliness and brings the couple closer together.

Responding sensitively means that sometimes the partner, who knows there is something wrong, has to bide their time. This is another anxiety in responding. There is an urge to speed up communication and allow the listener to intervene meaningfully. Patience is needed however until the partner is ready to reveal a particular part of themselves. Patience is another expression of love. If we see something clearly in our partner we want to tell them about it. But a hurried interpretation may simply open up all sorts of anxieties which our spouse is not ready to cope with. Thus a careful response is not necessarily one which reveals all that is felt by the listener. He or she may have to wait until the right time comes for interpretive disclosure. Many a spouse tells their partner what is wrong, after having listened to them, but fails to appreciate that their spouse is not ready to act on the interpretation.

Responding accurately means that the speaker feels received with as much understanding as possible. It means that burdens of corrective action or insight are not imposed without support or before the spouse is emotionally ready to tackle a particular issue. Interpreting at the right time is vital for all emotional dialogue, and not least for spouses who need to make each other feel that they really understand.

Criticism

Reference has already been made as to how frequently couples communicate with each other on the basis of mutual criticism. The failings of one act as the strength of the other and vice versa. A balance of frailty is established which leaves little room for any superiority. The partners retain an equilibrium of love dependent on their mutual inadequacies. Such love is very limited indeed, when it is primarily concerned with giving comfort to failure.

Growth of loving feelings means that mutual criticism recedes. Love is no longer a question of loving the inadequate. Inadequacy will always be present, but one way of reducing it is to ignore its manifestations and praise achievement.

Affirmation

Praising achievement is a reward for activity and results. This appreciation of the active part of the spouses is important. Far more important however is the affirmation of the person, who is unconditionally accepted with all their strengths and weaknesses. There are few relationships that reveal so much as that of spouses. Within a matter of years they can come to know each other very well. This knowledge will certainly reveal many limitations but at the same time will also show the strengths which exist and are in the process of being achieved. Affirmation confirms the attained and propels the spouse towards that which is about to be realized. Affirmation is vital for both.

Thus affirmation gradually ensures that the self-esteem of the spouse is both consolidated and expanded. The more love is shared by the couple, the greater is their strength to urge each other affirmatively. When hurt, their sense of goodness is large enough to overcome the pain and diffuse it. There is a constant battle in each one of us between good and bad experiences and whether the good will be overwhelmed by the bad. The value of affirmation is that the genuine love of self is increased and so the bad is absorbed and integrated by the good instead of the bad extinguishing the good.

Couples depend a great deal on each other for achieving the right balance.

Forgiveness

However good the listening, response and affirmation may be, it is inevitable that from time to time hurtful things will be said and done. With the passage of time these episodes should diminish as the couple get to know each other's vulnerable spots. But anger and misunderstanding can never be completely obliterated. When hurt has been caused, forgiveness and reparation are the natural sequences. Such forgiveness is not a shallow, superficial sign but a genuine response to the person who seeks it. Forgiveness can be offered and yet the misdeed is remembered and brought out at recurrent intervals to remind the spouse of their past conduct. This is not genuine forgiveness but the development of a hold over the spouse.

Sometimes the hurt spouse refuses to be pacified and withdraws into a sulk which can last for hours, days or even weeks. The refusal to accept repentance and reparation is a refusal to be human. Often it is the same person who sulks or never apologizes, whatever they have done. It is always the partner who has to initiate reconciliation. Such patterns are inimical to love and contribute to marital breakdown.

Genuine forgiveness between spouses is a sign of deep love and a reminder of the constant forgiveness that we receive from God. Human forgiveness is a channel of understanding divine love. It is a meeting between the human and divine in which the former is transformed by the latter. As the years pass by, the conflicts between the partners diminish and, on the occasions when they occur, forgiveness has a quality of depth which reflects and symbolizes the divine mercy.

Spirituality

The spiritual growth of spouses is essentially in their progress of love with each other, their children and others. This human love reflects the divine, and all the characteristics mentioned participate in an ever-deepening realization. But the awareness that this human love is a reflection of the divine brings the spouses in direct encounter with the source of all love, God. God is encountered by the developing personality, and gradually the mystery of persons in the Trinity is reached but never penetrated. The mystery is the complementary relationship of love between autonomous persons who are separate and one at the same time. Marriage gives some hint of the complementarity of two persons, a man and woman who are separate and yet from time to time become one. Marriage and the family as a community of love reflects the covenant relationship between God and man and directs the gaze to the central mystery of the Trinity where love permeates to differentiate and unite. So in marriage love differentiates and unites and the spouses grow in an awareness of God's immanent presence in their midst and his transcendence which is the ground of love for every spouse and every marriage.

Summary

Beyond sustaining and healing, a couple continue to grow over several decades. This growth transforms body into athletic and aesthetic physique, mind into wisdom, affect into deepening love. Communication is at the heart of affective growth which, by affirmation, facilitates the love of self and the most precious neighbour, the spouse. As parents they convey their love to their children.

References (Chapter 6)

1. Maslow, A.H., *Motivation and Personality*. Harper, New York, 1954.

2. Maslow, A.H., *Towards a Psychology of Being*. Van Nostrand, New York, 1962.

3. Smart, M.S. and Smart, R.C., *Children*. Collier-Macmillan, 1972.

4. Maier, H.W., *Three Theories of Child Development*. Harper and Row, New York, 1969.

5. Moreno, A., *Jung, Gods and Modern Man*. Sheldon Press, 1974.

CHAPTER 7

Permanence as Continuity, Reliability and Predictability

The contemporary onslaught on permanent commitments seems directly counter to the traditional view that evolving commitment is the appropriate form for marriage. This concept of permanence derives its roots from the Old and the New Testaments.[1] Permanence is symbolic of the covenant relationship between God and his people and is a constant challenge to the Judaeo-Christian tradition. During the period of the Old Testament divorce, however unwelcome, was permitted, and the New Testament left ambiguities which left open the door for some dissolutions and remarriages. In fact there has been a constant tension between permanence and divorce to this very day, and the reasons for permanence versus transience need constant re-examination. This will be carried out here in terms of continuity, reliability and predictability.

Continuity

One of the principal reasons for continuity of the marital relationship is the presence and care of children. Few would disagree that children need the continuous presence of their parents when they are growing up. Evidence for this has been offered in Chapter 3. The continuity of the presence of parents ensures that during their early years children are not subjected to frequent changes of significant attachments, but are allowed to identify with the masculine and feminine part of the parents from whom they receive socialization, stimulus to intellectual growth, physical care and emotional growth. The critics of marriage proclaim that children can be looked after by society[2] or by any caring adult. Cooper summarizes this thought in these words: 'We don't need mother and father any more. We only need mothering and fathering.'[3] It is up to the critics to show that their alternatives work consistently over a long time. No such evidence exists, and the successful communes throughout the world, and particularly those in Israel, maintain close contact between parents and children. The most widely prevailing view is that children need the continuing presence of their parents in their critical years of growth.

But what happens nowadays when people marry young and their children become grown up while the parents are still in their late thirties or early forties? And why should couples who have no children follow the same principle of permanence? The change in family construction, with the ensuing reduction in and early completion of the desired size, has raised new questions about permanency.

The three previous chapters devoted to sustaining, healing and growth have focused on the inward dynamics of the marital relationship. That is to say, in the depths of marriage there are requirements which demand the continuity of presence of the spouses, apart from their role as parents.

The art of sustaining means that the couple need continuity to learn each other's particular emotional anxieties which need special support. Gradually this support is taken for granted and the conditions are ripe for healing. Healing certainly needs continuity. Time is needed to feel secure, to expose one's wounds and receive healing. This is an exchange that takes place over years, and interruption often means that the process has to restart from the beginning. Growth is a journey of mutual exploration in which two people unfold their personalities and gradually learn the developing self of their partner. These three processes, of their very nature, need continuity. If this is the case, why do we have so many divorces?

The answer is that as the partners reach a particular phase of mutual negotiation their resources fail and instead of moving forward together, they begin to experience the partner as an obstacle. This is where motivation, persistence and awareness of the nature of the problem can combine to help them persevere with the challenge; where motivation is lacking they may give up and start afresh with someone else.

At the very centre of permanence is a precious truth, that continuity spares as much as possible the discarding of human beings, the partner as an object that can no longer be loved because we can no longer make sense of them. The covenant relationship reminds us that God never ceases to make sense of us by persistent love. We too need continuity to make sense of our partner. But, say the critics, continuity can simply be a dead relationship where nothing happens except two people co-existing behind a facade of social togetherness. Clearly the covenant relationship has to be animated by love, and continuity has meaning when the couple engage with each other, however minimally. But what if they cannot do even this?

Separation and divorce are available in all western societies with a few exceptions, such as the Republic of Ireland which does not have divorce. If divorce is chosen and a second marriage embarked on, the new relationship has to start afresh. All that has gone on in the life of the previous marriage is virtually excluded in the new one. So much is lost because it cannot be transferred to the new relationship. So many shared moments of discovery, disappointment, triumph, are locked inside the two people who have to start anew. So much human love is interred because it makes no sense to the new partner. But surely it is better to try afresh and have some sort of relationship than remain in a dead one; this is the appeal of divorce and remarriage. But intrinsic to the situation there is a loss, a loss of all the common experience of the first relationship. Whilst a second chance through divorce has its attraction for the adults (children are faced with different sets of difficulties), a relationship of continuity, however hard, keeps within the original relationship all the promise, effort, hard work, sacrifice and achievement. Neither person's endeavour is lost.

In order for continuity to be fruitful in negotiating the social and psychological depths of contemporary marriage, the understanding of permanency has to change from a blind commitment to an ever-living one which engages every part of the couple in realizing their sustaining, healing and growth.

Reliability

Continuity can be simply the maintenance of outward characteristics which do not engage the inner world of the couple. Continuity can be apathetic indifference to the world of the other or simply a convenient social and economic arrangement devoid of personal meaning. It can be a mutual dependence of infantile needs that have never been outgrown. But, granted that continuity is a life-giving encounter, the association of two persons alone is not enough. Sustaining, healing and growth need continuity but also reliability.

The divine covenant has the feature of God's reliability. Human covenants do not have such absolutes, but human behaviour must strive towards reliability if it is to remain authentic.

One of the key needs of the child is to have a framework of continuity within which key figures are reliable. They need to be reliable in the messages they utter, in their responses and in the way words and actions coincide. If parents say one thing and do another; if they promise something and deliver something else, or worse nothing at all; then the child becomes confused and its level of anxiety rises.

The same applies to spouses. A certain degree of reliability has to prevail. Spouses need to know that promises are meant and will be fulfilled, need to believe that what is proclaimed will be the general target for achievement; need to know that the utterances of each other are not empty boasts. Spouses are expected to be reliable in their work, their promises, their presence at the right time and right place, and to be honest. Just as God in his covenant with man acts in a reliable manner, so spouses need this quality in relation to each other.

But reliability is a quality which can lead to ossification and stagnation. It can lead to extremes of conservatism, where nothing is tried or allowed to happen, where change is taboo and reliability becomes a monotonous repetition. This type of behaviour is more akin to the rigidity of the obsessional personality. Such a person does not have the freedom to alter. Routine is the only safeguard against the anxiety of chaos. Such a spouse gradually becomes a bore who will not try anything new and is always finding fault and danger in innovation.

True reliability is not the dead hand of rigidity. Rather it springs from loving concern which ensures that the needs of the spouse are met. If the spouse is unduly anxious, then reliability by letting them know where one is, what is happening, avoiding prolonged absences without communication, helps to ensure that the fears of the partner are kept to a minimum.

But above all reliability is the part of love that will not fail to

answer when called. It means that the partners have created a
world for each other which ensures a loving presence no matter
what the difficulties or upheavals may be. Love is indicated by
reliable availability which can be called upon in all circumstances
just as God's love remains reliably available for mankind at all
times. So a loving reliability is, together with continuity, an essential
component of permanence.

Predictability

People can remain reliable in their love and yet be most unpredictable in the way they show it. Spouses expect a certain amount of
predictable behaviour from each other. The day is a structured
round of meals, work, care of children, leisure and other domestic
requirements. It is humanly impossible to construct continuously
new timetables, new patterns of behaviour. We come to anticipate
our spouse's behaviour with some accuracy. Our security, safety
and basic functioning depend on such predictable behaviour. We
need to know where we are and approximately what can be expected
from each other. In this way we can plan our lives with some degree
of certainty.

But once again inflexible predictability can destroy spontaneity
and the possibility of change, both of which are needed in the
expression of love. We all like pleasant surprises just as we hate
unexpected trouble. Predictability must not be the enemy of innovation in personal relationships, indeed a degree of uncertainty
gives pleasant surprise. The surprise may be expressed in a change
of job, house, different meal, different ways of showing appreciation,
but in a form that maintains curiosity and keeps discovery alive.
The same applies in our relationship with God; it has continuity
and reliability, but God's ways of responding to men are unique
and mysterious. The only thing that is predictable is that there will
be a response, its manner is part of the wonder of the covenant
between God and man.

Summary

Part of contemporary western society sees permanent commitment as a kind of yoke which imprisons couples in marriages which bury them alive. The bias against vows and commitment is a reflection of the increasing awareness that people change and as a result need new beginnings.

Because the Judaeo-Christian tradition has depended heavily on understanding marriage as a bond reflecting the covenant relationship between God and man channelled largely into the care of children, it has found it difficult to justify permanence now that children can no longer be regarded as the sole reason for marriage. But there is no incompatibility between authentic human and divine ways. When the possibilities of the modern companionship marriage are examined, it is found that sustaining, healing and growth need a framework of permanence lived as continuity, reliability and predictability. Instead of these characteristics being seen as destructive of human happiness, they are in fact the ground on which modern marriage thrives. In order for contemporary marriage to attain its expectations it needs permanency as the background within which couples and their children realize their potential but this potential needs to be clearly visualized and understood. It calls for effort, motivation and sacrifice from the couples, and for them to be supported by the whole community.

The permanence of the covenant between God and man applies yesterday, today and tomorrow. It does not alter. What is needed is to find the corresponding human dynamism; in sustaining, healing and growth we have a triad, backed by permanency, that has mobilized public expectation of marriage in this century and which reflects authentic human being.

References (Chapter 7)

1. Atkinson, D., *To Have and to Hold*. Collins, 1979.
2. Millett, K., *Sexual Politics*. Rupert Hart-Davis, 1971.
3. Cooper, D., *The Death of the Family*. Allen Lane, 1971.

CHAPTER 8

Sexuality

The relationship of married permanence, lived in continuity, reliability and predictability and tending towards sustaining, healing and growth has a central experience which unites the spouses in and through sexuality. The encounter of husband and wife is an embodied one. Their bodies and their masculinity and femininity are constant factors in the interchange between them. Sexuality is not confined to sexual intercourse but is a constant accompaniment of the relationship of the couple. The history of sexuality does not begin in puberty when genital sex becomes possible. Its roots are to be found at the very beginning of life from the time a boy or girl is conceived. This growth of the gender of the person, with all the social acquisition of what is regarded as appropriate for the two sexes, defines a great deal of how sexual life will be conducted later on. Placing the origins of sexuality at the very beginning of life is an important step for Judaeo-Christian thinking, in which the rules and regulations have been almost entirely concerned with adult genitality. Part of the contemporary controversy about sexual ethics lies in the fact that most of the force of tradition is allied to genital considerations, whereas sexuality begins much earlier in infancy and childhood.

The sex of the child is determined by genetic factors which in turn gradually shape parts of the brain which establish the correct hormone basis for the growth of the internal and external organs appropriate for each sex. By the time the baby is born its sex is clearly established and, with rare exceptions, there is no mistaking whether it is a boy or girl.

In the childhood years there are two prominent processes which further develop human sexuality. The first is the socialization of the child in its sexual gender. Societies allocate to each sex cultural features which begin to separate boys from girls from the very start of their lives. The way the sexes are dressed, the games they play,

the behaviour expected of them, begin slowly to differentiate attitudes and expectations.

It is in this area that a great social revolution is occurring.
Women are determined that the upbringing of girls will not be
narrow and confine them to the role of home-makers, childbearers
and, in general, assistants to men. There is a profound seeking of
equality of worth in upbringing even though roles may be complementary. At the extreme end of this attitude lies the belief that
women can do anything that men do, with childbearing being their
only specific function. Even here there are scientific researches into
test-tube babies which may make the womb unnecessary. We are
of course a long way from such happenings but the ideology of
equity is very strong.

The Judaeo-Christian tradition, which has been heavily conserv-
ative, need not be afraid of these developments. There is good
scriptural evidence that equality of worth is God's design for humanity. In the first account of Genesis the creation of man is
described.

> God created man in the image of himself,
> in the image of God he created him,
> male and female he created them. (Gen. 1:27)

In this opening declaration men and women are created in the
image of God and there is no fundamental distinction of value
between them. Both sexes are created in the image of God and there
is established from the very beginning of time a basic equality of
worth. In the New Testament Paul declares: 'All baptised in Christ,
you have all clothed yourselves in Christ, and there are no more
distinctions between Jew and Greek, slave and free, male and female, but all of you are one in Christ Jesus' (Gal. 3:27-8).

It may be no exaggeration to draw attention to the fact that,
despite Paul's various contentious remarks about women, he truly
understood their basic equality and worth in Christ and, as already
mentioned, he deserves to be made the patron of the Christian
movement of emancipation. It is true that only in our day and time
are the conditions ripe for realizing this truth, but the truth has not
been discovered by the modern world. It lay buried in the treasury
of Judaeo-Christian thought, and modern times are appropriate for
its implementation.

The upbringing of boys and girls in their expected masculine and
feminine gender should not contain an element of hierarchical sub-

ordination. The complementarity of the sexes is a matter of function
not of allocation of prime and secondary worth.

Childhood therefore is an important time of preparation for the
sexual gender or role of the sexes, and the home has a principal
responsibility in this matter. It is here that children receive their
first model through the way their parents live their lives, and inevitably they will absorb much of the way the parents act their sexual
roles. But this does not mean that the adult's future will be a simple
copy of their parental patterns. Other influences such as friends,
relatives, teachers, the media and society as a whole will exert their
influence.

The growth of sexual gender proceeds throughout the first and
second decades. Independently of this social phenomenon, there is
according to Freud an infantile sexuality which proceeds concur-
rently with the gender development. According to Freud the personality is influenced and shaped according to the influences of
sexuality and aggression. Neither of them are adult acquisitions.
They exist in early childhood and the course of the development of
these instincts is intimately related to the affective and sexual
growth of the individual.

Reference has already been made to this infantile development of
sexuality.[1] Freud maintains that infantile sexuality, or libido, is an
instinct which is focused in different parts of the anatomy called the
erotogenic zones. First there is an oral phase in which the mouth
is the prominent site of pleasure. The mouth and lips are lined with
smooth skin which gives pleasurable sensations when touched. The
baby concentrates on the mouth during the oral phase in the first
year of life. Then libidinal emphasis shifts to the anus and defecation
becomes pleasurable because the anus, like the mouth, is lined with
similar smooth skin. Finally the libido settles on the phallic zone
and the young boy has also to resolve the so-called Oedipus complex. This means that he has to abandon his sexual quest of mother
and, at the risk of being castrated (in phantasy), he turns to the
father and begins thereafter to identify with his masculine traits.

The close attachment of son to mother makes it likely that he will
learn a great deal of what femininity means, and some sexual
abnormalities are directly related to the boy's identification with his
mother, her affective and ordinary life becoming learned experiences
of the boy who continues to live through them, instead of moving
more closely to the father. 'Mother's boy' has entered our everyday
language and contains a truth that boys can identify more closely

with the mother and develop feminine attributes which may cause future difficulties in terms of homosexuality, fetishes, transvestism and transsexuality.[2,3] All these, except homosexuality, are rare conditions. The girl has to detach herself from the attraction which binds her to her father and identify with her mother. The ordinary proximity of mother and daughter makes this transfer of attachment easier. Freud maintains that after the age of five there is a latent period until puberty arrives, during which there is no further sexual development. But clearly, since sex is part of the embodied development of the person, the school years are a vital part of interpersonal encounter. During the school years and prior to puberty sexual growth consists of an increasing awareness of the body and the girl–boy relationship.

Puberty brings the secondary sexual characteristics. For the girl this means enlargement of breasts and menstruation, for the boy, growth of the genitals, male distribution of hair including the beard, a change in the voice and either spontaneous or induced orgasm with ejaculation of semen.

Adolescence

Puberty and adolescence overlap. Adolescence spans about a decade from around twelve or fourteen to the early twenties. These are the years characterized by further education, initiation into work, separation from home and establishment of relationships with the opposite sex. The establishment of heterosexuality is surrounded with much anxiety regarding the possibility of premarital intercourse. Traditionally the Judaeo-Christian tradition has condemned fornication, or premarital intercourse. The grounds for objection have been hitherto the safeguarding of life and care of the child, which needs a family structure. Furthermore the casual act of intercourse caused the loss of physical virginity which in previous times, and today in many parts of the world, is a serious loss.

These sexual principles, which were primarily centred on the needs of the child and the value of the wife, have altered radically in recent times. Widespread birth control has brought conception within men and women's control and virginity is no longer prized as something of great value. In the face of these alterations Christ-

ianity finds it difficult to put forward a readily understood case for
the continuation of premarital sexual abstinence. The care of the
child remains paramount and there is evidence that the use of
contraceptives is not uniform. Young people still have intercourse
impulsively without taking precautions. Overall however the number of women who had intercourse with their future husband[4] and
had not used contraceptives dropped in Britain from 38 per cent in
those marrying between 1956 and 1960 to 15 per cent in those
marrying between 1971 and 1975. Thus increasingly care is taken,
in having intercourse, to avoid pregnancy. Hence the value of premarital abstinence must be examined carefully and afresh.

First of all it is necessary not to pool together all premarital
sexual intercourse on the principle that the act is taking place out
of marriage. A much better classification is the type of relationship
which is present between the participants. Promiscuous behaviour
is defined by the absence of any relationship. There is simply a
meeting of bodies. Transient relationships are those in which the
couple get to know each other over a few days or even weeks prior
to intercourse. Here there is a slightly deeper encounter but it is
still a long way from a full one. Trial marriages have an even closer
link, but live on the understanding that the partners can go their
separate ways, and this prevents a wholehearted openness of each
to the other. Finally there are permanent relationships without a
marriage ceremony. Here the public dimension of the relationship
is denied. In some way all these relationships are incomplete.

Every sexual act has biological, social and psychological com-
ponents; biologically there is the realization of pleasure and the
possibility of initiating life; socially there is a declaration of the
existence of some type of relationship and psychologically there is
an encounter of mind, body and feelings. 'What is needed is a value
system of love which conceives human relationships as involving
the interaction of whole persons encountering mind, body and feelings in each other. When mind and feelings and particularly the
latter are ignored, there is a diminution of wholeness of both partners and therefore an inevitable dehumanization in the exchange.'[5]

The ethical ideal is to ensure that love is expressed fully and this
fullness is only met in a private and public declaration of commitment (of marriage) in which body, intellect and feelings are united
in an authentic personal encounter, open to life. The reason for
confining sex to marriage is to surround it with the appropriate
conditions which will engage the whole person in an exchange of

life-giving extending from the biological through to the social, intellectual and psychological. The deficiency of all other relationships is to be found in the fact that these encounters engage less than the whole person. But how many sexual acts even in marriage engage the whole person? This is a justified criticism, but human frailty must not become a norm. The norm has a richness which can only be captured by degrees. The traditional teaching safeguards this richness, now with fundamentally different reasons. These are not manufactured to preserve the teaching; rather they serve as the human possibilities which involve the whole and not the partial.

Sex in marriage

What defines marriage is a mutual private and public commitment of total availability of self in relationships which aim at life-giving. This life is found in children and in the enhancement of the quality of being of the partners. Partners meet constantly as embodied sexual beings who intereact according to their gender, role and upbringing and at intervals unite genitally. Clearly where new life is desired sexual intercourse has a special meaning. But what happens when new life is not initiated and birth regulation is used? Further, what is the meaning of the act when intercourse continues after the menopause or when the couple is infertile? Here traditional explanations are very weak indeed. They refer to the value of love in intercourse, the value of oneness, of uniting of persons, but these are broad hints which do not specify the meaning of intercourse as procreation did in the past.

During sexual intercourse the couple reduce their boundaries until they fuse into one and indeed become one. This is an intimacy which reminds us of the absolute closeness between baby and mother in which the body conveys a whole world of meaning. This world is not lost in adult intercourse. The intense preoccupation with the genitals has taken away emphasis from the fact that the oneness of coitus renews afresh trust, security and the sense of being recognized, wanted and appreciated.

Sexual intercourse is thus a body language. It is a language which embraces the gender and genitality of each spouse. As masculine and feminine persons the couple come together to prepare each other for intercourse. The body is caressed and kissed, feelings of appreciation expressed and gradually tension rises which calls for genital union and ultimate orgasmic relief. The care with which intercourse is undertaken is part of the life-giving to each other. There are numerous complaints of hasty, ill-prepared, uncaring acts which repudiate love. This is what critics of marriage seize on. They maintain that all Christianity is concerned with is to confine intercourse to marriage with little concern about its quality. By and large this criticism has been justified. There has been no parallel tradition emphasizing the quality of sexual intercourse similar to the insistence of the teaching against fornication and adultery.

Given that coitus is a life-giving encounter, which is undertaken with care to prepare and arouse each other so that both reach an orgasm if possible, what is its further meaning? As a body language it has the following possibilities:

(i) It is a means of thanksgiving. Couples can thank each other not only for the act they have just experienced but for their mutual presence. They can say with or without words, 'Thank you for being here; I am grateful for your presence yesterday and the day before and all the time we have been together.'

(ii) It is a language of hope. Through intercourse a couple can reassure each other that they are wanted and appreciated and that they would like to stay together in the future.

(iii) It is a means of reconciliation. Every couple knows that many quarrels and arguments are partially resolved or finally reconciled in an act of love.

(iv) It is the most economic means by which the sexuality of each other is reinforced in a unique way. The couple acknowledge each other's masculinity and feminity through one of the most powerful means of reinforcing the sexual identity.

(v) Intercourse is a recurrent confirmation of the personhood of each other.

(vi) It is the means through which sustaining, healing and growth are affirmed.

(vii) It is the means through which permanence is reinforced and finds regularly one of its most powerful meanings.

The Judaeo-Christian tradition found the principal meaning of intercourse in new life. There is little doubt that children are a marvellous expression of God's invitation to married couples to join in his creative activity. Clearly nowadays the overwhelming majority of sexual acts are consciously and deliberately non-procreative independently of what means of birth control are used. These non-procreative acts have now become undoubtedly the majority. There is a need to evaluate the meaning of coitus when it is non-procreative.

This is where an element of contemporary society has seized sex merely as a source of pleasure, and the pursuit of pleasure is equated with love. There can be no greater mistake, because as we have seen sex engages the whole person in a continuous relationship. There has developed a polarity between those who advocate sex for its pleasurable aspects only and those who condemn pleasure and still insist that children are its main justification. Both groups are mistaken. The pursuit of pleasure alone dehumanizes; the pursuit of sex primarily in terms of procreation reduces its existential meaning. It is this meaning which now needs consideration, because sexuality has reached a stage where new life can be created on a number of intended occasions, whereas the rest of the time which can span over fifty years, it is the non-procreative, intrinsic meaning of sex which is sought. To realize its full meaning, care is needed with love-making and a concentrated awareness of the meaning of one's spouse.

Coitus is a moment which reflects one extreme end of the polarity of closeness and distance between the couple. It is a reminder of the relationship of the Trinity which makes its members both one and also completely autonomous. So the couple reach peaks of unity and then disengage and return to their separate complementarity.

Sex is one of the most powerful means of life-giving. On a few occasions it is used deliberately to give a new life and on every occasion acts as a renewal of the life of the couple and through them of the family. Marriage safeguards the expression of this potential and in turn sex protects the nature of permanent love.

Fidelity

An extension of the criticism of modern marriage is the conviction that, if a monogamous marriage is to be preserved, then the relationship of the spouses cannot be exclusive. Extramarital relationships are advocated for all sorts of reasons but principally on the grounds that a couple need alternative contacts to enrichen their personal and sexual lives. Here is the considered view of a well-known American psychiatrist, 'In my 38 years of psychiatric practice I have seen many people who have benefitted from, and whose marriage has been helped by, an affair. I came out in favour of affairs after seeing this a good many years ago and observing the positive results, while seeing only an occasional case that came to grief.'[6] The opinion expressed that little harm follows an affair is questionable. Many a marriage goes through much distress and unhappiness as a result of an affair. Indeed on some occasions it may be the direct or indirect cause of marital breakdown.

The traditional Judaeo-Christian view is against adultery, and indeed the Old Testament contained provisions for stoning the adulterer or adultress to death even though in practice this may have been rarely carried out.

> The man who commits adultery with a married woman:
> The man who commits adultery with his neighbour's wife must die; he and his accomplice. (Lev. 20:10)

But why such severity? One reason is the same as the forbidding of fornication, namely the paternity, care and protection of new life. As for the wife, she was part of his possessions. At the spiritual level marriage was seen as a symbol of the covenant relationship between God and man. This was a relationship *par excellence* of fidelity, and Israel was castigated repeatedly for her adulterous excursions into the practices and religions of the surrounding alien countries. The covenant relationship discloses that it is of the very nature of love to have relationships that are faithful.

At the existential level which we have been examining, infidelity is an act of betrayal which arouses in the partner the anxiety of prospective loss. The spouse feels repudiated and forsaken, compared unfavourably with somebody else, unable to meet the needs of their partner. The proclaimers of the freedom of infidelity reiterate that all would be well except for the nuisance presence of jealousy. It is jealousy that needs eliminating not infidelity.

But at the very centre of jealousy lies the common human fear of losing a significant person. Jealousy is the fear and insecurity of loss. The threat of loss is a permanent feature of the human scene and in attempting to abolish it one meets the resistance of an irreducible sense of being human. There is no way of eliminating jealousy until and unless the person concerned ceases to matter.

Then there is no jealousy because the significance of the person has been surrendered. There come moments in marriage when jealousy ceases because the spouse no longer matters.

But what happens when the spouse is still loved and he/she is unfaithful? Traditionally the act of adultery made the adulterer technically responsible and guilty. But the more we examine the occasions of adultery the more we realize that they are by no means always a unilateral and deliberate flouting of fidelity. The 'innocent' spouse may have contributed a good deal to their partner's behaviour. Withdrawal from coitus, lack of demonstration of affection, systematic invalidation, all ultimately cause exasperation and the seeking of an alternative relationship. Whenever infidelity has occurred, it is important for both partners to review their intimate lives. The explanation may not always be found in such a search but the evaluation of the relationship will certainly clarify the situation and assist the future.

Friendship

The advocates of extramarital relationships have grasped part of a truth – that married couples need friends as well as each other. In our society friendships of the same sex are viewed with suspicion and frowned upon. Part of the contemporary freeing of human relationships is the extension of friendship. Men and women find themselves side by side at work, and from such encounters friendships can spring up which assume deep meaning. Such friendships provide extensions to the home encounters and enrich the life of all concerned.

But how are friendships to be conducted in such a way that they do not finish up in bed? A friendship has to be distinguished from a marital relationship. Marriage requires the fullest possible availability of the spouses to each other and their family. It is very difficult to remain fully available to two people simultaneously. Friendship accepts limitations, with the clear understanding that the centre of attention is directed to the spouse and the children. It accepts sexual abstinence because the true meaning of intercourse belongs to the intimate relationship of marriage. A number of people try to have their marriage and an affair at the same time. The result is that justice is not done to either relationship. But what about the situation in which the marriage is only sustained because there is an alternative affair? These situations do exist, and indeed have existed for a long time. They express a half-way situation between separation, divorce and the continuity of the marriage. They remain fragments of full relationships.

Friendship however allows an interaction of personalities, a testing of views, a trustworthy communicating about one's feelings and views, and all genuine friendships endow a mutual enrichment. But there are both gains and duties in friendship. It is important for example that the spouse knows of the friendship, particularly a heterosexual one, and that such friendship does not arouse an excess of anxiety. It is important that the spouse of the friend knows of the existence of the friendship and if possible all the four people become friends. The closer the friendship the greater is the care needed that it does not develop a marital quality. In particular, friendships should not be used as sounding boards for recurrent criticism of the spouse. Marital difficulties should be settled between the spouses otherwise the friend can easily become the alternative spouse.

Above all, the true mark of friendship is to ensure that what belongs to the marriage is not denied. Thus time, availability, new experiences, concern and affection which belong to the intimate relationship of marriage must not be reduced at the cost of the spouse. What can occur with a friend are aspects of sustaining, healing and growth that cannot be easily promoted between spouses, and here friendship plays an invaluable part as the basis of interaction is widened.

The advantages of friendships are multiple but so are the risks. As the sexes mingle and mixed friendships become more common, the gain from such freedom will need an equivalent degree of watchfulness, discipline and regard for the integrity of the friend.

Children

Books of a previous generation would have placed children at the head of a chapter on sexuality. Their position here is not an indication of indifference or devaluation. Children remain precious living realities of the love of the spouses for each other and for their offspring. Their creation, nurturing and care will remain a high priority in every family.

The results of psychological research have shown that the welfare of children is intimately related to the stability and happiness of the parents. The parental relationship is vital for the wellbeing of the children. Up to recent times a great deal was said about procreation and too little, if any, about the wellbeing of the parents. Such wellbeing is vital for the transmission of the characteristics and values that children need. These are stability, care, security, love, masculinity and femininity. The emphasis is slowly but steadily changing from numbers to quality in the upbringing of children.

A number of marriages, of the order of 10 per cent are infertile through sterile factors in either spouse.[7] Scientific advances are being made continuously in this field and the number of involuntary infertile may be expected to decrease in the future.

There remains a small number of couples who have deliberately chosen infertility. These couples have often been berated for being selfish and materialistic. Certainly some may be so, but there are others who, having had a good hard look at themselves, find they have no vocation for children. They may find babies frightening, they may not have motherly instincts, they may be terrified of having their freedom curtailed or they may simply know that parenting is not for them. Each couple need to assess carefully their reasons, which may vary from selfish to well-justified ones. Not everybody is fit or ready to be a parent, and children's homes all over the world are a living reminder that some parents are so only in name. The preoccupation with procreation, without a concurrent appreciation of the complexity of parenting, has emphasized new life without a comprehensive insight about the suitability of parents to bring up children. As children acquire increasingly more value, western society is moving away from indiscriminate childbearing to responsible parenthood where parents, and the parents alone, can assess their ability regarding the size of the family from none to many children depending on their resources.

Birth regulation

The principle of birth regulation has been accepted by all Christian denominations. In other words the spouses have been given the responsibility to assess the degree of co-creativity with almighty God. They err when they are neither generous nor responsible enough. There remains the argument of what methods are permissible. All denominations other than Roman Catholics have reached the conclusion that they can use a wide range of mechanical and hormonal contraceptives and, when sterilization is included, 80 per cent of the now-married women have used contraceptives.[8] The fundamental argument of Catholic theology is that every sexual act should remain open to new life. In the words of Paul VI, 'The Church, nevertheless, in urging men to the observance of the precepts of the natural law, which it interprets by its constant doctrine, teaches as absolutely required that any use whatever of marriage must retain its natural potential to procreate human life.'[9] As far as Roman Catholics are concerned this remains the teaching of the Church and they cannot and must not ignore it unless they have seriously considered the matter and reached alternative conclusions in their conscience. Such deliberation is not common and there is overwhelming evidence that large numbers of Catholics simply ignore this proscription.

There are many reasons offered for adopting alternative solutions. None of them have found favour with the Church and this matter is a deep wound which divides the Roman Catholic Church.

For the sake of completion it is important to add that the use of the infertile period has made important advances in the last twenty years and the use of temperature methods and the testing of vaginal mucus have given extremely satisfactory results. Thus one must distinguish the theological grounds for the teaching of the Church and the practical consequences of using different forms of birth regulation. It is very possible that the infertile period will gradually offer such advantages that it will be widely used for its own sake. This is not the situation at present, but on the other hand no contraceptives exist which have all the criteria of safety and effectiveness. Thus there remains the double task of pursuing the theology of contraception, and finding the means which respect human nature, are safe and effective. Ultimately the theology of the meaning of intercourse will be found in a penetrating examination of human love and sexuality. This has begun only recently and needs a world-wide consensus before the time is ready for any substantial change. In the meantime there is bound to be some continuing tension between the received and the emerging. What is vital is that obedience to the Church should remain, whilst fundamental prophetic discussion continues. It is vital to avoid mutual recrimination and casting doubt on the loyalty of those who are examining more deeply the nature of sexuality. Development of thought is as necessary as obedience, and the tension between law and love is as old as the beginning of Christianity and Paul's writings.

There is also a fear that if the Church's teaching is modified on contraception, this will be a step toward the acceptance of abortion. There is little evidence that one will follow the other. The underlying issues are fundamentally different and opposition to abortion is infinitely greater in all communities. It is totally inadmissible to pool all sexual problems together. Masturbation, fornication, adultery, contraception, abortion, divorce, homosexuality, rape, etc. are all distinct entities, and much harm has been done in the past by pooling them together.

Summary

Human sexuality is a process which grows with the personality. There is an infantile and adult form and both play a significant part in the experience of adults. Coitus is the adult experience, and this is a life-giving force, on a few occasions deliberately creative of life and on every occasion having the possibility to give life to the couple. This life is most completely experienced within marriage, which is the relationship that most fully facilitates life-giving. When sexual intercourse is intrinsically procreative, the parents assume responsibility for the size of their family and for the use of methods of family limitation consonant with the dictates of their informed conscience. All sexual activity outside marriage has some meaning but it is partial and incomplete.

References (Chapter 8)

1. See ch. 3.

2. Allen, C., *A Textbook of Psychosexual Disorders*. Oxford University Press, 1962.

3. Masserman, J.H. (ed.), *Dynamics of Deviant Sexuality*. Grune and Stratton, 1969.

4. Dunnell, K., *Family Formation 1976*. Office of Population Censuses and Surveys, 1979.

5. Dominian, J., *Proposals for a New Sexual Ethic*. Darton, Longman and Todd, 1977.

6. Spurgeon English, O. and Heller, M.S., 'Is Marital Fidelity Justified?' in *Sexual Issues in Marriage*, ed. L. Gross. Spectrum Publications, New York, 1975.

7. Glick, P., 'Updating the life cycle of the family'. Paper read at the annual meeting of the Population Association of America, Montreal, 1976.

8. Dunnell, *Family Formation*, p.42.

9. Paul VI, *Humanae Vitae*.

PART III

The Life Cycle of Marriage

CHAPTER 9

Courtship

In Part II of this book covered by chapters 4 to 8 an exploration was carried out of the possible forms of human relationship arising from the nature of contemporary marriage. In Part III, the following four chapters, consideration will be given to some of the complex realities facing the married in various stages of their life-cycle.

Marriage has often been interpreted as an institution whose essential features are static. In fact the partners and their children who live through several decades of married life find it anything but static. Couples go though courtship and then become a married pair, have children whose growth spans two decades and, as they depart, the couple return to a one-to-one relationship. Each phase has its own unique features, and social scientists have tried to capture as richly as possible the constituents of each one.

In a classical life-cycle description by Duvall[1] of the USA an eight-stage process has been proposed. Stage 1 describes the couple without children; stage 2 from the birth of the oldest child to 30 months; stage 3 covers the phase of the first child from 30 months to 6 years; stage 4 studies families with schoolchildren with the oldest child between 6 and 13; stage 5 the oldest child is now between 13 and 20; stage 6 the family has young adults; stage 7 is concerned with middle-aged parents ('empty nest' to retirement) and the final stage 8 covers the period of retirement to the death of one partner.

In this book a shorter version proposed by the author will be used.[2] This is a three-phase cycle with each phase being examined for the prominent social, physical, emotional, intellectual and spiritual systems. The three phases of marriage are:

Phase 1 – the first five years, approximately from the mean age of marriage (25.1 for men and 22.8 for women) to the late twenties or early thirties;

Phase 2 – from 30 to 50;

Phase 3 – from 50 to the death of one spouse.

In this chapter courtship will be examined.

Courtship – social characteristics

One of the well-documented factors of modern courtship is the freeing of choice from family and community pressures. The wide mixing of the sexes permits, in theory, a wide range of choice. 'In theory' is added because, despite a seemingly unlimited range of choice, people usually find themselves choosing their friends from the proximity of the neighbourhood. Extensive studies both in the USA and in Britain have shown that future spouses are not only drawn from people living near but also from those who have similar characteristics. The tendency for men and women to choose in each other characteristics similar to their own has been defined as 'assortative mating'.[3]

GEOGRAPHICAL PROPINQUITY

If social similarity is one of the keys of selection, then it could be expected that couples court and marry within a narrow radius of where they live. Studies in the USA of engaged and married couples whose place of residence was checked have found that approximately 50 per cent of the couples, who met, dated and ultimately married, lived within thirteen or fewer standard blocks of each other.[4] This geographical propinquity has also been noted in Britain.[5]

This finding is not surprising. Although men and women work away from home and may meet there, after work they return to their residential community. It is there that their leisure time will be mostly spent, the social mixing takes place and friendships develop. The immediate locality forms a boundary within which many selections of future spouses occur.

AGE

There are some courtships which are continuous friendships from childhood. The majority however begin in late teens and early twenties. Dating as such begins earlier but the stage of falling in love is a later development. Research evidence suggests that there is a high degree of similarity in age of couples so that courtships and marriages with a high age discrepancy are rare occurrences. In fact, in England and Wales in 1977, the mean age at marriage[6] for men was 25.1 and for women 22.9. Since marriages under 20 are particularly vulnerable to marital breakdown, it is important to know how many men and women marry at that age. In the same year 9.4 per cent of men and 30.3 per cent of women married under the age of 20. This is a small reduction on previous years but still a very high percentage as far as women are concerned. As already noted in chapter 6, emotional growth continues in the twenties and thirties and the younger the age at marriage the more likely it is that such development will occur later on, putting the marriage under stress.

SOCIAL CLASS

Similarity of age is matched by similarity of social class. There has been a tendency however for such similarity in marriage partners to become less marked in recent years.[7] Within social class categories, there is a strong similarity in Social Class I, a drop in Social Classes II and III and a rise again in Social Classes IV and V.* As with other factors the future stability of the marriage is linked with similarity of social class. The reasons are obvious. Similarity of social class tends to give a common approach to life. The things that are of interest and that matter are likely to be shared and the risk of conflict reduced. In a study of 4,858 marriages in Britain, covering all social classes, only 315 instances were found where the

---

Social class– census definition
The following five broad categories of social class are based on the unit groups of the Occupational Classification:
    Class I Professional and similar occupations.
    Class II Intermediate occupations.
    Class III Skilled occupations.
    Class IV Partly skilled occupations.
    Class V Unskilled occupations.

man married a woman of lower social and educational background and 134 women married a man below their social standing.[8] Such mixed marriages risk the fate of all mixed marriages of being more vulnerable.

RELIGION

Religion is a strong binding force and many studies have shown a tendency for marriages to occur between people of the same faith.[9] The rate of intra faith marriages (between members of the same Christian denomination) depends of course on the availability of co-religionists. Mixed marriages* have been shown to be more vulnerable in their outcome.[10] But, as with social class, there is a decline in intra faith marriages.[11] The decline in endogamy for social class and religion is part of a tendency already noticed which has reduced the accepted role criteria of the past and has encouraged an emotional affinity at the cost of social cohesion. These tendencies have important implications for all churches who deal with mixed marriages and have to provide pastoral care for the broader needs of a Christian household including different denominations. Marriage remains sacred and holy for both partners and the symbol of the relationship of God and his people needs bringing out as the uniting principle between them.

COMPLETION OF EDUCATION

After age at marriage, the age of completion of education shows a very high level of association between spouses and is a powerful determining factor in selection of deep friendships that lead to marriage.[12] Coleman concludes from his study

> that similarity of terminal age of education without similarity of class is a more decisive direct determinant of marital choice than is similarity of social class without similarity of terminal age of education. Or put in another way, that similarity in educational attainment makes it easier to marry across class barriers than does class similarity in the face of educational incompatibilities.[13]

*In the context of this book 'mixed marriages are those of Christians of different denominations.

Summary

As far as social characteristics are concerned there is good evidence that similarity plays an important role in courtship in defining the group of eligible men and women. Clearly there are exceptions and this is an important matter. If the exceptions are few and go against the general trend then they can be expected to remain unsupported by the community and be particularly vulnerable to the stresses and strains of marriage. Thus in the past marked deviations from the norms of endogamy were risky propositions regarding their outcome. On the other hand, if the exceptions are part of a larger trend, e.g. to marry someone of a different faith or different social class, then the discrepancies will not elicit too much disapproval by society and the couples will not be at such risk.

These social changes in courtship are akin to those described regarding the roles within marriage. Just as the roles are becoming less rigid and are being replaced by an engagement of a deeper layer of the personality, so strict endogamy may be giving way to different criteria for courtship selection depending primarily on age and education rather than social class and religion. If this movement gathers momentum, then marriage will have to be supported more than ever by the internal resources and cohesion of the spouses rather than by the external supports of the community. Alternatively the community has to reappraise the needs of the married and support them according to changing criteria of the internal dynamics of marriage.

Courtship – psychological factors

The social variables mentioned above define the group of eligible people from whom an ultimate choice will be made. The factors which operate in this definitive choice are not clear. Physical attraction, the meeting of emotional needs, and other unknown elements all combine to narrow down to the person with whom courtship finally proceeds to an exclusive commitment to marriage.

PSYCHOLOGICAL SIMILARITY AND COMPLEMENTARITY

On the basis of social similarity early research also indicated psychological similarity, that is to say that spouses are attracted by similar psychological traits, and evidence has been brought forward to substantiate this view.[14] The personal needs which couples seek in marriage are love and affection, confidence, sympathy, understanding, dependence, encouragement, intimate appreciation and emotional security.[15]

A point of some importance arises here, namely that assortative mating has not only the possibility of bringing together stable personalities free from vulnerable traits but also the opposite. This theme will be pursued further in chapter 13 where the causes of marital breakdown will be considered. But the theory of similarity of psychological traits remains a prominent one.

Another theory is that of complementarity. The author of this view, Winch, maintains that, although the field of eligibles is dictated by social similarity, the final choice is made on the basis of complementarity, or that opposites attract each other.[16] For example a dominant spouse marries a non-dominant one, one who needs nurturing is attracted by someone who gives succour, or one who needs to be an achiever marries someone whose need is to abnegate. Complementarity is an attractive theory, but so far extensive studies do not give more than minimum support for the idea although in practice the features described can be seen.

So far attraction has been considered in terms of similarity and complementarity. A third view[17] suggests that in addition to conscious motives, unconscious ones also play their part, that partners may select each other because their feelings and emotions which are unconscious fit with each others. Thus a self-rejecting person may marry someone who is critical, and the deprived someone who is undemonstrative and rejecting, in other words partners are chosen to meet an internal world of development that is incomplete or hurt and the partner is chosen unconsciously because they appear to fit in with the unconscious system of emotional development. These liaisons and marriages tend to be unstable because sooner or later the real needs of the couple emerge only to find that neither partner has the resources to meet mutual needs.

In brief the personal choice may be made on the basis of similarity, complementarity, strong unconscious factors or any combination of these characteristics. There is still plenty of room for research on marital choice in order to define it more accurately.

INTELLIGENCE
One factor seems to suggest similarity and that is the intelligence of the courting and married couple. The evidence is fairly strong on its nature although it is more important in Social Classes I and II rather than in classes III, IV and V. [18]

Duration of courtship

Short courtships carry a higher risk of marital instability and possibility of marital breakdown. In an extensive study of 520 divorced and 570 continuously married people the difference and consequences between periods of courtship are shown clearly.[19]

TABLE 1

	Divorced (520) %	Continuously Married (520) %
Less than 6 months	6	1
6 months but less than 12 months	14	7
One year but less than 2 years	39	34
Two years plus	41	57

Whilst there can never be an exact period of courtship that would suit everyone, it is clear that hasty marriages are more vulnerable to divorce. This is not surprising. The pursuit of a commitment for the length of marriage needs a fairly careful knowledge and evaluation of the type of person the future partner is and this takes time.

Turbulence

One of the features that has emerged in studying courtship is its quality as a predictor of marital stability. Stormy courtships with frequent severe quarrels and separation predict a tendency that may continue in marriage. In the study already quoted there were more courtship break-ups among the subsequently divorced than the continuously married.[20] The same applies to broken engagements.

Another feature of significance is the opposition of parents to a pending marriage. The divorced appear to have had more objections from their parents to the future daughter/son-in-law. If these objections persist, they are likely to cause further tension between those courting, and the spouse concerned will start marriage with an important support system missing. Children want to protect the good name of their parents, even if the latter are behaving awkwardly. This leads to arguments between the young couple, and later on in marriage the question of in-laws can become a prominent problem.

Premarital sexual intercourse and cohabitation

There is little doubt that the incidence of premarital sexual intercourse is high and has become progressively more common among those who are courting at the level of an agreed understanding that they will marry or live together. Table 2 which is based on a national sample of married women, shows there to be a marked increase in the incidence of premarital sexual intercourse amongst women with their husband-to-be.[21]

TABLE 2

Proportion of women of all ages first married in different years who reported premarital sexual intercourse with their husband-to-be

Year of marriage	% having had sexual intercourse.
1959–60	35
1961–65	47
1966–70	61
1971–75	74

Table 2 documents clearly the rise of premarital sexual intercourse in the last twenty years in Britain, a phenomenon which is also occurring in other parts of Western society.

As the proportion of women who have premarital sexual inter-course increases, so does cohabitation with the future spouse. The percentage of women who cohabited with their husband prior to marriage increased from 1 per cent to 9 per cent between the years 1956 and 1975. Of those who admitted cohabiting, 26 per cent reported a period less than 3 months, 15 per cent between 3 and 5 months, 24 per cent six months but less than a year, indicating that two-thirds of those who cohabit do so for less than a year. 20 per cent-report cohabitation for between one and two years and the remaining 15 per cent had lived together for two years or longer.[22]

The trend towards a greater incidence of premarital intercourse and cohabitation is a concern for the Judaeo-Christian traditions. The concern is not entirely a matter of confining coitus within marriage. Many cohabiting couples are married in all but name. Such couples often ask what does a piece of paper add to their love for each other?

The fact remains that society needs clarity about human rela-tionships. It needs to know who is related to whom, who accepts responsibility for the care of children, who owns property and who is committed in an enduring manner so that they cease to be treated as single people. Marriage has a private and public dimension and the forfeiture of the latter not only confuses and threatens society but denies the couple any support they might claim as a result of being married.

Another danger in the so-called trial marriages is that the absence of a public declaration leaves room for the couple to repudiate each other more easily. In fact strictly speaking these are not marriages at all, because the couple deliberately allow escape doors if their relationship does not work. A public commitment adds strength to the motivation to work hard to sustain the relationship.

There is a final point about premarital intercourse, a point of fundamental value. Coitus is not the most appropriate means of exploring the suitability of a relationship. It is the quality of per-sonal interaction which is so crucial for the stability of marriage. Sexual intercourse is a means of sealing the discovery of appropriate mutuality not the means of discovering it. Coitus is too narrow a base to reveal real insight about future harmony. But what about cohabitation? On the surface the appeal of this position is high, but whilst couples are on trial they have a very good reason to remain at their best and impress one another. It is not possible for them to be fully frank, for the fear of rupture remains a haunting thought. Marriage with its solemn personal and public avowal gives a very much stronger infrastructure within which a couple can act as their true selves.

It is also possible that those who praise cohabitation are the very people who personally find closeness and permanency very difficult. They see commitment as an experience of suffocation, as a prison, and so they prefer to cohabit as this allows some of the advantages of marriage without having to experience the anxiety of a permanent commitment. They praise the freedom of a private arrangement because they cannot tolerate the sense of being trapped. Thus it is important to examine both social and psychological reasons when cohabitation is being offered as the appropriate answer to the contemporary problems of marriage.

PREMARITAL PREGNANCY

The presence of premarital pregnancy enchances the possibility of divorce. This is a finding that has been verified repeatedly.[23,24,25] In England and Wales there has been a sustained reduction of pregnant brides since 1967 particularly for brides aged 18 to 22. This reduction has been accompanied by an increase in abortions.[26]

From the Christian point of view a decrease in premarital pregnancy *is* desirable as a preventive action to marital breakdown but not at the cost of abortion. For those who accept abortion there is no problem.

Summary

Courtship is a complex and vital period which gives a lot of opportunities for education and support of the future couple. There is a great deal not known, but there is also a substantial knowledge which can be used here and now for the prevention of future marital breakdown. Thus age, education, social class, premarital pregnancy, duration and character of courtship are all statistically related to marital breakdown. These risks can either be eliminated or care taken to give such marriages extra support.

References (Chapter 9)

1. Duvall, E.E., *Marriage and Family Development.* Lippincott, Philadelphia, 1977.

2. Dominian, J., 'Marital Therapy' in *Introduction to the Psychotherapies* (ed. S. Bloch). Oxford University Press, 1979.

3. Coleman, D.A. in *Equalities and Inequalities in Family Life* (ed. R. Chester and J. Peel). Academic Press, 1977.

4. Clarke, A.C. in *American Sociological Review* (1952) 17, p.17.

5. Coleman, p.30.

6. *Population Trends*, No.16: *Mean Age at Marriage.* Office of Population Censuses and Surveys, HMSO, 1979.

7. Coleman, p.34.

8. Glass, D.V., (ed.). *Social Mobility in Britain.* Routledge and Kegan Paul, 1954.

9. Coleman, p.35.

10. Landis, J.T., 'Marriages of Mixed and Non-mixed Religious Faith' in *Selected Studies in Marriage and the Family.* Holt, Rinehart and Winston, 1962.

11. Coleman, p.37.

12. ibid., p.38.

13. ibid., p.44.

14. Burgess, E.W. and Wallin, P., *Engagement and Marriage.* Lippincott, New York, 1953.

15. ibid., p.199.

16. Winch, R.F., *Mate Selection, a Study of Complementary Needs.* Harper, New York, 1959.

17. Dicks, H.V., *Marital Tensions.* Routledge and Kegan Paul, 1967.

18. Coleman, p.28.

19. Thornes, B. and Collard, J., *Who Divorces?* Routledge and Kegan Paul, 1979.

20. ibid., p.65.

21. Dunnell, K., *Family Formation 1976.* HMSO, 1979.

22. ibid.

23. Christiansen, H.T., 'Time of the First Pregnancy as a Factor in Divorce' *Eugenic Review*, 1963: 100, 119.

24. *Population Trends*, No.3. Office of Population Censuses and Surveys, HMSO, 1976.

25. Thornes and Collard, p.77.

26. Thompson, J., 'Fertility and Abortion, Inside and Outside Marriage', *Population Trends* No.5. Office of Population Censuses and Surveys, HMSO.

CHAPTER 10

The Early Years

The first phase of marriage lasts approximately five years, from the middle twenties to about thirty, five crucial years during which the couple have to form a stable relationship covering five parameters, namely the social, physical, emotional, intellectual and spiritual. Evidence will be presented in chapter 13 suggesting that this phase in marriage is of paramount importance to its viability. The couple have been in love during their courtship, a state of heightened emotional and sexual expectation and idealization of each other, which is followed by loving. Loving means availability and willingness to establish a minimum relationship in all the parameters involved. When this minimum does not exist the marriage can hardly be said to have got off the ground. The establishment of these parameters requires sustaining, healing and growth, and whenever appropriate these requirements will be allied to the concrete tasks facing the couple.

Social dimension

The social issues facing the couple are the setting up of a home, distribution of household tasks, finance, relationship with relatives and friends, work and leisure.

SETTING UP A HOME
Most couples will wish to establish a residence of their own and this is more often achieved by the higher socio-economic group and those who marry after the age of twenty.[1] Their economic resources allow them to do this instead of living with relatives. The import-

ance of having a home is considerable, so that the couple can establish their separate life and have the opportunity to experiment, make mistakes, and rectify them without the attendant supervision of relatives.

Setting up the home was traditionally the wife's task, but now both spouses share and contribute to this. It is an exercise of mutual support in which the couple adjust and adapt to each other's aesthetic and practical sense of what is appropriate. There may be differences in preference of colour, furniture, decoration and establishing a balance between the parts of the house that are to be shared and space for temporary withdrawal by the individual spouse.

DISTRIBUTION OF HOUSEHOLD TASKS

In the not too distant past the whole responsibility of running the home was placed firmly on the shoulders of the wife. Now the wife is very likely to be working during these early years and a sharing of household responsibilities is an important part of setting up a home. The husband is increasingly expected to shop, cook and do his share of household tasks. Most husbands are prepared to promise to do these chores before they are married; the question remains whether they will do so in practice and how much. There is still a tendency to leave much of the housework to the wife.

Here is an important part of sustaining. The wife, now and also in the future, may wish to pursue her academic career or remain in an interesting job. She may also want to look after her house and have children. The combination of the two careers requires a good deal of sustaining by the husband who not only needs to take his share in the housework but also encourage his wife when life becomes difficult and demanding for her. He may also need to help her cope with some of her guilt feelings about being a mother and a full-time worker. Clearly the couple have to ensure that the children have sufficient caring access to them, but with understanding and support the appropriate arrangement can be achieved.[2]

FINANCE

During this phase and up to the time the first child arrives both spouses are likely to be working and there are few financial difficulties. Mention has already been made that money carries its own intrinsic economic value and at the same time is a powerful symbol for love and healing. There are people, whose upbringing was relatively deprived, who find it very difficult to spend money on themselves. For them money is a security rather than a unit of spending. Such people tend to use their money entirely for the family and find it very difficult to think of themselves. Often however there is a disgruntlement at this inability and the spouse can do a lot of healing by encouraging their partner to spend some money on their own needs in an independent manner. In this way the deprived person begins to feel that they are good enough to have money allocated for themselves.

When the first baby arrives the likelihood is that for a while the wife will cease working. Then she will become entirely dependent on her husband who has to make his contribution appear willing and spontaneous. Money now becomes a channel of loving availability.

RELATIVES AND FRIENDS
The concept of leaving one's relatives and cleaving to one's spouse is a very old one. 'This is why a man leaves his father and mother and joins himself to his wife, and they become one body' (Gen. 2:24). The separation is far more than a physical one. The spouses, who hitherto had their parents as the central focus of their life, have now to switch and make each other that centre. This is a difficult detachment which is quite a challenge for some men and women. If a wife or a husband is over-attached to their parent, there will be difficulty in severing the umbilical cord. The spouse of such partner has to show patience, demonstrate to him/her that they are a reliable alternative and gradually allow their partner to get accustomed to them as their central reference. Parents may find it very difficult to let go of their children and may continue to telephone and visit far more frequently than is required. Again the spouse can help the partner to distance themselves without rejecting the parents or feeling unduly guilty about not consulting them, nor contacting them.

Sometimes both spouses are held in the tight grip of their parents and show excessive dependence on them. This is a situation that needs far more help and may require a counsellor to act as the main support whilst the spouses are discovering the possibilities of trusting one another.

Couples have also to agree on which of the friends they had prior to marriage are to continue playing an intimate part in their lives afterwards. Not everyone will be acceptable to both spouses and some may have to be dropped, particularly ex-girlfriends and boy-friends. But some who were known for many years, even from schooldays, are retained and sometimes effort and sacrifice is needed on the part of the spouse who did not know them before in order to accept them. Jealousy plays an important part here, and care needs to be taken to avoid battles about friends. What needs to be established is that those who matter are retained by both spouses and the rest, who are a threat to the marriage, gradually relin-quished.

WORK

As far as the husband is concerned, marriage rarely interrupts the continuity of his work pattern and so in some senses the impact of matrimony is not such a social upheaval. The wife also works until the arrival of the first baby. In the census of 1971 in England and Wales there were 69.6 per cent economically active women at the beginning of marriage, dropping to 27.9 per cent after six years and then rising again to 59.7 per cent after twenty-four years of mar-riage.[3] These figures show the high rate of work before babies arrive and the gradual return to high levels of employment as the children grow up.

One of the perennial questions regarding the mother's employ-ment is the possible adverse impact on children. The general con-census is that, provided adequate substitute care is available, there is no research evidence of damage for the preschool child.[4,5,6] Never-theless there remains a strong intuitive belief that mother should be around, if possible, in the preschool years and there to receive the child on return from school in the primary years.

LEISURE

The period of courtship will have established sufficient similarity for the couple to know what sort of recreation they enjoy together. Sometimes the wife may wish to learn to be interested in predom-inantly male games such as soccer, cricket or rugby, but on the whole the couple will have common interests. Time together will be considerable prior to the arrival of children but greatly circum-

scribed thereafter. This is where the husband can help the wife by
baby-sitting, and naturally they need a relative or friend to babysit
for both of them. After children arrive time together is precious and
arrangements need to be made to realize it. Sometimes one spouse,
often the husband, does not like to socialize or has few friends of
his own. Both these difficulties need help from the spouse to extend
the horizon of their partner.

Physical dimension

The early years of marriage, before the children arrive, are a unique
time to get to know each other. Good health is essential for this and
this is generally present. In a few instances a debilitating disease
may start soon after marriage and keep the partners apart physically
and emotionally. The sustaining needed for such a couple is considerable. They have to support each other during the illness, sacrifice sexual fulfilment during this time and be prepared to start
when the physical illness is over.

Sexual satisfaction is very important in these early years. Couples
are likely to have had some sexual experience with each other but
now they are in a situation where they can approach each other in
a relaxed and comfortable manner. It takes about a year for a
couple to settle to a satisfactory rhythm of sexual life. Research in
the United States reports that 82 per cent of wives married for less
than a year find their sexual life good or very good, and this figure
increased to 88 per cent when the wives could communicate fully
with their spouse about their reaction and feelings.[7] This leaves 12–
18 per cent dissatisfied, which agrees with an English study which
found that 12–21 per cent of wives were initially sexually
dissatisfied.[8]

Sexual satisfaction is much more than obtaining an orgasm.
Foreplay, that is to say the preparation for intercourse, is a time
when the couple make it particularly clear to each other that they
are recognized, wanted and appreciated as spouses. The combination of erotic physical touch and appropriate words allows a meeting
place between adult and infantile needs. This is a time when the
couple regress, retreat to earlier forms of joy and excitement and
gradually come together with the total oneness that they experi-

enced as young children in the arms of their mother. The prelude
to physical oneness is an emotional unity where the I and You
dissolve and the couple lose their boundaries of self and become
one.

To achieve this they need to feel completely relaxed and to trust
in each other's commitment. When the body and mind are thus
prepared, the genitals are ready to receive and complete the physical
union. In the process of achieving this it may be necessary to
overcome the tense reaction of one spouse. Such closeness and
intimacy may be threatening to one partner for whom it conveys a
paralysing loss of control, a sense of disgust, or a combination of
both. These feelings need to be understood and gradually eliminated. The need for good communication is important to explain
anything painful but also to guide each other to what is pleasurable.
Part of the retreat into early patterns of infant–mother unity is also
the conviction that mother knows what is good for one without
being told. In intercourse there is a return to this conviction that
the spouse now knows intuitively what the other wants. But of
course they do not and so communication is vital. Such communication directs the partner to the sites which are pleasurable, to the
quality of touch that is desired, the degree of arousal prior to genital
entry and the type of physical exchange that produces a satisfactory
orgasm. Occasionally intercourse will be very pleasurable without
an orgasm for the wife, but an attempt to achieve a mutual orgasm
will certainly enhance the pleasure.

The biblical term for sexual intercourse is 'to know' and it can
be seen that sexual intercourse has a series of layers which are
gradually penetrated. There is personal recognition at the level of
erotic attraction. Sexual attraction brings the husband and wife
together and allows them to recognize each other in depth right
back to the earliest phase of life in infancy. The physical embrace
and intimate closeness removes boundaries and allows a personal
union to occur which is completed by the genital one. Now they are
addressing each other physically but in the depths of their body
they find each other and acclaim the joy of the past, present and
future. This encounter with life is also ultimately an encounter with
God, the author of life, and in the midst of intercourse the total
surrender of each to the other is a recognition of the oneness of the
Trinity, the oneness of the covenant between God and man, and
the oneness of Christ and the Church. Thus coitus embraces the
whole range of human experience from the physical through to the

spiritual. Oneness is achieved from separate persons who belong to one another and intercourse is a recurrent reminder of the oneness and separateness of all relationships, from the Trinity, through the Incarnation to human relationships.

Emotional dimension

Sexual intercourse is one form of emotional expression. Emotional communication continues at other times and during these early years of marriage it holds a central place in the relationship of the spouses. The couple need to feel recognized, wanted and appreciated at other times than when they are having sexual intercourse. This caring revolves round acknowledgement which is expressed in appropriate communication. There are plenty of everyday activities which need caring communication. Couples may have different rhythms of activity and rest, and so times of going to bed and rising may need adjustment. Some want a really warm bed and others find heat unbearable. The times meals are taken and the type of food may clash. Above all, the time spent together and the time each needs for themselves has to be structured. Communication is vital for all these arrangements.

'Communication' does not mean mere exchange of information. As the couple get to know each other's moods, needs, sensitivities and anger points, they learn how to respond with care and sensitivity. Some spouses need immediate attention and cannot bear frustration otherwise they feel hurt and rejected. Communication is a matter of conveying inner needs to each other and reassessing the mutual understanding of each other. This is where the wounds of the past have to be met. One spouse may find criticism, however well meant, intolerable. Another may need active and recurrent affirmation to feel that they are on the right course. Still others may find expressing their angry feelings very difficult and they keep them inside only to have a major outburst about something trivial or withdraw in a sulky mood. All these reactions will become material for the early exchanges in marriage.

Such communication of course needs time and this is where a couple who are both working may find it difficult to sit down and have a heart-to-heart talk but there can always be found some time if the couple really want to converse. It may be that one spouse or both finds it very difficult to express their feelings and makes all sorts of excuses to avoid such an encounter.

The distribution of power and the resolution of conflict are of vital importance in egalitarian relationships. This applies particularly to marriages of the upper socio-economic group. With marriages in the lower socio-economic group the remnants of patriarchy still remain and such couples still think of the husband as the principal partner who earns the income and takes decisions whereas the wife runs the home.[9] Such a patriarchical home tends to reduce overt conflict because the partners know where they stand with each other. Conflict is more likely to appear in egalitarian relationships where every major decision has to be reached on the basis of consensus. Repeated unresolved conflicts are a threat to the marriage. Tempers may rise in the process of settling an issue and this may be followed by verbal and finally physical aggression.[10]

Intellectual dimension

The normal period of courtship ensures that the way a couple look at life is likely to be similar, but not identical. Couples are likely to be of similar intelligence, similar backgrounds and to approach questions with an outlook and an interest which is likely to lead to harmony. Views on religion, economics, world events, political orientation, artistic interpretation are likely to be shared experiences, but not always. Even in normal courtships there may be facets of outlook which are not shared. In fact the more egalitarian the relationship is, the more likely it is that partners will have distinctive approaches to life but this adds to the richness of the exchange. It only raises difficulties when one partner cannot bear to have their views challenged and interprets this as a personal affront.

Even more serious difficulties arise when a couple marry in a hurry and have not had the time to get to know each other. They may find to their horror that in fact they have very little in common. These are people who needed desperately to get away from home or to find some meaning in life, hence the rapid decision to marry. It is only afterwards that they discover how little they have in common. This is not an insurmountable problem provided they do not start blaming each other for the deficiencies.

Spiritual dimension

The word spiritual can be interpreted in two ways, firstly as the direct impact of religion on the life of the couple and secondly as the value system they share. As far as the Judaeo-Christian tradition is concerned, the essential feature is that marriage is holy and sacred, and more specifically in the Roman Catholic tradition it is a sacrament and therefore an active channel of grace. This really means that the experiences of the couple, the social, physical, emotional and intellectual, are all events which actively carry grace or the life of God. The married have the opportunity to see and experience God and Father, Son and Holy Spirit in the everyday life events which encompass them.

Sometimes priests complain that the modern family has ceased to pray together. Prayer is a powerful means of reaching and responding to God, the transcendental God. But in their every moment of relating to each other, couples participate in the divine life. The most menial to the most powerful mutual event is a prayer, a prayer addressed to the immanent God present in each other. Marriage is a powerful sharing of the life of God and, although it needs to be supplemented by the other sacraments, it contains an inherent source of grace which is activated by the interaction of the spouses. This intrinsic access to the life of God, which is love, is the privilege and responsibility of every couple.

The spiritual which connects the human with the divine presence allows those who have such faith to participate in a unique dimension of being, a force which transforms the whole existence of their life.

Others do not see God in this specific revealed manner of the Judaeo-Christian tradition. Rather they depend for their spirituality on a set of humanistic values which are very similar to the Christian ones. The bridge that connects the two is love, love expressed as care, concern, truth, justice, support for the helpless, and for the dignity of the human being. The way the couple treat each other is a major part of the value system that guides their life. They rely on reason and common sense and values which are still part of a traditional Christian society.

Youthful marriages

Attention has already been drawn to the vulnerability of teenage marriages. Such married couples tend to belong to the lower socio-economic group, to have more commonly a premarital pregnancy, and to have no accommodation of their own. The fact that the mother ceases earning when she is pregnant places the couple in a precarious financial situation. Altogether brides under the age of twenty tend to have a combination of problems which may overwhelm them, and the rate of divorce is high in this group.[11,12]

Children

The number of women pregnant at marriage in Britain rose from 13 per cent in the group who married between 1956–60 to 22 per cent for those who married in 1971–5. Thus premarital pregnancy has increased overall but has fallen among the under-twenties, primarily through abortion. Premarital pregnancy in the under-twenties still remains high with a level as much as double that of premarital pregnancies in all other age groups.[13]

The timing of the children after marriage shows a postponement of immediate childbearing.[14] Wives remain at work for some time before they have their first baby. Excluding premarital pregnancies, only 9 per cent of those married between the years 1971–74 had a baby in the first year compared to 15 per cent of those of those married between 1956 and 1960. Even more impressive is the fact that of those who married in the seventies only 26 per cent had a child in the second year compared to 45 per cent of those who married between 1956 and 1960. Similar differences are noted in the third year of marriage.

The advent of the first child changes both the social and psychological structure of the home. The wife becomes a mother and often leaves work, and the husband becomes a father who has now to support his wife and child emotionally and economically. It is not surprising that such major changes may produce an upheaval in the household. The obvious points are that the baby demands a lot of attention which is withdrawn from the couple. It is thus a time of relative deprivation and stress. It is in fact a psycho-social crisis and may temporarily cause considerable difficulties, not least the presence of fatigue. A study of 1,296 mothers with infants under one year found that they spent half as much time again doing housework as mothers whose youngest child was a teenager.[15] Such fatigue permeates the whole relationship of the spouses and may affect emotional and sexual communication.

As for the child during these early years, the primacy of importance is physical and emotional care. The child remains utterly dependent on the parents for survival and for acquiring the resources to feel recognized, wanted and appreciated. It is during these years that trust and autonomy will be established and enough separation from parents will occur for the child to be able to cope with aloneness for progressive periods. These are also the years when the child is coping with the first steps of intellectual growth and needs to be stimulated with language, objects, toys and games to begin to get familiar with the order of things. But above all these are the years when the parents provide a facilitating framework for reliable emotional growth.

References (Chapter 10)

1. Ineichen, B. in *Equalities and Inequalities in Family Life*, ed. R. Chester and J. Peel. Academic Press, 1977.

2. Rapaport, R. and Rapaport, R., *Dual Career Families*. Penguin, 1971.

3. Britton, M., 'Women at Work'. *Population Trends* No.2. Office of Population Censuses and Surveys, HMSO, 1975.

4. Rutter, M., Tizard J. and Whitmore, K. (eds.), *Education, Health and Behaviour*. Longman, 1970.

5. Douglas, J.W.B., Ross J.M. and Simpson H.R., *All our Futures*. Peter Davies, 1968.

6. Rutter, M., and Madge, N., *Cycles of Disadvantage*. Heinemann, 1976.

7. Levin, R.J. and Levin, A., *Sexual Pleasure: The Surprising Preference of 100,000 Women*. Redbook, 1975.

8. Thornes, B. and Collard, J., *Who Divorces?* Routledge and Kegan Paul, 1979.

9. Aldous, J., *The Development Approach to Family Analysis*, vol 2. University of Georgia Press, Athens (USA), 1974.

10. Gayford, J.J., in *British Medical Journal*, 1975, 1, 194.

11. Thornes and Collard, p.71.

12. Ineichen, p.53.

13. Dunnell, K., *Family Formation 1976*. Office of Population Censuses and Surveys, HMSO, 1979.

14. ibid., p.12.

15. Walker, K.E. in *Family Economics Review* (1969) 5, 6.

CHAPTER 11

The Middle Years

The second phase of marriage, between the ages of thirty and fifty, lasts much longer than the first phase. These are the years during which the children complete their education and start to leave home. At the same time spouses go through significant social and psychological shifts of which the most prominent is the change in personality. For the Judaeo-Christian tradition of permanency in marriage these years are of particular importance, because, even when a marriage appears to be stable and satisfactory in its early stages, much misunderstanding and conflict may erupt in this phase, leading sometimes to ultimate breakdown. These marriages are very hard to categorize. Were there problems from the very start, or did difficulties emerge with the development of the relationship? Very often when we look at marriages in this second phase we find problems which continued from the first five years of marriage as well as the emergence of new ones.

Once again the second phase will be described in terms of the social, physical, emotional, intellectual and spiritual dimensions.

Social dimension

During these twenty years the married will tend to stabilize the place where they live. They may have to move for reasons of work but couples will try to keep changes to a minimum consistent with their work or career. Frequent change of accommodation presents its own problems, particularly for the wife, who has to make and break friendships. Sometimes moving house can be most traumatic with the loss of familiarity of the building, the surroundings and friends.

The internal arrangements of the household will have been established by now and the contributions of husband and children to
running the home will be partially based on the working arrangements of the wife and the social structure of the household. Some
husbands help a great deal, others much less. But if the wife is
working, and increasingly she is likely to be doing so during these
two decades, then she certainly needs help if she is not to be
overwhelmed by fatigue. Occasionally there is a reversal of working
roles and it is the wife who goes out to work and the husband who
stays behind and looks after the home and the children. Such
reversals of roles are not common but they indicate the flexibility
permitted in society at present.

A particular feature of these two decades is social mobility, up-
wards or downwards. Downward social mobility is the result of
chronic ill health, (physical or mental), gambling, drinking or ir-
regular work. Upward social mobility is the result of success at
work. If this success has been achieved in business, it is possible for
the husband to surround himself with a new group of friends and
interests which no longer include the wife; sometimes it is the other
way round. There is now an alienation of interests between the
spouses. In particular if the wife has worked hard and made sacrifices to promote her husband's interests, only to discover at this
stage that she is redundant in his life, the consequences are particularly painful for her.

Research shows that people in class III (non-manual) are more
prone to divorce than those in classes I or II or IV.[1] One of the
reasons for such a propensity to marital breakdown is the uncertainty of people in this group, in which upward mobility creates
divisions between spouses and also produces uncertainty about
friendships which belonged to both in the past and may be abandoned and those of the future which attract only one of the spouses.
The impermanence of the social network operates against stability.

As far as the managerial and professional social classes are concerned, the forties are a significant period. This is the time when
some people recognize that they have reached the peak of their
career which is below their hope and expectation or else they have
attained heights they cannot cope with. In either case there will be
social and psychological stress. However the majority of men and
women accept the limits of their working advance with sufficient
insight to expect neither more or less. The only upheaval in these
circumstances is an early loss of job due to redundancy.

Physical dimension

The health of the overwhelming majority of married couples remains good during these two decades. A certain amount of cancer
and heart disease may nevertheless appear, the former particularly
in women and the latter in men. Chronic post-puerperal depression
syndromes may be present and reduce the availability of sex, intimacy and leisure. The syndromes remain from the first phase of
marriage and may be extremely corrosive to the stability and happiness of the marriage.

Marital happiness is closely related to sexual satisfaction. In an
American study of 100,000 women, 94 per cent of the wives, who
admitted being 'mostly happy', declared their sexual life good or
very good, and conversely 53 per cent, who reported a poor sexual
relationship, were mostly unhappy in their marriage.[2] A British
study[3] found that, in a stably married population, 96 per cent of
women and 98 per cent of men claimed that the sexual side of their
life had both started and continued satisfactorily or that earlier
difficulties had been resolved. On the other hand, 38 per cent of
divorced women and 30 per cent of divorced men whose initial
sexual relationship had been good said that it had deteriorated later
on.

The sexual difficulties during these years will be the initial ones
of the first phase which have not improved and are now becoming
unacceptable. The complaints may be of persistent dysfunction at
the genital level but are more likely to be of an unsatisfactory
attitude to coitus. Wives will complain that their partner is selfish,
inconsiderate or cruel. Selfishness and cruelty include failing to
show affection before intercourse, reaching a climax too quickly,
denying the wife an opportunity to reach hers, making love when
drunk, forcing intercourse against the wish of the wife, assaulting
her prior to coitus and persistent demands for some form of sexual
variation. The husband will complain that the wife is cold, rejecting
or not interested in sex.

In addition to these difficulties, sexual life may suffer as a result
of an extramarital affair. The incidence of such affairs was calculated by Kinsey to be 26 per cent of women by the age of 40 and
50 per cent of men.[4] These figures, from the United States in the
early 1950s, need updating.

There is plenty of evidence that many marriages negotiate one or more extramarital affairs without irreversible damage to their marriage. After the initial shock, the couple come to some understanding which involves change in the relationship and a better adaptation. There are circumstances however when the underlying structure of the marriage is already so fragile that an extramarital relationship is sufficient to bring about an irretrievable breakdown. This is much more likely to happen when the marital relationship has been deteriorating for some time and the extramarital relationship is an indication of the feeling of need for a new partner. The story in the Gospel of St John (John 8:1-11) shows clearly that adultery is a serious matter but not an indication for killing the person concerned. It is an occasion for forgiveness and a new beginning.

Adultery requires an examination of the reasons behind it. One reason has been already described, namely a deteriorating relationship which is no longer supplying the minimum needs of the couple. In this situation the couple have to look seriously at their problems and, if necessary, seek help. Adultery in these circumstances is a dire warning which needs heeding.

There are men and women who indulge in extramarital relationships when their own sexual life is unsatisfactory or missing. Once again this is a warning that attention needs to be given to the repairing of sexual function, and nowadays there is a great deal more help available in this area than ever before.

There are however spouses who have regular extramarital relationships in the presence of a satisfactory sexual and emotional life in their marriage. These are men and women who have a lot of sex in their own marriage and yet seek more outside it. On the surface they appear selfish, self-centred, sexually indulgent beings in whose favour very little can be said. They appear insatiable, even though their affairs are transient and purposeless.

Recent work[5] has tended to show that sexual behaviour is linked with the personality. The stable extrovert with a high sexual drive is likely to have an excessive need for intercourse. This intercourse, like much of the extrovert's behaviour, is frequent and shallow and does not engage any depths of the partner's personality. Such a make-up has a very high threshold for sensory stimulation and a great deal of emotional excitement is required in order to make an impact. The extrovert appears to be having a fine time, but in practice such a person needs frequent and intense stimulation to be aroused, an arousal which is not retained for long and therefore needs constant repetition. The extrovert has endless affairs, all of which mean very little, since he is propelled by a make-up which yearns for excitement. This does not mean that extroverts cannot restrain their behaviour, but it is more difficult and the apparent instantaneous gaiety is an unceasing seeking for a reliable and retainable experience.

The instability of the extrovert can extend to the introvert who has a low sexual drive, strong inhibitions, feelings of guilt and difficulties in meeting people of the opposite sex and is likely to try fleeting sexual relationships which do not endure. Finally there is the sexual activity of the person whose emotions are deeply buried and who appears on the surface cold, calculating and unable to maintain any close relationship. Such a person has intercourse as a desperate attempt to break through the grip of alienation which keeps them at a distance from others. Such men in particular can tolerate warm contact for a very limited period and sex is a way of breaking down their isolation.

All these categories of extramarital activity make it very difficult to put all adultery in the same group. Christ avoided condemnation, but his direction to go away and try to sin no more, or to overcome the human difficulties, is something which is much more easily accomplished when the personality is examined in depth.

Emotional dimension

As with sexual difficulties, continuation of emotional problems such as noncommunication, little time spent together or persistent unresolved conflict, may continue in the second phase. Now that the patterns are seen to persist, the relationship begins to deteriorate seriously. Most marriages however adapt and cope with these problems. The particular emotional difficulties of this phase are those that involve change in the personality.

1. DEPENDENCE–INDEPENDENCE

The first feature that is likely to change is the degree of emotional dependence that one spouse has on the other. Emotional dependence means that the spouse, for example the wife, looks up to her husband for guidance, clarification and decision making. In a sense he is still an extension of a powerful parental figure. Gradually however her dependence lessens. She wants to try more and more to live her life on the basis of her own evaluations and decisions. Her husband, seeing this growth, has to encourage it and adapt to the new level of independence in his wife. Most husbands do just this and a new level of mutual autonomy emerges. This does not mean that dependence is no longer needed, but it does mean that it is a mature form which leans on the husband but does not disintegrate if he is not there, or if he does not know some particular answer. Mature dependence is an expression of sustaining without removing from each other the freedom to run their own life.

Some husbands or wives find the emergence of their spouse unacceptable. They have been accustomed to wield power and they cannot share it now. The spouse's independence is a threat to their own position and they cannot tolerate it. By opposing the changes they antagonize the spouse who gradually feels imprisoned and suffocated. Anger spills over into the sexual field and intercourse is refused by the angry partner. This in turn leads to arguments and very soon the marriage is in turmoil. Such a marriage needs help before it is too late and the independent partner decides that they cannot live with their spouse any more.

2. CLARIFICATION OF IDENTITY

As the formerly dependent partner withdraws from the influence of their spouse they begin to think, feel, act and evaluate life from their own point of view. They no longer see things the way their partner does. They change their values and priorities, they become clear as to who they are, what is their purpose in life and what they want to do with it. This is where conflicts within marriage may occur. The spouse may decide they do not wish to be married, that they are in the wrong vocation, with the wrong person, living the wrong sort of life. Their partner may remain a friend but becomes incomprehensible as a spouse. Clarification may occur slowly or rapidly in the thirties or the forties. Such situations puzzle outsiders who have seen only a stable marriage and have not been able to understand the internal turmoil taking place in the depths of the emerging personality.

3. SELF-ESTEEM

The absence of autonomy and clarity of identity has meant that the spouses possess very little of themselves. They act with their bodies but these still belong to their parents or parent substitutes, they think with minds but the thoughts are those of others, they feel but their feelings are those which they accepted as appropriate from various sources of influence. It is only with the gradual removal of these external influences and the acceptance of the self as belonging to one's self that self-esteem rises. The spouse begins to feel worthy of attention. What is praised actually belongs to one's self and is lovable because what is loved is truly one's self. Praise, affirmation and love can be accepted and reciprocated because the person who receives and gives no longer lives by kind permission of others. The transformation of Pinocchio was from a wooden toy to a real boy; the transformation of each one of us is from delegated existence and worth to self-acceptance and possession of a lovable self.

The part that each spouse can play in the emergence of their partner is considerable. Instead of being sources of retardation and inhibition, partners who are empathetic to the changes in their spouse can facilitate the process.

These changes can make or break a marriage and are part of the growth process which can be a prolonged crisis in the life of a marriage, leading either to satisfactory mutual growth or to the wreck of the relationship. Support for marriage needs to reach the depths of such changes. Such assistance is one of the challenges of contemporary marriage.

Intellectual dimension

The essential point of the second phase of marriage is that the deeper layers of the personality are seeking expression. The couple begin to relate with parts of themselves that were hitherto undeveloped, unacceptable or unconscious The single most important feature of this phase is the change in outlook, attitudes, opinions and values. A common example is that a husband may change his priorities from work orientation and drive for success to the importance of living, relating, feeling and interacting with others. He may wish to take up another occupation concerned with the church, social work or some form of caring. The same may apply to the wife. Political views may change and indeed all that is valued may gradually alter. The important thing is that the changes are congruent and that the spouses can accept the alterations in each other.

Spiritual dimension

Religious conflict may arise from conflicting attitudes over birth control, sterilization and abortion. To some Christian consciences some or all of these actions are seriously reprehensible and if the spouse insists on any of them there may be a serious spiritual clash.

Independent of this special form of conflict, the emergence of the personality may also result in the abandonment of the faith in which a person was brought up. Such faith, if not effectively integrated in the personality, may become meaningless and another alien influence which has to be discarded. Surprisingly the rejection of a formal faith may be accompanied by a considerable interest in God. Such loss of practising faith may lead to conflict regarding the religion of the children.

But in most marriages it is the ever-deepening interaction of sustaining, healing and growth which gradually unveils the springs of love of the couple. As the love deepens so the spiritual sources of this dynamic entity influence their life. The connection between love, mystery and God may not be clear but spouses recognize the connecting link or the presence of something which transforms them whenever they are conscious of its presence.

Children

These twenty years see the entry of children into school and spans the school years. Intellectual growth is well known and is the chief interest of the school. The parents contribute their part to the intellectual growth of the child by appropriate stimulation. Parents in particular are responsible for facilitating the growing autonomy of the child, the fruition of their sexual gender and the capacity to feel lovable. The capacity to love and be loved is largely internalized from the atmosphere which children imbibe in the home. This readiness to love has to integrate with the awakening of physical sexuality at puberty, and the parents have the responsibility to prepare for both.

Ultimately adolescence is reached and presents the final phase of separation between the growing person and their parents. Adolescents may still remain at home whilst they are learning how to cope with life after school, in further education or work, or they may depart. The ability to leave home, cope with work and form relationships with the opposite sex are the major challenges of adolescence.

In the process of achieving these objectives some tension with parents is inevitable, but the anticipated turbulence is not necessarily what will happen. Most homes negotiate adolescence with minimum trauma.

References (Chapter 11)

1. Thornes, B. and Collard, J., *Who Divorces?* Routledge and Kegan Paul, 1979.

2. Levin, R. and Levin A., *Sexual Pleasure: The Surprising Preference of 100,000 Women*. Redbook, 1975.

3. Thornes and Collard, p.102.

4. Kinsey A.C. *et al.*, *Sexual Behaviour of the Human Female*. W.B. Saunders, 1953.

5. Eysenck, H.J., *Sex and Personality*. Abacus, 1978.

CHAPTER 12

The Later Years

The third phase of marriage extends from about the age of fifty till the death of one spouse, which statistically is likely to be the man. Death however may not intervene for twenty to twenty-five years, and so there ensues a third phase in marriage which is the product of our age with its increasing health and medical advances. These are the years when the couple face each other, once again alone.

Several studies have tended to show that marital satisfaction begins to fall soon after marriage and particularly when the children arrive, remains at a low ebb and increases again in this phase when the children have left.[1,2]

Although events in this phase overlap with the previous one, they will be considered primarily as a third-phase phenomenon.

Social dimension

During these years the main social events include the husband's work position, the illness or death of the parents of the couple and the marriage of the couple's children.

The job of the husband has been referred to already. The forties overlap with the fifties and the husband is now fairly clear that he has reached the limits of his professional advance. Workmen in the lower socio-economic group have reached their peak a long time ago in their twenties and their thirties, and their means of advance are rises of their salaries. The professional and managerial classes not only have reached the limits of their advance but they may also be made redundant or have to retire early.

In these circumstances it is the wife who has to be sustaining. She has to restore the self-esteem of her husband if his ambition has been greater than his talents. At such moments the husband feels low, insecure and his self-esteem is reduced. The wife has the task and responsibility of restoring confidence in her husband by making him feel worthy of love independently of his achievement. The same support is needed if he has to retire early or has been made redundant. All these circumstances are exceedingly traumatic and, having lowered the self-esteem of the husband, radiate further in their negative impact. The husband may become irritable, full of complaints, and may lash out verbally and sometimes physically. In deep despair such a man may turn to drink and even to a suicidal attempt. The task of the wife is to heal the wounds of apparent uselessness which overwhelm her husband. Demonstrations of affection, sexual intercourse, encouragement and the maintenance of hope, where this is realistic, can maintain the spirits of the husband until a solution of the job situation is reached.

During these years the couples' parents are likely to become sick and/or die. Spouses have the responsibility to look after their sick parents and occasionally to provide room in their own house for the survivor. If the couple are united in the presence of a good relationship, they will assist each other to give support to their aging parents or in-laws. If on the other hand there is marked tension between them or with their parents or in-laws, the presence of illness or entry into the home by the elderly relative may become a source of tension.

The arrival of an elderly parent in the home often coincides with the marriage of the children. However as already mentioned, the children may decide to have extensive premarital sexual intercourse, to live with their boy/girlfriend and refuse to marry, at least temporarily; such behaviour may shock and prove a source of marked parental distress. In particular if the mother does not approve of her daughter's boy friend, then the marriage may go ahead without parental approval.[3] This is a particular loss to brides in the lowest social class, where traditionally there is a deep bond between mother and daughter.

Normally, where good will exists between the parties and the family, all these problems are negotiable. Grandparents are either accommodated in the spouse's home or have their own abode and are visited frequently. Children are usually on good terms with their parents and indeed a new relationship now emerges with them as they become adults.

The departure of the children leaves the parents with greater freedom and a renewed interest in each other. Until retirement, earnings are high and the costs reduced, thus encouraging time together for the spouses who may want to travel and visit unknown places, people and situations. This is also the time when new hobbies may be acquired.

Finally retirement arrives for the husband, and this may coincide with that of the wife. Most men are prepared for their retirement. Some are not; indeed they may consciously refuse to recognize the pending event and when it comes it takes them by surprise. Occasionally the point of retirement is very painful, particularly if there are no alternative ways of spending time. Such a person may be overcome by an excessive anxiety or even depression.

Thus this phase of marriage sees the departure of the adolescents from home, leaving alone the spouses, whose own parents may need their help. But in any case they have some freedom to do things which please them and which they may not have been able to do before.

Physical dimension

This is the phase where illness makes frequent appearance. A fundamental fear surrounding illness at this stage is the danger of the ultimate loss of the partner or the consequences of a crippling disease. The attitude to illness varies amongst couples. There are husbands and wives who find it very difficult to nurse their partner. Indeed they find the passivity and helplessness of illness a source of anxiety and disquiet. They feel obliged to attend to their sick partner but there is a reluctance, not from indifference, but from fear of illness. In such a situation the sick spouse may be bitter, particularly if they are seldom sick and, on the rare occasions when they need this type of sustaining, it is not forthcoming.

Again it is easy to reach hasty conclusions about the apparent selfishness of the reluctant spouse. If illness frightens, then they tend to run away from it. But why should it frighten them? Because they are fearful not only that they might catch the disease itself, or that they will be inept attenders, but their own sense of independence is threatened. Anybody in need is a threat to their unrecognized needs to be looked after. This attitude to illness is often present from the very start of marriage but it may only reveal itself during this phase when the frequency and severity of illness are more common. Sometimes it is the sick person who cannot accept help because their independence is threatened. Sickness is in fact a return to childhood dependence which may be totally unacceptable. Such a person resists nursing care, which they call fuss, because they feel that they are losing their adulthood and turning into helpless children.

The sexual life of the couple in this phase has received a lot of attention in recent years. For centuries sexual intercourse was seen primarily for procreation and the life-cycle was that of marriage, procreation and when the children grew up and were ready to marry, the parents died. Increasingly sex is seen as a uniting, loving experience which has a significance beyond the reproductive years. Thus the menopause of the woman, which occurs approximately at the age of fifty, is not a signal for cessation of intercourse. The menopause has no effect on the frequency or enjoyment of intercourse, but wives with previous difficulties have now a reason to rationalize their dislike of sex.[4] A small group of women, calculated by Kinsey to be of the order of 11 per cent, had not had an orgasm or enjoyment of sex with their husband after twenty years of marriage.[5] These are however the exceptions, the overwhelming majority of couples enjoy their sexual life which continues in the sixties, seventies and even the eighties.[6]

The main threat to sexual intercourse does not come however from the wife in this phase but from the husband whose impotence level begins to rise during these decades. Kinsey calculated that 6.7 per cent of men were impotent by the age of 50, 18.4 per cent by 60, 27 per cent by 70 and 75 per cent by 80.[7] Sometimes impotence can occur in the forties with men who have had a poor sexual drive and infrequent intercourse throughout their life.[8]

Thus there is evidence that biological factors play a prominent part in the reduction of sexual drive and in the associated impotence. Indeed the prognosis for function is poor if the impotence has been continuously present from three to five years.[9,10,11] Despite the difficulty of helping couples with impotence problems in these years, there is still hope of improvement if seeking help is not delayed.

This phase of marriage is not spared extramarital activity. Indeed ageing may stir up anxiety about sexual effectiveness and both spouses may indulge in such behaviour. In a study in the United States half of the husbands whose children had left home expressed a desire for an extramarital affair and a quarter had one.[12] In another study, also in the United States about one-third of all wives had had extramarital affairs. [13]

Thus the overall picture of sexual activity in this phase is that of reduced incidence but with a very wide margin of continuity and enjoyment. Adultery involves about a quarter of husbands and a third of wives. As in all stages of marriage adultery should be taken seriously and examined. It is often saying something loudly and clearly to the partners. Instead of burying the episode, it needs understanding and, if possible, a repairing of the cause. The cause may be a deteriorating relationship or insufficient sexual activity. In either case steps can be taken to improve the situation. The threat of loss of the spouse, which adultery brings forth, is a damaging anxiety which needs allaying as soon as possible

Emotional dimension

One of the patterns of marital difficulty which emerge during these years is closely linked with occasions of adultery. This is the pattern in which the departure of children leaves the parents alone, but even worse without a meaningful relationship between themselves. This of course is not a common phenomenon but when it occurs it is particularly painful.

This problem is specific to the third phase, but there may be difficulties outstanding from the first and second phases. In particular the emotional movement of independence from dependence, clarification of the identity and the rise of self-esteem may be continuing for a small minority during these years.

For the majority of couples these are the years where a synthesis of opposites takes place, a view which is owed to Jung.[14] Thus increasingly the inferior or lesser side of the person, or the shadow, is integrated with the conscious reality ego. The feminine side in man fuses with the dominant masculine reality and the masculine side in women with their feminine reality. Men mellow with the years and women assume some of the qualities of men. 'Thus to achieve wholeness in man, as in the deity, the opposites are cancelled out; good and evil, conscious and unconscious, masculine and feminine, dark and light are raised to a synthesis expressed by the *coniunctio oppositorum.*'[15]

This psychological integration of opposites, leading to the concept of self which is a wholesome unity of the personality, occurs to various degrees in this phase. Couples draw together as their integrated selves meet each other. There is now a much greater understanding and empathy as their personalities have conscious access to the whole of themselves.

Thus for the majority of couples this third phase is an enjoyable one as companionship and sharing of leisure activities increase[16,17] and as the mutual emotional communication deepens to a growing sense of oneness.

Furthermore the married life of their children assumes an importance, especially with the arrival of grandchildren. Parents in good relationship with their children assist in baby-sitting to relieve some of the pressure of parenting. Grandparents have the pleasure of looking after their grandchildren without the responsibility of parenthood. This is an arrangement that is convenient to everybody. But the support of the married child goes well beyond this into a continuous social, emotional and material sustaining until the time comes when the roles are reversed and it is the children who look after the elderly parents.

Intellectual dimension

The synthesis referred to at the emotional level also occurs on the intellectual plane. The couple transform their knowledge and skills into wisdom. This distillation of knowledge makes communication much more meaningful. Interests may flourish and, in addition to doing things together, there may also be diverse interests which are pursued on their own.

Spiritual dimension

The transformation of knowledge into wisdom with the integration of the self leads to new openness, values, attitudes and needs. The spiritual acquires a new sense of significance as the material needs have been met. Men and women start second journeys[18] in which service to others plays a more important role than monetary gain. Men may change their vocations in the forties and fifties and become priests, social workers or engage in voluntary work in the community. Women, likewise, having completed their childbearing, may start helping others. It is important that these spiritually orientated values are shared by both spouses, otherwise rifts of interest may develop.

With advancing years the search for God or an equivalent transcendental force deepens. It is a deep quest for the meaning of life. The relationship between the spouses has given a feel, a taste of the immanence of the divine in the love shared. There is now a quest for the origin, the transcendental reality, which seizes and energizes the couple during these years.

It is often thought that the search for God at this age is a desperate insurance project. Men and women are afraid to meet their end without faith. This is far from the answer. Many die without a formal attachment to any religion but with a thirst for the divine partially satisfied.

Marriage, with its manifold opportunities for love and pain, sacrifice and joy, hurt and forgiveness, provides the essential ingredients for directing the soul to its source and these are the years when there is a definite movement towards this destination. This does not mean that earlier phases of marriage do not lend themselves to such a discovery. But there are many other urgent priorities which dilute the intensity of the quest. There is a need for a certain withdrawal from the world to seek its creator and saviour and these years encourage this.

Death of spouse

The third phase ends with the death of one spouse, often the husband. There is a natural period of grief, which in some cases becomes severe and turns into a depression, but this is rare.[19] More often there is a grieving process and then little by little the spouse is remembered from the images which have been internalized over the married years. These images are pictorial and affective and a powerful memory remains which subsequently consolidates itself. Anniversaries are a sharp reminder of the deceased, and within the Christian tradition there are the feasts of All Saints and All Souls which are reminders and which celebrate the reality of the unity of the living and the dead under the supreme rule of God Almighty. For those who have faith, prayer is of course a constant means of communication between the living and the dead because, in faith, life does not end – it is transformed into a mystery of relationship between the individual and God.

Children

In this third phase the children have become adults who have a new relationship with their parents. The majority of the children will in turn marry and, as time passes by, there will be a gradual reversal of roles of dependence. It is the parents who will become emotionally and sometimes materially dependent. The cycle of life in the family conserves, as far as is possible, the continuity of relationship between one generation and another in a ceaseless, changing relationship of love.

Summary

The three phases of marriage with their individual characteristics are a reminder that marriage is a dynamic unfolding process with its own distinctive features in each phase. The viability of marriage depends on the continuing realization at a minimum level of these various dimensions.

References (Chapter 12)

1. Rollins, B.C. in *Journal of Marriage and the Family* (1974) 36,271.

2. Walker, C. in *Equalities and Inequalities in Family Life* (ed. R. Chester and J. Peel). Academic Press, 1977.

3. Thornes, B. and Collard, J., *Who Divorces?* Routledge and Kegan Paul, 1979.

4. Ballinger, C.B. in *British Medical Journal* (1976) I, 1183.

5. Kinsey A.C. *et al.*, *Sexual Behaviour in the Human Female*. W.B. Saunders, 1953.

6. Masters, W.H. and Johnson, V.E. in *Middle Age and Ageing* (ed. B.L. Neugarten). University of Chicago Press, 1968.

7. Kinsey, A.C., *Sexual Behaviour in the Human Male*. W.B. Saunders, 1948.

8. Ansan, J.M. in *British Journal of Psychiatry* (1975) 127, 737.

9. Johnson, J. in *Journal of Psychosomatic Research* (1965) 9, 145.

10. Cooper, A.J. in *British Journal of Psychiatry* (1968) 114, 719.

11. Cooper, A.J. in *British Journal of Psychiatry* (1969) 115, 709.

12. Johnson, R.E., 'Marital Partners during the Middle Years'. Ph.D. dissertation, University of Minnesota, 1968.

13. Levin, R.J., *The Redbook Report of Premarital and Extramarital Sex*. Redbook, 1975.

14. Moreno, A., *Jung, Gods and Modern Man*. Sheldon Press, 1974.

15. ibid., p.60.

16. Hayes, M.P. and Sinnett, N. in *Journal of Home Economics* (1971) 63, 669.

17. Orthner, D.K. in *Journal of Marriage and the Family* (1975) 37, 91.

18. O'Collins, G., *The Second Journey*. Villa Books, Dublin, 1979.

19. Dominian, J., *Depression*. Collins, 1976.

PART IV

Marital Breakdown

CHAPTER 13

Marital Breakdown

From the Old Testament, right through the New Testament, and in the tradition of Christianity, marital breakdown and divorce have been seen as violations of the basic nature of marriage which, as a covenant relationship, should remain inviolate. Nevertheless breakdown of individual marriages has continued, and in this chapter there is an examination of the contemporary situation of this topic. The first three parts of the book have outlined the possibilities of the positive outcome of modern marriage; in this section a complementary part of the picture is described. This is the world of marital upheaval, conflict and suffering, as relationships which started with intense hope fade into disillusion and a sense of failure.

Demography

What is the incidence of marital breakdown? There is no way by which this information can ever be known with complete exactitude. What is known with certainty is the number of petitions and divorces which occurs annually. These figures are known for England and Wales.

A quick perusal of Table 1 reveals a steady rise throughout the century until 1947 when there was a leap in numbers reflecting the disturbance of the war years. After this rapid rise the number of divorces fell but not to the previous incidence. Then in 1961 numbers began to rise and since then have never abated reaching 143,000 in 1978, falling slightly in 1979, but rising again in 1980. Careful inspection shows that the rise accelerated after 1971.

TABLE 1

Petitions for dissolution and annulment of marriage and divorces.
Selected dates for England and Wales.

	Petitions	Divorces
1911	902	650
1921	2,848	2,733
1931	4,784	4,013
1941	8,305	R6,368
1947	48,500	60,254
1951	38,382	28,767
1961	31,905	25,394
1971	110,900	74,400
1972	110,700	119,000
1975	140,100	120,500
1976	146,400	126,700
1977	170,000	129,000
1978	163,600	143,700
1979	163,900	138,000
1980		148,200

(Reference – Registrar General)

The year 1971 saw a major change in the law. Up to then divorce was obtained on the basis of the matrimonial offence. The matrimonial offence was a concept by which marriage was seen as a contract, certain offences against which could provide the basis for its dissolution. These offences consisted of adultery, desertion for three years, cruelty and five years' admission to a hospital for mental disease. In 1969 the Divorce Reform Act was passed which came into operation in January 1971. Under this act the sole ground for divorce was the irretrievable breakdown of marriage. The bases for irretrievable breakdown are: adultery which the petitioner finds intolerable to live with; unreasonable behaviour of the spouse with which the petitioner cannot live; desertion or living apart for two years and the spouse's consent; or living apart for five years with or without consent of the spouse. This act which sees marriage essentially as a relationship has been a model which has spread round the world. It certainly makes divorce relatively easy even though economically it is more exacting, as the law has continuously changed to ensure the economic well-being of the wife and children. Husbands have often to maintain two households, that of their first marriage and also of the second, and often their resources do not easily accommodate such expense.

The increase in divorce in England and Wales in the last twenty years is mirrored both in Europe[1] and in the United States.[2] In the last ten years the divorce rate in England and Wales[3] has approximately doubled for the ages above 25 and trebled for those aged under 25. The increase in divorce rates throughout Western society is a cultural phenomenon of the greatest significance.

When does this breakdown occur? Up to recent times the calculation was made on the basis of the time that divorce occurred, the *de jure* duration. But in fact couples cease to cohabit before their divorce and it is the *de facto* duration that matters.

Studies in the United States, in Europe and in Britain show that a great deal of breakdown occurs in the first five years of marriage. Thus Monahan, summarizing the findings of other investigators and his own, places the highest incidence of separation in the first year followed by the second.[4] In Sweden an analysis of the annual risk of divorce up to forty years after marriage showed that divorce increases from the time of marriage reaching a peak four years later.[5] In Britain Chester found that 38 per cent of divorcees had ceased to cohabit by their fifth year of marriage but only 16 per cent had divorced during that time.[6] A more recent study found that 34 per cent of divorcees had separated by the fifth year although only 11 per cent had obtained a divorce; by the tenth anniversary 60 per cent of couples who subsequently divorced had already separated.[7] Thus there is strong evidence that whilst divorce can occur at any time during the marriage cycle, the first five years account for nearly 40 per cent of separations and the rest are spread over the whole cycle with a peak after twenty years of marriage. The same study[7] found that independently of when the divorce took place, 80 per cent of divorced women and 59 per cent of divorced men thought that serious marital difficulties had started by the fifth anniversary of the marriage.

Thus as far as preventive work is concerned the early years of marriage are crucial, and wives in particular appear to be far more sensitive to the presence of serious problems than husbands. This is another important point in the work of prevention; so often a wife knows that things are not right at the beginning of the marriage, but neither the husband nor their priest nor counsellor pays attention to her complaints. Gradually her hopes are eroded and the

time soon passes when useful intervention can take place because
the motivation to fight for the marriage is lost.

MACRO-SOCIAL REASONS

What are the reasons for this steep rise in marital breakdown in the
last two decades? At the heart of every marriage that breaks down
lies a social, physical, emotional, intellectual or spiritual incompatibility, either singly or in combination. What differs from age to
age is the variety of grounds that contribute to such incompatibility.
In this section the current global reasons are considered.

At the head of this list must come woman's emancipation and
therefore the consequences of a changing man-woman relationship.
For thousands of years there has been a patriarchical structure in
which the man had the superior position. Marriages were fashioned
in a hierarchy of relationship in which the husband was the head
and the wife the subordinate member of the partnership. The actual
working out in practice of this social relationship must have varied
from marriage to marriage. In some marriages the husband was the
titular head whilst the wife really exercised power. But such power
was circumscribed within the household. In public and within society as a whole the man remained the leader. Furthermore there
were social and economic constraints which made it difficult for the
wife to leave her husband since she relied on him for support.

It is only in our day and time that woman's emancipation has
taken a leap forward and that society is rapidly recognizing the
equality of worth of the sexes in their dignity and rights. The
privileges of the man are slowly being reduced and the husband-
wife relationship has expectations of a life of equality.

Such equality makes heavy demands on communication, mutual
respect and the need for sharing responsibilities. These changes
have been embraced with such rapidity, in the last quarter of a
century, that they have outstripped preparation, education and
support for such a style of relationship. In brief, expectations run
well ahead of the resources of couples to operate such massive social
and psychological changes, and the consequences are large-scale
incompatibilities which are no longer accepted as a legitimate cross
but are reacted to with divorce and change of partners.

The large-scale entry of women into the labour force means that
they have an economic independence which no longer coerces them
to live in intolerable personal situations. The advent of widespread

birth control also means that another factor that tied women to their homes, namely multiple pregnancies, has gradually been eliminated. The present-day family is small and children arrive usually when they are deliberately planned. The result is that women have a much greater degree of personal freedom and the ability to return to remunerative work with its accompanying independence.

Deeper expectations are not confined to the social level. As already described in Part II of the book, the gradual erosion of fixed roles brings couples to an intimacy which engages a deeper layer of their psychological being. This is a layer which has been influenced by a century of psychological development in which the psyche's impact on the personality is being increasingly understood and appreciated.

These psycho-social developments have coincided with a period of rapid detachment from official religious institutions. In particular the binding commitment of vows has been diluted and continuity is no longer seen as a virtue. As already discussed, continuity answers some of the person's deepest needs, but currently the disposable is in ascendancy and time will be required to appreciate that social, emotional and sexual expectations in marriage are best served with continuity. In summary, the whole of Western society is being swept by ideological changes. These changes ultimately impinge on marriage which is the institution that carries the collective burden of all these changes.

MICRO-SOCIAL REASONS
Within the major factors described above there are specific ones which have been identified as having their own adverse effects. These are age at marriage, pre-marital pregnancy, housing, social class, education level, and religion.

1. *Age*
The relationship between age at marriage and outcome has been studied extensively. The results are fairly uniform and clearly indicate that youthful marriages are risky propositions.[8,9,10] The situation is summed up in *Population Trends* thus:

> There is a very much enhanced risk of divorce at any given duration if the bride is under 20 years of age at marriage. For example 9 per cent of all marriages contracted in 1963 had ended in divorce by 11 years of marriage duration; but where the bride

was under the age of 20 years at marriage, 16 per cent had ended in divorce at the same marriage duration, compared with only 8 per cent where the bride was aged 20-24 at marriage. The much higher risk of divorce of younger brides is enhanced still further if the groom is also under the age of 20 at marriage.[9]

Whilst youthful marriages are at greater risk not all of them end in divorce, so there must be some factors which aggravate the age element and others which are supportive. Two factors further increase the risks of youthful marriage. These are premarital pregnancy and belonging to socio-economic Class V. It is known that both these characteristics, which are of themselves risky elements, are found in excess in marriages with spouses under the age of 20. On the other hand the presence of support from parents, good housing conditions and sturdy personalities are advantages which will protect some couples from the higher risks in this age group.

Why are youthful marriages risky propositions? The fact is that whilst men and women complete their physical and intellectual development before the age of 20, emotional growth is certainly not completed, and since marital success is intimately related nowadays to emotional stability, incomplete emotional maturity is a responsible factor. Some young people who find themselves in confusion about their personal identity, i.e., who they are, where they are going, what they want to achieve with their life, marry in order to acquire the status of a married person. Unfortunately a ring on the left hand does not by itself produce clarity of identity, and the marriage may be given up in a short time after it has served its purpose of being a bridge between adolescence and adulthood.

2. *Premarital pregnancy*
Reference has already been made to the adverse element of premarital pregnancy. Work over a number of years by Christensen in the United States had established that the presence of premarital pregnancy increased the risk of divorce.[11] Other studies[12,13] have confirmed this finding. The reasons for this phenomenon are multiple. For some couples the pregnancy binds them before they are ready for marriage. Such hurried marriages may lack accommodation, adequate financial provisions and even kinship support. Another factor is that the presence of the baby diverts attention from the spouses in the important early years, preventing the formation of a strong bond between them.[14]

As with the factor of age, not all marriages with premarital pregnancy end in divorce. These are the couples who had a long courtship and their pregnancy is deliberate. These are also marriages which have parental support, less premarital problems and less postpuerperal depression.[15]

However, independently of the outcome, those with premarital pregnancies tend to have a higher sexual drive before and during marriage and extramaritally. This suggests a personality profile tending towards an extrovert make-up with a certain compulsion towards higher sexual activity with shallow personal relationships.

3. *Housing*

It is part of the desire of most newly married couples to be able to go to their own separate accommodation where they have the privacy and comfort to establish their own relationship. Research evidence of the housing history of a divorced population[16] indicates that many such couples had to start their marriage by sharing and being in conflict with those with whom they shared during the first year of marriage. In addition the divorced population moved more frequently than the continuously married, and these changes were not planned but were haphazard and impulsive. Such changes meant that the couple had to uproot themselves frequently, interrupting their contact with neighbours and friends, and had to start afresh. These interruptions are stressful for the couple but particularly for the wife, who is denied access to the support and security of her immediate environment, because as soon as she established a network of friends she has to uproot herself.

4. *Social class and education*

Repeated studies in the United States have shown an inverse relationship between social class and divorce. That is to say the lower the socio-economic group the higher is the risk of divorce, and the same applies to education level. Studies in Britain are few. An early one[17] showed no such relationship. A recent study by Gibson[18] confirmed this finding, but it was noted that social classes V and III (non- manual) were more prone to divorce, a finding which has been exactly replicated in another study.[19]

What are the reasons for the finding that implicates social classes V and III (non-manual)? Social class V has a loading of divorce-prone factors such as youthful marriages, a higher incidence of premarital pregnancy, unsatisfactory housing and poor financial conditions. The proneness to divorce in this social class is understandable. As far as social class III (non-manual) is concerned these factors do not apply. But this social class is not securely attached. Its members do not clearly belong to the class above or below them and therefore the social supports are weak. Furthermore, if the husband is the person who has achieved economic success, he may fraternize with acquaintances who are not meaningful to his wife. She may think that he is abandoning her and what she stands for, in fact sacrificing her for a world she is equipped neither to share nor understand. Gradually she feels alienated from her husband who is considered to be climbing beyond his resources, in fact getting too big for his boots.

Education level, which plays such an important part in the United States with the recurrent inverse findings, does not play such an important part in England and Wales.

5. *Religion*

The religious adherence of a couple, if similar, is likely to provide an additional strength to the motivation of working hard for the preservation of the marriage. Also there are likely to be less contentious matters such as conflict over contraception, abortion, sterilization, religious education of children and the values the couple wish to pursue. Mixed marriages have been associated with divorce in the United States.[20] The absence of any religious attachment in either partner was found also to be associated with proneness to divorce,[21] a finding which has also been confirmed in England and Wales.[22] Adherence to a faith need not be expressed in church attendance, but, when it is, it is associated with greater marital stability, a finding both in the US[23] and in the UK[24] These findings accord with the position of Christian and Jewish denominations which emphasize indissolubility. Furthermore, if the couple are active church attenders, they are more likely to be highly motivated to preserve their ideals of marriage.

However, these barriers to divorce are likely to become less strong as society becomes more and more secularized, and the relationship of faith to divorce needs consistent examination. There is no doubt that increasing numbers of both faiths are resorting to divorce, and so the protection of religious faith appears less strong than it was.

First phase (first 5 years of marriage)

The factors mentioned above have been studied repeatedly and a consensus of their importance has emerged. So far the adverse influences have been examined in terms of global events, reinforced by specific social circumstances, but there is a third element, namely specific features in each phase of marriage in the social, physical, emotional, intellectual and spiritual dimensions. These elements have been subject to repeated clinical observation.

SOCIAL DIMENSION

The social elements are the separation from parents, setting up home and the financial distribution of responsibility for running it, the handling of premarital friendships and the pursuit of work and leisure. The difficulties associated with all these features have already been described in the chapters dealing with the various phases of marriage. Here there is a brief recapitulation of the main points and some expansion of particular issues.

1. *Separation from parents*

The effective separation from parents described at the very beginning of the Bible is paramount to the well-being of marriage. Spouses want to separate from their parents to whom they return in due course.

2. *Household arrangements*

The traditional household arrangements were centred on a distribution of responsibility in which the wife had the main share of running the home. Increasingly the husband is expected to participate in running the house, particularly when the wife is working which is so often the case nowadays. Difficulties surround the contribution of the husband. Sometimes promises made during courtship are not kept after marriage. As a result the working wife or mother gets excessively tired and resents the fact that her husband escapes lightly as if he were still a bachelor. The distribution of work appears grossly unfair and the husband's inability to assist is interpreted as a demonstration of not caring.

3. *Financial arrangements*

It is rare for money arguments to be absent in the presence of marital conflict. If in fact money becomes a major topic of contention, it can have deep and lasting negative effects. The wife complains that her husband is mean and irresponsible, and the husband counterattacks that his wife is a poor housekeeper or unduly spendthrift on her personal appearance. The wife in turn complains that her husband drinks or gambles or cannot cope with money.

Occasionally the husband fails completely to take charge of the bills that come. Letters are put aside or not opened. Reminders appear and are ignored. Finally there are court threats. A sensitive wife finds all this repudiation of responsibility difficult to tolerate. She becomes increasingly anxious and possibly insecure. She urges her husband to act and he either reassures her that all is well or complains that she nags him. Finally, in desperation the wife may offer to take over the payment of bills and thus takes a role which is traditionally held by the husband. While her confidence returns if she knows that financial responsibilities have been discharged, she resents having this burden placed on her shoulders.

Although conflict over financial matters may remain throughout enduring marriages, marked disagreement in the early years of marriage may influence the wife to leave if the atmosphere of financial irresponsibility becomes an intolerable stress.

4. *Friends*

Difficulties over previous friendships can arise in certain circumstances. Firstly, as with the parents, one friend or more may retain a central prominence in the life of one partner and their influence may be resented by the other. Sometimes there is a pattern in which a particular friend may have had an affair with one of the spouses. The other spouse may become tormented, comparing the meaning and sexual capacity of this friend with themselves. Questions are asked repeatedly of how the husband or wife compares with the premarital encounter with this friend. The questioning may be prolonged and repetitive. This questioning may last far into the night and the weary spouse may admit to details which further fuel the curiosity and insecurity of the partner. Whatever is revealed is insufficient, and the questioning continues, not so much out of the desire for objective information, but for reassurance that the husband/wife compares well with the predecessor. Sometimes the predecessor is an ex-wife or husband who is thought to be still influential. Such persistent questioning gradually erodes marital trust and can be the beginning of the end of the marriage.

Another problem is the marriage when one spouse has a wide

circle of friends and the other very few, if any. The attendance on the spouse's friends may be resented, and dependence on them may provoke jealousy, rudeness and rejection of them. Such a lonely husband or wife may wish to detach their partner from their circle of friends and reduce them to the same isolation as themselves. In this way both partners may become recluse, isolated and subjected to the strains of a suffocating world circumscribed by each other's company.

5. *Work*

The early years of marriage see the continuation of work by the husband. Marriage does not interfere with the working routine of the husband. Most wives work as well for a period prior to child-bearing. Some 70 per cent of married women work in the first year of marriage in England and Wales, and this percentage drops to 30 per cent by the fifth year.[25] This drop is undoubtedly due to child-bearing, which takes the wife out of work for a variable period. The feature that stands out for the working wife is her tiredness in combining work and household duties unless the husband helps.

Work however is not only a means of economic independence on the part of the wife. It is also a powerful means of preserving her self- esteem which is realized through the sense of immediate reward of accomplishment, the feeling of doing something of value and the friendships and stimulation that work provides. When all this is given up for childbearing and rearing, the world of the wife becomes circumscribed and this is the time when she needs the attentive presence of her husband more than ever. If this is not forthcoming, a sense of being uncared for and unloved descends on her.

6. *Leisure*

Ideally leisure includes a balance between the time spent together and the need for aloneness which is a time of recharging. Each couple begins to work out their leisure activities, with the husband for example maintaining his interest in sport and/or attending the pub and the wife visiting friends and participating in her own hobbies and interests. Separate activities need to be matched by combined outings to the pub, films, theatre, concerts, visiting friends and relatives.

Such a balanced pattern of socialization may be disturbed when one spouse increasingly restricts the freedom of the other and ex-pects their partner to give up their leisure pursuits and stay at home. This reduction of mutual leisure activity may be compounded by the lack of desire to do anything together. A partner who is thus restricted feels trapped and imprisoned as their social activities become increasingly curtailed. They feel confined and resent their isolation. They become homebound and are subjected to the hus-band/wife's insecure hold over them. The spouse who is unwilling to go anywhere and meet others often treats their partner as an object which is there to meet their neurotic needs. The unwilling spouse may have marked or hidden phobic tendencies, finding it very difficult to go out and meet people, and gradually prevents their partner from having their freedom.

PHYSICAL DIMENSION

The first few years of marriage are crucial for establishing sexual rapport. Repeated studies show that marital satisfaction is accom-panied by an equivalent sexual one. In a study (already quoted) in the United States of 100,000 women, 84 per cent of the wives who said they were 'mostly happy' also felt that their sexual life was good or very good. Conversely those who reported unhappiness also felt that their sexual life was unsatisfactory.[26] In a study in England and Wales of 520 divorced men and women, 79 per cent claimed an initial sexual satisfaction, whereas 88 per cent of 570 men and women with continuing marriage experienced satisfaction.[27] Thus some 12–20 per cent start their marriage with sexual difficulties. These problems may be divided into those that involve the quality of lovemaking and the presence of sexual dysfunction.

The quality of lovemaking depends on sensitive appreciation and on accurate response to the spouse's need. This means a careful appraisal of the occasions the partner wants sex, careful preparation in which emotional and bodily contact is made and the ability of the spouses to tell each other what they need and how they want love made to them. A husband may lack sensitivity, cut short the preliminaries of lovemaking and fail to see that his wife is not satisfied. She in turn may avoid expressing criticism in case she hurts her husband. In this way a poor sexual relationship is estab-lished from the very beginning. In addition to this insensitivity of the actual lovemaking, husbands often and wives sometimes may make love under the influence of drink, acting roughly and lacking bodily hygiene.

Beyond these clumsy patterns of lovemaking, the couple may face actual dysfunction at a genital level. The most obvious dysfunction at this stage is non-consummation.[28] In this pattern of dysfunction what often happens is that the couple avoid having sexual intercourse during the courtship, often on moral grounds. After marriage, intercourse is attempted during the honeymoon. The husband attempts penetration and meets a rigid wall in the opening of the vagina which makes penetration impossible. The wife is holding herself tightly and may shout with pain. The husband, eager to avoid hurting his wife, gives up. This is a pattern which is repeated until the couple ceases trying. This common problem is followed by another pattern if low sexual drive is present in either spouse but particularly the husband. This means that intercourse is only attempted every few weeks which may leave the other spouse very dissatisfied. Other rarer problems in this phase of marriage include premature ejaculation, fluctuating impotence on the part of the husband and inability to enjoy sex or absence of orgasm on the part of the wife.[29] Sexual variations are rare causes of marital breakdown with the exception of homosexuality.

All these difficulties may appear at the beginning of a marriage. In the past, when the social structure of mutual roles were emphasized rather than the emotional and sexual content of the relationship, these deficiencies in the sexual life would have been accepted without complaint and certainly not as a reason for marital breakdown. Nowadays expectations of personal fulfilment run high, and sexual disappointment is a powerful factor in subsequent marital breakdown.

EMOTIONAL DIMENSION

The emotional requirements of the couple in these early years is to establish a relationship in which both partners act as adults and give and receive love. For example, instead of the spouse being recognized as a husband or wife, they are sometimes treated as a mother or father. Such a projection may be due to the presence of a dominant parent on whom there was a marked dependence. This pattern is carried over into marriage where the spouse is made to behave as a parent. The projection may be conscious but is often unconscious. The partner on the other hand may need to feel like a parent figure, to be in control and to treat their spouse as a dependent child. This is known as collusion, which is an unconscious matching of needs or roles that fails to do justice to the relationship as it should be realistically. Clearly such collusive relationships are vulnerable because sooner or later the reality has to emerge, and the marriage may not be able to stand the transformation.

Apart from projection, couples have various degrees of personal sensitivity. Thus one spouse may find close relationship difficult and yet expect a good deal of affirmation. These are men and women with high needs of being loved and a low tolerance to disappointment, frustration, rejection or criticism. They have little capacity for disappointment. They find it difficult to trust and their hopes vanish quickly. The ability of the marriage to contain such a vulnerable spouse depends on the resources of their partner. If the partner has a high level of understanding and affection and is persistent in their loving, they may overcome their partner's reticence and deepen their trust. If on the other hand the spouse responds to such sensitivity with lack of demonstration of affection and little availability, has himself/herself a low threshold to frustration, loses their temper frequently or withdraws for long periods, then the presence of one or more of such features exhausts the trust and hope of the vulnerable partner. Drink and gambling makes any relationship difficult but particularly such a sensitive one.

The theory of attractive similarity means that vulnerable people do attract each other. Where two very deprived people come together in matrimony they try to extract from each other qualities of love that are not available. Sometimes the combination is of a shy, deprived person with a partner who is truly loving. To the astonishment of the loving partner, their spouse finds it difficult to accept their love however deprived their background may have been. This astonishes the loving spouse who is yearning to give love but is far more aware of criticism and rejection. This combination of limited ability to respond to love with an enormous capacity to respond to criticism is a recurrent pattern that can destroy the marriage. Its roots are to be found in the background of the individual who grew up with low affirmation and high rejection experiences. Much as such persons yearn to be loved their self-rejection and sense of unworthiness make it difficult for them to believe that others truly want to love them. This is a pattern which is eminently suitable for healing. The loving partner has to persist until the other trusts that they really mean the love expressed. Gradually there is a second opportunity to learn how to be loved and this is achieved in the presence of a spouse who will not be put off. The problem becomes further complicated if the loving partner becomes tired, feels rejected and withdraws. When their spouse is more ready to receive love, they are no longer prepared to give it, and a vicious circle of mutual rejection is set up.

A sensitive, empathetic ability to recognize the needs of the partner is a requirement for modern marriage. Wives on the whole have a greater ability to feel their way into their husband's needs, whereas husbands often find it difficult to listen to and appreciate the inner world of their wives. If the wife feels persistently misunderstood or not understood at all in her social, physical, emotional, intellectual and spiritual needs, then sooner or later she will feel that she is living with a stranger, in fact she becomes very lonely in the presence of her spouse who does not enter her inner world.

INTELLECTUAL AND SPIRITUAL DIMENSIONS

Normally a couple are likely to have similar intellectual and spiritual goals. When these vary markedly then marital breakdown is a distinct possibility.

CHILDREN

The advent of the first child is of great significance to a marriage. It often means the withdrawal of the wife from work and her complete economic dependence on her husband. In the early months of the baby's life, tiredness, irritability and temporary loss of sexual activity are situations that most young couples experience to a greater or lesser extent. These features are accompanied by a reduction in leisure and time spent together unless there are reliable baby sitters.

One feature which stands out as far as the wife is concerned is a postpuerperal syndrome of depression. Most mothers get temporarily depressed, the so-called maternal blues which may last from a few hours to a few days.[30] A small number of these women do not recover and they join another group whose depression starts on the tenth postpuerperal day. The condition in this latter group may persist for weeks, months or years. The wife remains irritable, agitated, tired, disinterested in sex and gradually begins to change in her personality. From being a happy contented person she drags herself around, looking prematurely old, unable to get close to her husband, feeling chronically tired and without any sexual interest.

Naturally, unless the husband clearly understands the condition, he finds the situation increasingly intolerable.

This postpuerperal syndrome may be aggravated by social factors. Stopping work, as already mentioned, deprives the wife not only of her wages but also of the company and support of friends and the rewards of work. There are some women who find rearing a young child incredibly difficult and who long to return to work to save their sanity. For some women the availability of reliable baby-minders, creches and preschool nursery classes are urgent requirements, as an early return to work is essential for them.[31]

Second Phase (30 to 50)

These two decades span the period of marriage during which the children are growing, the professional husband is promoted and the wife returns to work. But at the heart of this period lies profound social, emotional and spiritual change. These are the years in which the person gradually withdraws from accumulated external and internal influences and emerges as a self-directing person in their own right. The emergent feelings, attitudes and values may be radically different from those held when the marriage began. The change involved is often compatible with continuity of the relationship, because both partners are changing in a fairly uniform manner. If not, the unilateral emergence of one spouse may lead to such an alienation between the couple that continuity is impossible.

SOCIAL DIMENSION
Apart from social mobility and its consequences already noted during these years, the children are growing up and when the parents reach the forties, the period of adolescence is reached. Here additional strain is thrown on the parents, particularly if the mother has had excessive responsibility for looking after the children. She may find that she could cope when they were young but not in their adolescence. A reluctant father is dragged in to control and discipline the children who resent his arrival on the scene at this late stage. Family friction is high and, if there are additional problems present, the marriage may experience marked difficulties.

The forties are the years during which the parents of the spouses may fall sick and die. The surviving parent may have to be accommodated in the marital home, and this can produce a good deal of strain if this step is not mutually agreed.

These are the years when wives will return to work in large numbers. It is up to the husband to give additional help to ease the strain on her. Most husbands do just this, but a few do not, and this may lead to excessive fatigue for the wife. These are the circumstances when some wives feel that the only role they provide is to be an effective economic and housekeeping unit. The feeling grows of not being appreciated or loved but being used as a skivvy. Such reactions may lead to looking elsewhere for appreciation, which, if found, may lead to marital breakdown.

PHYSICAL DIMENSION
This phase is not marked by any new sexual problems. The continuing presence of sexual difficulties from the first phase now begins to impinge. Husbands and wives may come to realize that initial difficulties are not transient. A sense of marked frustration and disappointment sets in in the thirties. A feeling that sex is not going to improve begins to take hold. In this atmosphere of disappointment, extramarital affairs may occur in order to find out what sex can be like. If the extramarital experience is good, it may start the process of basic separation between the spouses. A rewarding extramarital experience may restore the self-esteem of the spouse who is no longer prepared to return to the desultory efforts of their partner.

Another important feature of this phase has already been mentioned, namely a protracted postpuerperal syndrome which makes sex extremely rare or non-existent. This is a situation which causes havoc in the marriage and needs urgent attention.

EMOTIONAL DIMENSION
Emotional change can be marked during this phase. The movement from dependence to independence with differentiation of the self and growth of self-esteem is marked. In the past such changes made no significant difference to the continuation of marriage. Nowadays growth in one spouse needs corresponding response in the other

and if this is not forthcoming marital breakdown may ensue. Such breakdown forms a major contribution to divorce.

INTELLECTUAL AND SPIRITUAL DIMENSION

If the thirties is the decade of change from dependence to independence, the forties is a time when the differentiated person begins to integrate the various parts of self. Conscious and unconscious, the good and the bad (shadow), the masculine and feminine parts, the angry and controlling elements, all the ambivalences within the self begin to be resolved and integrated. This brings peace and integration in the individual, who may now change their goal in life.[32] They may want to change jobs, move away from materialistically orientated work to a humanitarian vocation. There is a new sense of awakening of the spiritual dimension, and life may take a new course with an inner peace which steers a new pattern of life. All this is not threatening to the marriage unless the partners fail completely to share the aspirations of their spouse.

Third phase (from age 50 to death of one spouse)

SOCIAL DIMENSION

The process of self-actualization and differentiation of self, which begins in the forties, continues in the fifties. This is the time when the new awarenss of self may lead to a new career with all the uncertainty that this implies for the wife. Such an upheaval may be intolerable to her. Men who have made a success of their business, civil servants who retire early, all these categories of persons may wish to start afresh. Often the wife will be agreeable but sometimes not.

This change affects only a few. The majority will be concerned in completing the last phase of their work, with some having to face early retirement and redundancy. Both can be a shock to the husband whose self-esteem is threatened. His feelings of inferiority may invade his private life and he may become irritable, snappy, depressed and unable to perform sexually. He needs every bit of support he can get from his wife in this situation. If the wife is critical and hostile, the marriage may come under severe strain.

PHYSICAL DIMENSION
Some of the problems of the previous two phases may continue into this one with gradual cessation of intercourse. But usually intercourse continues at a reduced frequency but without difficulty. The main problem which may cause marital breakdown is permanent impotence of the husband and refusal of the wife to have intercourse after the menopause.

EMOTIONAL DIMENSION
Perhaps the single most important pattern of these years is the emotional pattern related to the departure of children. Their exit leaves couples on average twenty to twenty-five of further life together. But for some couples the departure of the children is the eclipse of their own relationship. These parents may have been deliberately waiting for the children to grow up before they leave. For others however the empty-nest phase, as this period is described, takes them completely by surprise. After the departure of the children, the couple look at each other and to their suprise they see a stranger. Despite the fact that they have lived together, eaten and slept and made love, they have failed to forge a reliable emotional bond. One or both had lived their lives through the children and not one another, and when the children depart they have little or nothing in common except the memories of bringing up their children, which is not enough to keep them together.

INTELLECTUAL AND SPIRITUAL DIMENSION
As already suggested this phase overlaps with the last one. It is a period of reassessment of the ultimate values of life. Intellect is turned into wisdom and this wisdom reshapes the priorities in the life of the couple. A problem exists only when these priorities diverge widely between partners.

Summary

Marital breakdown has been presented in this chapter as a major social disruption occurring in the whole of Western society. The factors range from large-scale social changes in the man–woman relationship, through individual adverse social factors, finally aggravated by problems in the interpersonal relationship which vary in various phases of the life-cycle. Knowledge of these factors, if used effectively, can – and already does – help couples to adopt practices that will prevent the breakdown of marriage.

References (Chapter 13)

1. Chester R. (ed.), *Divorce in Europe*. Martinus Nijhoff (Social Science Division, London) 1977.

2. Glick, P.C. and Morton, A.J., 'Perspectives on the Recent Upturn in Divorce and Remarriage', *Demography* (1973) 10, 301.

3. *Population Trends*, No.18. Office of Population Censuses and Surveys, HMSO, 1979.

4. Monahan, T.P. in *American Sociological Review* (1962) 27, 625.

5. Dahlberg, G., *Acta Genetica et Statistica Medica* (1948-51) 1–2, 319.

6. Chester, R., 'The Duration of Marriage to Divorce', *British Journal of Sociology* (1971) 22, 172.

7. Thornes, B. and Collard J., *Who Divorces?* Routledge and Kegan Paul, 1979.

8. ibid., p.71

9. *Population Trends*, No.3. Office of Population Censuses and Surveys, HMSO, 1976

10. Glick, P.C., *American Families*. Wiley, New York, 1957.

11. Christensen, H.T., 'Time of the First Pregnancy as a Factor in Divorce', *Eugenic Review* (1963) 10, 119.

12. Thornes and Collard, p.71.

13. *Population Trends*, No.3.

14. Pohlman, E.H., *Psychology of Birth Planning*. Shenkman, Cambridge, Mass., 1969.

15. Thornes and Collard, p.71.

16. ibid., p.81.

17. Rowntree, G. and Carrier, N.H., 'The Resort to Divorce in England and Wales 1857-1957', *Population Studies* (1958) 2, 188.

18. Gibson, C., 'The Association between Divorce and Social

Class in England and Wales', *British Journal of Sociology* (1974) 25, 79.

19. Thornes and Collard, p.37.

20. Landis, J.T., 'Marriage of Mixed and Non-mixed Religious Faith' in *Selected Studies in Marriage and the Family*. Holt, Rinehart and Winston, New York, 1962.

21. Landis, J.T., 'Some Correlates of Divorce and Non-divorce in the Unhappily Married', *Marriage and Family Living* (1963) 25, 178.

22. Thornes and Collard, p.52.

23. Goode, W.J., *After Divorce*. Free Press, Chicago, 1956.

24. Thornes and Collard, p.52.

25. *Population Trends*, No.2. Office of Population Censuses and Surveys, HMSO, 1975.

26. Levin, R.J. and Levin A., *Sexual Pleasures: The Surprising Preference of 100,000 Women*. Redbook, 1975, p.52.

27. Thornes and Collard, p.97.

28. Friedman, L.J., *Virgin Wives*. Tavistock Publications, 1971.

29. John, D., *Sexual Dysfunction*. John Wiley, 1979.

30. Pitt, B., 'Maternity Blues', *British Journal of Psychiatry* (1973) 122, 431.

31. Rapaport, R., Rapaport, R., *Fathers, Mothers and Others*. Routledge and Kegan Paul, 1977.

32. O'Collins, G., *The Second Journey*. Villa Books, Dublin, 1979.

CHAPTER 14

Consequences of Marital Breakdown

Until very recently the main concern of society and parliament regarding marital breakdown has been the development of divorce laws which could liberate unhappy men and women locked in impossible marriages who could not establish alternative legal unions because the divorce laws did not permit it. After the Second World War this problem caused great concern, and in the course of the 1960s divorce laws began to emerge throughout the Western world which departed from the traditional fault-finding basis to the concept of irretrievable breakdown. Essentially divorce could now be granted when marriage, treated as a relationship, was no longer viable as such. In England and Wales the new act based on these principles was passed in 1969 and became effective in 1971. The rate of divorce was increasing before this, but it accelerated subsequently, although the first slight fall was observed in 1979. During the seventies the growth of divorce has given us an opportunity to look at the consequences in some greater detail. Is there a price to be paid for divorce? This question will be answered in terms of the impact on the spouses, their children and the state.

Impact on spouses

If it is remembered that modern marriage is essentially an emotional attachment forming an affective bond between the couple, then the breakdown of this bond will produce a series of symptoms indicated by anxiety, anger and depression, and that is precisely what has been found in a large-scale study of divorced women.[1] This relates to marriages which have been in being sufficiently long to allow an emotional interaction between the partners who will therefore feel the loss of each other.

As far as anxiety is concerned, a spouse whose partner has left may rush about frantically to discover where their departed spouse has gone. If they find him/her, there may be a dramatic scene of accusations and counter-accusations, mixed with crying, pleading, threatening and cajoling. The departure may not be sudden but threatened over a period of time during which anxiety rises and becomes tension. The tension is manifested in physical complaints such as headaches, loss of sleep, loss of appetite or sometimes the converse, an excess of food intake with increase in weight. The partners may become irritable and this irritability may be accompanied by increased smoking and drinking. Irritability is also associated with snappy behaviour, outbursts towards and punishments of the children which are not remotely deserved. The slightest irritation is exaggerated and any noise unbearable. Anxiety may also be experienced in marked sweating, palpitations, abdominal aches and pains and change of bowel rhythm. At the same time attention and concentration begin to deteriorate. The husband looks at his work and can neither concentrate nor function with any sense of initiative. He is distracted and far away when at home where the future looks gloomy. The wife is also distracted and prone to accidents at home as her attention drifts from cooking, ironing and cleaning to her future. She wanders aimlessly in the shops and finds that she forgets easily, sometimes even the purpose of her visit. On rare occasions she may leave the shop without paying and be caught for shoplifting, which makes life even more complicated than it is already.

This widespread irritability may be associated with anger, and during the days, weeks, months preceding the ultimate rupture, the couple may have flaming rows. All the accumulated bitterness will explode in frequent quarrels which resolve nothing and simply become channels of abuse. The same ground is covered over and over again and the arguments become bitter recriminations which flare up into fights. Sometimes the fights are not simply confined to verbal abuse but may become exchanges of physical blows. When one of the spouses or both are under the influence of drink, much trauma can be inflicted. Doctors, casualty departments, relatives and friends see results of these bloody exchanges. Sometimes the couple are too ashamed to show their wounds to anybody else and there is much physical damage which goes undetected.

The irritability and anger may in fact trigger off or aggravate all sorts of physical complaints. Headaches have already been mentioned, pain in the back of the head and back, abdominal pains, irritation of the skin, aggravation of asthma, of diabetes, epilepsy, peptic ulcer, irritable bowel, raised blood pressure, pains in the chest and left arm (sometimes confused with angina), hot and cold feelings, bowel disturbances, disturbances of periods and sexual problems also occur.

In addition to anxiety and anger, many people suffer from depression in this situation. In addition to one or more of the symptoms described, these men and women feel miserable, life appears empty; they lack energy, weep, ignore their appearance and may begin to feel that life has no meaning.

All these symptoms come under the category of psychiatric complaints and one study showed that marital problems was the factor most commonly associated with psychiatric illness for women and came second after work for men.[2] Other recent work has shown that marital problems and divorce are a common cause of depressive illnesses.[3,4]

Depression, with its accompanying sense of desperation and futility, is not infrequently a prelude to attempted suicide (or parasuicide as it has come to be called in Britain) or suicide itself. There is overwhelming evidence that marital breakdown is associated with both. A study of self-poisoning in 68 married men and 147 married women showed that marital disharmony was a major precipitating factor for 68 per cent of the men and 60 per cent of the women.[5] In a selection of 130 people taken from a wider sample of 577 cases of attempted suicide in Oxford, 83 per cent of the married men and 68 per cent of the married women complained of marital problems.[6] Those who repeat their suicidal attempt have a higher risk of ultimately killing themselves. In two studies of repeated suicide attempts, separation or divorce were some of the features present.[7,8] When one considers that each day at least a thousand people in the world commit suicide[9], then marital break-up is an important contribution to fatality, and its reduction an important measure of preventive medicine.

These symptoms of anxiety, anger and depression may last for a few weeks, months or even years. Some people cannot get over the loss of their departed spouse and years later still feel their departure acutely. These are men and women who have been heavily dependent on their spouse for emotional support, and the departure of their partner leaves them isolated, empty and lacking meaning. For them divorce is the equivalent of a total and irrevocable loss. The majority of men and women recover their equilibrium after a period of time, but this may be variable and there is little doubt that marital break-up, separation and divorce are a major contribution to ill health.

Impact on children

The impact on spouses is sufficiently severe to ensure that separation is not undertaken for trivial reasons. Indeed, if the dissolution of marriage leaves the partners untouched emotionally, doubt would have to be cast on whether such a couple have ever experienced a real affective bond. For the children the matter is different. Almost invariably they have formed emotional bonds with their parents and they find themselves in a situation where they have to lose the presence of one parent through no fault of their own. Nobody asked them if they wished to be brought into the world and indeed when they were born probably both parents were committed to them. Then one decides to depart and the children find themselves in a one-parent situation against their wishes.

Children reflect parental stresses by producing their own manifestations of difficulties.[10,11,12] These difficulties can be at home, at school or in society. At home the children may manifest emotional problems such as irritability, clinging to parents and crying. Sleep disorders may appear, with the young children finding it difficult to settle down in bed, wanting mother or father to remain close to them. There may be a return of frightening dreams, of nightmares and of bed-wetting. At school there is a severe drop in attention and concentration. The child may be a source of disturbance, attention-seeking or clinging. Both at home and school there may be abdominal pain symptoms, difficulties with eating, headaches, aggravation of established disorders and a generalized restlessness. As far as social disturbance is concerned, children may play truant, steal, lie, be destructive and show undue aggression.[13] Severe parental discord has such an impact that it is strongly associated with these conduct disorders even when the home is unbroken.[14]

How long does it take for these disturbances to settle down?

The evidence seems to suggest that it takes about two years for the children of divorced parents to catch up with children who remain in intact families.[15] Whilst the acutely distressing manifestations of children may be attenuated over a period of two years, widespread problems remain. Children are often given to the custody of their mothers, and fathers cease visiting very soon after they depart. If the father continues to visit the children, there may be recurrent emotional scenes particularly when the children are young. They find it difficult to go back to mother at the end of the weekend. They had a specially good time with their father and they want it to continue. There are often emotional scenes and sometimes the children return to their mother distressed. This may be interpreted by the mother as a sign that the children are unhappy with their father and she may make difficulties about further visits. Another source of difficulty for the wife may be the presence of another woman, indeed the one who displaced her. She may not wish the children to go to the husband's home if such a person is present. Sometimes she may find the attentions of the 'other woman' threatening, as if she might steal the affection of the children.

But beyond all these details lies the brutal fact that most children want and need two parents. The regular absence of one is a source of distress and, however well they adapt – and human beings do adapt to the most challenging situations – the loss is not easy to compensate.

These immediate distressing features are reasonably well documented. The long-term impact of divorce on children is less clear. Neurotic illness, alcoholism, depression, personality disorder, sexual difficulties and antisocial behaviour have all been thought at one time or another to be connected directly with broken marriages. The evidence is certainly not unequivocal, and in no sense can the claims be substantiated. There is no doubt that disturbed childhoods are associated with these conditions, but the part this plays is not exactly clear and, in the process of trying to amass the damaging evidence of divorce, the greatest care must be taken to evaluate the findings correctly. At the clinical level all these conditions are occasionally related to divorce in childhood but the links between the two need further careful examination. It is possible that the potential damage is contributed by the disturbance in the marital relationship and not the divorce itself, but the latter may make its own specific contribution.

As far as the influence of divorce on the children's capacity to form stable marriages in adult life, the evidence is once again contradictory. Early American research showed that there is indeed a vicious circle, with the divorce of parents contributing statistically to an increased vulnerability in the marriages of the offspring.[16] Recent British research does not however confirm this.[17]

Impact on relatives

It is natural for a couple in marital distress to turn to their relatives for help and support during the difficult times of a pending marital breakup. Parents are torn between the happiness of their child and the welfare of the marriage and that of the grandchildren. If they belong to a generation who believed in the inviolate permanence of marriage, the threat of a divorce in their child's life is a major shock. For them it is the marriage that matters. For others trying to evaluate the stories of their child and son/daughter in law is a nightmare. They may identify completely with their offspring and the justice of their cause or they may see that both spouses are contributing to the problem. Their advice may be sought and they may find themselves in a dilemma as to what to say. If the trouble continues for a long time, the strain may be considerable. They may have to house their son/daughter temporarily, look after the grandchildren and generally be supportive at a time when they were expecting to be free of parental duties.

One-parent families

The increase in divorce has inevitably meant an increase in one-parent families. Their number in England and Wales has steadily risen. The Finer Report[18] calculated that in April 1971 there were some 620,000 one-parent families involving approximately one million children. In 1976 the figure grew to 750,000 one-parent families constituting 11 per cent of all families with dependent children involving one and a quarter million children.[19] The latest figure (1980) suggests that one-parent families have increased further to some 900,000. One-parent families include single and widowed women but the majority are the result of marital breakdown.

These one-parent families are largely women with children and a small proportion of divorced and separated fathers with children. Life is hard for these women and men. They are still recovering from the shock of separation or divorce. In addition they have either to work and look after their child/children or stay at home and be completely dependent on social security. They are often lonely, and the single person who has been married finds it very hard to find a place in the community. As Christians they are not sure whether they are welcomed in their parish. As single people they may be a social embarrassment. They often constitute a threat to a married couple, either of whom may feel that the single person has designs on their partner. Thus these men and women feel socially alienated and their self-esteem takes a plunge.

Economically the single parent, particularly the woman, may be in serious economic difficulties and not have a secure abode. The combination of social disadvantages of little money, social isolation and no secure housing, places these parents on the fringe of the community. Single-parent groups such as Gingerbread support these parents and give them a chance to recover their confidence and dignity.

As will be noted below there is a high rate of remarriage, and the difficulties of the single state are mitigated as the family is reconstructed. Some problems of course are carried into the second marriage.

There is evidence that until another intimate relationship is reconstructed, the single person remains particularly vulnerable to suicide. Whilst the suicide rate for the married is 9.9 per 100,000 of population, there is an increase to 47.9 per 100,000 among the divorced. But for those who are married and live apart, which includes a great number of single-parent families, the figure[20] reaches an astronomic proportion of 204.4 per 100,000.

Thus in every respect, economically, socially and from the point of view of survival, the single parent remains handicapped and vulnerable.

The public cost

So far a description has been given of what might be termed the private cost of marital breakup in terms of health, suicide risks, impact on children, social and economic distress. This goes on continuously in the community and is evident only to the sufferers and their immediate entourage. This is the hidden cost. There is also a public cost measured in terms of the supplementary benefits to separated, divorced and single mothers, the cost of taking children into care and legal costs. In 1977 these amounted to nearly 600 million pounds. If there is added the cost of absenteeism from work, doctors' time, prescriptions and hospitalization, then clearly a sum of one billion pounds is involved, a sum which is constantly rising with inflation and the number of single parents involved. At a time of widespread economic difficulties throughout western society, this is a large sum of money which could be reduced by appropriate preventative work.

Second marriages

The rate of remarriage is very high, of the order of 60 to 70 per cent. In 1968 remarriage of both parties constituted 6.5 per cent of all marriages, and when the marriage was the second for one only the figure rose to 10.4 per cent. Thus some 17 per cent of all marriages in that year had a partner celebrating a second marriage. In 1978 this figure increased to 35 per cent.[21] This is a new and important social phenomenon. About half the people divorcing in a given year remarry within five years, the bulk soon after divorce.[22]

These are marriages to which spouses bring their previous experiences and, most important, the wife brings her children. If both spouses bring their children to their second marriage, then the newly constructed unit has to cope with adaptation between spouses, between children, and between children and step-parents. All this can be done successfully and, in the presence of patience and good will, the family unit survives and prospers.

But it is not surprising if the second marriage does not prosper. The couple have to overcome the habit of comparing their new spouse with the previous one. Their expectations have to be curbed to reality. A new beginning is not going to be an instant answer bringing happiness and contentment. If first marriages have to be worked at to succeed, second ones need this approach even more.

A source of possible conflict is the presence of children. If one spouse has children, generally the wife, the new husband has to accept these children as his own. There are many men who do just this; there are others however who cannot come to terms with their step-children. If both are parents, then they need to avoid showing favour to their own children at the expense of their spouse's. A rare but special problem is the presence of a handicapped child which confronts the step-parent with particular adaptation issues. A less rare problem is the marriage of a man/woman with grown-up children to a partner who has no children. Such a person may feel left out of the closely knit community of children and parent and may resent this. If in fact he/she has to exercise discipline over the adolescent children of their partner, they may appear harsh and rigid. Finally there is the problem that arises when there are children from the second marriage who may be preferred to those from the previous one. All these complications are becoming apparent as second marriages increase in numbers.

Are these second marriages more successful than first ones? An early assessment of this question indicated that second marriages were stable and successful. As the number of remarriages increases, so does their rate of breakdown. The early conviction that second marriages are immune from breakdown is no longer tenable. Second marriages are vulnerable. A great deal of work will have to be done however to indicate which second marriages are serious risks. Statistical analysis does not show this; it only reflects totals of dissolutions.

It can be speculated for example that marriages of divorced young people are likely to be more stable second time round as they have progressed in maturity. Similarly spouses who have moved from dependence to independence, from identity confusion to identity clarity, from lack of self-esteem to confidence are likely to choose spouses who now correspond with their level of growth and maturity. However, individuals who harbour traits of persistent immaturity, are unable to feel loved or give love, are prey to the slightest criticism or have persistent tendencies to aggression, alcoholism and gambling, are not likely to be more successful in subsequent marriages, unless they marry someone who has the ability to tolerate their shortcomings. Thus second marriages usually work when the spouses have similar degrees of maturity or one of them is far more tolerant and accepting of their partner's shortcomings. In the absence of these changes, second marriages turn to third and subsequent ones. This has come to be known as serial polygamy and is the very opposite of the covenant relationship of a stable one-to-one commitment. In third and subsequent marriages there is increasing likelihood of finding the small percentage of extremely vulnerable men and women who do not know how to give or receive love.

Theological implications of divorce

The theological implications of divorce are complex. All Christian denominations agree that the teaching of Christ is clear on this matter. Indissolubility is the divine norm and every other alternative is a distortion of this standard and yet marriages continue to break down in Christian denominations. A recent survey in England and Wales showed a divorce rate for Roman Catholics which is similar to that of the community at large.[23]

How do Christians cope with marital breakdown? The word 'Christian' has been used because discipline varies amongst the denominations. As far as the Roman Catholic Church is concerned, church tribunals first set up in the Middle Ages continue to function today. These tribunals do not exist in the reformed Protestant tradition.

These tribunals hear cases and give nullity dispensations on the grounds of diriment impediments, irregularities of juridical forms, and defective consent.[24] According to present legislation, the following are diriment impediments: age, abduction, crime, spiritual relationship, impotence, sacred orders, marriage bond, vow of chastity, consanguinity, affinity, public decorum and disparity of cult. The irregularities of juridical forms means a violation of the rules laid down by the Church as to how the marriage should be carried out. Defective consent refers to the fact that each of the partners must will to marry, and to marry one person; that is to say, the person must give his consent freely, give assent to the essential characteristics of Christian marriage and this assent is given to a specific individual. The question of proper consent is of paramount importance, since one of the widest grounds for nullity nowadays is what is technically called lack of due discretion.

In an early paper by the author[25] the following point was made. 'Each party in offering themselves, offers a self who undertakes to love, provide help and sexual satisfaction and to be a parent. These are commitments undertaken at the time of the contract, but, unlike other contracts, the ability to discharge the requirements resides in personality characteristics which are beyond the conscious grasp of the person. In other words, spouses may offer to each other, in perfect faith, aspects of themselves which, in practice in the actual existential reality, are found to be totally wanting, rendering the promises null and void. One cannot offer in a contract something one does not possess, and that which is lacking can only be seen in the actual relationship itself, not before. 'In this paper it was argued that there are marriages which are so only in name because the psychological resources of loving are not present.

Some eight years later the Canon Law Society of Great Britain and Ireland issued a pamphlet on the Church's matrimonial jurisprudence.[26] This document picked up the teaching of Vatican II. Commenting on this teaching it says:

> This teaching clearly sees marriage as a mutual self-giving of the two persons with a view to a permanent, exclusive and procreative relationship. It is brought into being by their irrevocable personal consent, this and this alone is the 'conjugal love' of which jurisprudence takes cognisance. Those who by reason of a personal constitutional deficiency, are not capable of just such a partnership, are consequently incapable of marriage . . . modern jurisprudence has come to realize that one of these exceptions is that of a person who, perhaps by reason of grave disturbance of the mind or of the personality, is at the time of the marriage, not capable either of evaluating adequately what marriage involves or of fulfilling the inherent and essential obligations of the married state.

Although these developments are of recent origin, the ideas behind the principles of due discretion have been present in the Church for some thirty years. Nevertheless both the Church tribunals and the principles of due discretion have come under attack.

The Church tribunals and the principles of nullity do not find favour with the Church of England. In 1978 the Church of England published its second document on the question of marriage, divorce and remarriage.[27] In reference to the practice of nullity the report had this to say, 'We do not think that this Roman Catholic practice offers a way forward which the Church of England could or should follow.'[28] As far as 'could' is concerned, the report makes the reasonable case that, since there is no tradition for such tribunals in the Church of England, problems of organization and procedure could complicate matters. As far as 'should' is concerned, this document, in common with other thought in the Anglican circles, does not really approve of the principles of nullity particularly those based on due discretion. Since this is one of the few areas in which there is ecumenical divergence, it is worth exploring the grounds offered for the criticism.

The document says: 'We know of no general agreement among theologians, psychologists or the general public about what constitutes psychological maturity or immaturity of any age.' This statement is true as far as it goes. The fact is that, when a careful examination of marital breakdown is made, patterns emerge which are obvious and recurrent.[29] The absence of any agreement on the subject is due to the massive neglect of this area of work and the poor co-operation between theology and the behavioural sciences. One of the great assets of the Roman Catholic Church tribunals is that intimate communication between theology and the behavioural sciences is being established and marital breakdown is no longer the mystery that it has been hitherto. It is vital for the Churches to understand the nature of marital problems and to distinguish between the marriages that are viable but difficult and those that are not viable. In this way the Christian community can accumulate the knowledge and expertise to discern marriages that are capable of surviving and those which have never been marriages from the very beginning. Such a knowledge will have wide repercussions for training, education, pastoral support and the ultimate preservation of the Christian ideal of indissolubility. If a Christian community accepts all marital breakdown, then it has no means of discriminating between the marriages which should have survived and those which could not survive because the essential ingredients were never there, nor of encouraging and helping the viable marriages.

Marriage tribunals have a chance of working towards these goals and, in the view of the author, are a powerful contribution to the general raising of the understanding and the standard of marriage. This of course means that Roman Catholic tribunals must change

in their constitution with mandatory inclusion of members of the
laity and psychological experts and with the issue of regular reports
as the basis of understanding nullity. The joint efforts of the
Church's jurisprudence and theology will raise the level of understanding of the nature of marriage, will have important repercussions on pastoral work and contribute to the viability of marriage.

The Anglican report also considers as unsatisfactory procedures
which call into question the validity of a relationship which may
have been in existence for many years. There is little doubt that in
practice that is exactly what happens. There is an external appearance of marriage and an emotional alienation which reaches the
surface only after many years of marriage.

Finally there is criticism that nullity can be given on the grounds
of immaturity at the time of the marriage but not in respect of
subsequent immaturity. With few exceptions all such immaturity is
present at the beginning of marriage independently of the time it
manifests itself. Indeed immaturity only shows when stress is sufficient to bring it forth.

This report, like the first one,[30] made recommendations compatible with remarriage in the church of a divorced person. This re-
commendation came close to implementation but has not been
accepted so far. There is no doubt that, with the absence of remarriage in the Church, the discipline of the Church of England is one
of the hardest in Christendom. In the absence of tribunals which
grant nullity and of any remarriage in church, the members of the
Church of England who are divorced and wish to remarry in Church
cannot do so unless the priest violates the canonical position. However, at the time of printing, the General Synod has announced a
change in this position by accepting remarriage in the Church.

Nonconformist churches have more flexible rules and remarriages
of divorced people are permitted. Indeed Anglican communities in
other parts of the world have modified their position towards greater
flexibility.

As far as the Eastern Churches are concerned, they too maintain
the ideal of indissolubility but in practice, with regret, allow second
and even third marriages in church. The theology of marriage in
the Eastern Churches has always placed the love of the couple at
the heart of the 'ends' of marriage although such a language is not
used. In the context of this theology and in the economy of grace,
second and third marriages are permissible. It should be remembered of course that Eastern and Western traditions moved quite

differently in general, and in particular the enormous impact of the theology of the Middle Ages on marriage did not affect Eastern Christianity.

The tension between the ideal of indissolubility and the reality of marital breakdown affects all Christianity, and the various denominations have different ways of coping with the reality from the Roman Catholic tribunals and their work on nullity, through the reformed and Eastern Churches with entirely different traditions and disciplines. At the heart of the matter lies one complex theological issue – namely the teaching of Jesus in Matthew which says, 'It has also been said: Anyone who divorces his wife must give her a writ of dismissal. But I say this to you: everyone who divorces his wife, except for the case of fornication, makes her an adulteress; and anyone who marries a divorced woman commits adultery' (Mat. 5:31-32). This clause has been the subject of endless exegesis ranging from those who see it truly as an exemption to others who deny it. By and large Roman Catholics have denied the exemption significance whilst other traditions have favoured this interpretation. One of the most detailed recent studies, with an extensive bibliography, is the book *To Have and to Hold*.[31] This matter will not be considered here because nothing less than another book can do justice to it.

Pastoral care

As far as the Roman Catholic Church and indeed all Churches are concerned, the challenge is how to take care of the divorced with, on the one hand, compassion and inclusion in the life of the Church and, on the other, the absence of scandal and giving the idea that such a fundamental Christian teaching has been repudiated.

One of the most obvious ways of ensuring that divorce does not occur is to ensure that there are no provisions in the secular law for it. The Roman Catholic Church relied on this principle for a long time, predominantly in Roman Catholic countries. One by one these countries are introducing divorce and this approach is becoming extremely restricted. Even when there are no laws of divorce, this in no way means that marital breakdown does not exist. Whether the laws of divorce make it easier for couples to break up their marriages is a matter open to dispute. Clearly the law sets a framework of reference, a social atmosphere. The forces which lead to breakdown are so ubiquitous however that they ignore the absence or presence of the law and indeed the latter often reflects a basic tendency in society. Be that as it may, most Western countries have divorce laws and there are millions of divorced Roman Catholics.

As with contraception, it is important to ensure that divorce and remarriage do not alienate people from the Church. These are men and women who need particularly the support of the Christian community. They need the sacraments and to have access to God and prayer. It is essential for the Roman Catholic Church to ensure that those who have not received a dispensation of nullity, and therefore the permission to remarry, are not ignored or excluded from the life of the Church. Essentially this means that on the one hand they should be enjoined to come forth and participate in the sacramental life including communion and at the same time the congregation must be left in no doubt what the teaching of the Church is and continues to be. In this way adults and children remain within the orbit of the life of the Church and receive the comfort and support they need. The care of the divorced must be an exercise of love and the Church, following its master, must show the way.

The evil of divorce

The traditional teaching of Christianity has been that divorce is evil. Unfortunately the word evil, as in so many sexual issues, tended to be a label for the people involved. In this chapter and in this book as a whole we can see that there is much evil in marital breakdown expressed in human suffering, distortion and damage. But the divorced are often caught in circumstances beyond their control and they are victims of forces, social and psychological, which they neither comprehend nor command. They are overwhelmed by circumstances which are often beyond their capacity to contain. This in no way means that they are not free people, doomed by destiny. It simply means that, as new levels of expectation are sought in marriage, these take people by surprise as they have been neither prepared nor educated for them. One of the real problems facing Christianity is that it has tended to indict the divorced, having done very little in practice to prevent marital breakdown. A new age is dawning when the Church is beginning to realize what a neglected sacrament marriage is and how much effort is needed to care for it tenderly and constructively.

Thus the relationship of evil and divorce remains. The world may talk about the 'creative' divorce, and indeed for some couples a divorce is a passport to freedom from misery and destruction. But all divorces contain a great deal of human misery and pain, and this is where the evil resides, an evil which is now becoming clearer as the numbers of the divorced rise astronomically.

This rise in divorce gives the Church an opportunity to pay particular attention to marriage and to communicate with the world not primarily on the basis of condemnation of laying guilt on the shoulders of the divorced but rather sharing their suffering and showing that indissolubility is the reality that respects not only the divine law but human integrity.

Summary

Some twenty-five years ago, when the liberalization of divorce laws was the principal aim, there were thinkers who considered divorce a creative enterprise. Gradually a picture is emerging that the consequences of marital breakdown are manifold and severe for everyone concerned.

References (Chapter 14)

1. Chester, R., in *British Journal of Preventive Social Medicine* (1971) 25, 231.

2. Sheppard, M. *et al.*, *Psychiatric Illness in General Practice.* Oxford Unversity Press, 1966.

3. Briscoe, C.W. in *Archives of General Psychiatry* (1973) 29, 119.

4. Paykel, E.S., *et al.* in *Archives of General Psychiatry* (1969) 21, 753.

5. Kessel, N. in *British Journal of Medicine* (1965) 2, 1265.

6. Bancroft, J. *et al.* in *Psychological Medicine* (1977) 7, 289.

7. Bagly, C. and Greer, S. in *British Journal of Psychiatry* (1971) 119, 515.

8. Morgan, H.G. in *British Journal of Psychiatry* (1976) 128, 361.

9. World Health Organisation, *Prevention of Suicide*. W.H.O., Geneva, 1968.

10. Rickman, N. in *British Journal of Psychiatry* (1977) 131, 1221.

11. Rutter, M. in *Proceedings of the Royal Society of Medicine* (1973) 66, 1221.

12. Graham, P. and Rutter, M. in *Proceedings of the Royal Society of Medicine* (1974) 66, 1226.

13. McCord, W. and McCord, J., *Origins of Crime – a new evaluation of the Cambridge-Somerville Study*. Columbia University Press, New York, 1959.

14. Rutter, M. in *Journal of Child Psychology and Psychiatry* (1971) 12, 233.

15. Hetherington, E.M., Cox, M. and Cox, R., Family Interaction and Social, Emotional and Cognitive Development of Children following Divorce in *The Family: Setting Priorities*, ed. V. Vaugh and T. Brazelton. Science and Medicine, New York, 1975.

16. Landis, J.T., *Social Forces* 34 (3), 213.

17. Thornes, B. and Collard, J., *Who Divorces?* Routledge and Kegan Paul, 1979.

18. *Finer Report on One Parent Families*, HMSO, 1974.

19. *Population Trends*, No.13. Office of Population Censuses and Surveys HMSO, 1978.

20. Dominian, J., *Marital Pathology*. British Medical Association and Darton Longman and Todd. 1980.

21. *Population Trends*, No.20. Office of Population Censuses and Surveys, HMSO, 1980.

22. *Population Trends*, No.16. Office of Population Censuses and Surveys, HMSO, 1979

23. Hornsby Smith, M. and Lee, R.M., *Roman Catholic Opinion*. University of Surrey, 1979.

24. Brown, R., *Marriage Annulment*. Geoffrey Chapman, 1970.

25. Dominian, J. in *Ampleforth Journal* (Spring 1968) LXXIII, Part. 1.

26. Canon Law Society Trust, The Church's Matrimonial Jurisprudence, 1975

27. *Marriage and the Church's Task*. Church Information Office, London, 1978.

28. ibid., p.80.

29. Dominian, J., *Marital Pathology*.

30. *Marriage, Divorce and the Church*. SPCK., 1972.

31. Atkinson, D., *To Have and to Hold*. Collins, 1979.

CHAPTER 15

Prevention of Marital Breakdown

The traditional stand against marital breakup was the presence of strict anti-divorce laws, coupled with a moral teaching and social values that condemned both marital breakup, divorce and remarriage. In these circumstances which prevailed in western society until very recently, divorce and remarriage were disapproved of both socially and religiously. Thus it was not easy for men and women to part in the face of such combined opposition. This did not mean that all marriages thrived or were compatible. Indeed the constant criticism of indissoluble marriage was that it kept together couples whose relationship had died and who either parted or lived under the same roof without emotional or sexual contact. The drive towards easier divorce was an attempt to free people from the shackles of impossible situations. The freeing of men and women so as to give them a second chance was the main motive behind the liberalization of divorce. During this phase, primarily in the 1950's and 1960's, divorce was conceptualized as something positive and creative, and the opposition of Christianity to it as something dogmatic and inimical to human authenticity.

Gradually, as divorce has increased, it can be seen that its aftermath is not without intense and sometimes protracted complications and difficulties. As the previous chapter has shown, there are adverse short-term and possible long-term consequences; as well as there being a private cost, there is also a public one. A picture is beginning to emerge which indicates that it is indissolubility that reflects most accurately human aspirations and integrity and that divorce is truly a deviant expression. Christianity has the task of convincing society that its opposition to divorce is not mere dogma but a human necessity. But in order to do this it must also show that it does not want to keep couples glued together out of social and economic necessity, in other words that sustaining, healing, growth and emotional and sexual fulfilment are compatible with permanency. In order to do this, a new conceptualization of marriage is needed with the necessary training, support and education for it, leading to the prevention of marital breakdown.

Ideology

What sort of marriage needs preserving? The Christian answer is that all marriages should be. But the next question is vital, namely when is a marriage a marriage? To answer this question adequately is to accept that what constitutes marriage is in a stage of transition. On the one hand, there are marriages in which the externals of permanency, children and fidelity matter, these are the traditional goods of marriage enunciated by St Augustine. On the other hand, there is an emerging marriage in which the interior world of the couple constitutes the essential mark of its being. It has been emphasized throughout this book that this movement from external to internal reality, expressed in the realization of the potential of feelings, emotions and sexuality in a relationship of equality of worth, is the contemporary ideal. Its realization varies from couple to couple, but there is not the slightest doubt that it is affronts against these aspirations that ultimately press people to terminate their marriage. These aspirations are intimately related to sustaining, healing and growth which are profoundly Christian values. So that the emerging pattern of marriage is in no way anti-Christian, indeed it gives couples an opportunity to realize a much deeper layer of their being, of love reflecting that of God.

Thus there is a need to protect the internal dynamism which ultimately governs the viability of marriage. This does not mean that social factors do not play a part. For example it is only in the presence of economic wellbeing that couples can give their attention to the deeper quests in their being. It is only in the presence of an equality of worth of the sexes that the emerging marriage can succeed. It is only in the absence therefore of economic, social and political turmoil that there is sufficient stability for marriage to realize its new expectations. From now on there will be a subtle interaction between social stability, economic wellbeing and this new type of marriage. These have been largely the conditions for the last thirty years which have seen such profound changes in the ideology of marriage.

It is this type of marriage whose quest is a deeper realization of self that needs protection as it emphasizes personal relationships of love. Wherever love has an authentic opportunity of growth, Christianity has a deep interest, for God is love (1 John 4:8), and in preserving these marriages it is not colluding with an abstract myth but with an unfolding of God's design for man.

Research Findings

The research findings of the last fifty years have been directed to the definition of those factors which adversely affect companionship marriage, as the emerging marriage has come to be called. In other words, the factors which damaged traditional marriage in the past were economic instability and lack of leadership on the part of the husband, incompetence and poor housekeeping on the part of the wife and infidelity on the part of either. The research that is emerging identifies social and psychological factors which impair the inner dynamic interaction. These factors have been mentioned before but are here referred to again with the associated possibilities of prevention.

SOCIAL FACTORS

1. *Age*

There is a consensus of findings that marriages under the age of twenty are more vulnerable. In terms of the traditional pattern of marriage it did not matter when a couple were married. Age did not impair the capacity to work, be fecund and minister physically to each other. But age does matter when there is an encounter of personalities who are looking for mutual understanding at an emotional level. The younger the spouses are the more likely it is that there will be identity confusion, and with the passage of time they will become different people needing entirely different personal complementarity.

At the practical level there are a number of ways of preventing this type of youthful marriage. The Church and society should emphasize the dangers of youthful marriage and make sure that the facts are well established in education. Another way of preventing this type of wedding is to avoid marriage on the basis of pregnancy. Marriages forced as a result of a pregnancy are dangerous propositions. Gradually this fact is being grasped, but one way of dealing with the difficulty is through abortion. This is unacceptable to the Christian conscience. In any case the natural results of such terminations are largely unknown in the impact they have on women's lives over the years. Assisting the girl to have her baby in circumstances where she is not humiliated nor rejected is an essential human and Christian objective. The baby can be kept or offered for adoption, and the serious mistake of forcing a marriage when the couple are not ready for it is avoided.

The danger of early marriage has been appreciated and a percentage of couples live together before marriage. Once again Christianity cannot support this solution. The discussion of the reasons against cohabitation belong to a book on human sexuality; here one point will be made. It is held that living together is a good preparation for marriage as well as a sexual outlet for a period in life when the sexual drive is high. On the surface this seems an ideal solution. But whatever experience cohabitation gives, it is not the same as marriage. The fact is that its total experience is surrounded by the ultimate knowledge that the couple could split up if they so desired with minimum inconvenience. The freedom alters the whole reality of the experience. There is no doubt that for some couples the preliminary living together facilitates ultimate marriage, whilst for others it does not do so, indeed when some couples get married emotional and sexual problems begin. One can see the case that can be made for insecure couples to live together and facilitate their growth towards marriage, but this can also be done by a suitable courtship.

Another approach is for state and Church to raise the minimum age of marriage. This may mean that some couples live together. It may be interpreted as an attack on the freedom of the individual. The fact is that if the state has the right to lower the legal age of marriage, it can also raise it. Similarly the Church can impose its own conditions for Christian marriage.

However the fact remains that, as the law and Christian practice stand at the present moment in Britain and elsewhere, couples can get married under the age of 20. Some of these marriages belong to social groups where early marriages are the norm and there is an implicit support for such an event. The real danger lies in youthful marriages which belong to socio-economic groups where it is not possible to give the support they need. This is where preventive work can be done by ensuring that any youthful marriages that are vulnerable are supported by the Church and the community. This can be done in the course of preparation for marriage, when such couples are tactfully reminded of the dangers and the need to seek early help.

2. *Premarital Pregnancy*
Evidence has accumulated that premarital pregnancy is also an adverse loading factor. In particular the strain on the marriage is increased if the couple marry young as well. It used to be thought that an early pregnancy completes and fulfils a marriage. Nowadays it is realized that time is needed for the couple to get to know each other and integrate their life before a baby arrives. For this to be achieved an effective method of birth regulation is needed and couples should be trained to use the infertile period from the time sexual activity begins. Christianity insists that intercourse belongs to marriage, but if it is anticipated then care should be taken to avoid a pregnancy. Abortion is not an acceptable Christian solution and if there is a premarital pregnancy the support of the community is vital to avoid an enforced marriage.

3. *Socio-economic group*
There is evidence that marital breakdown is more frequent in the U.S.A. and Britain in the lower socio-economic groups. These groups have a tendency to be associated with early marriages, premarital pregnancy, poor housing and economic prospects, and therefore they are loaded with adverse factors. Clearly the fact that men and women have a low station in society does not mean that they are any less human or debarred from marriage. It does mean however that they need special support. When marriage is taken seriously, the community will appreciate that it has responsibility for all the disadvantaged, and these social classes run special risks in marriage. The community could very easily make special provisions for work, housing, care of children and the Church give personal support.

4. *Housing*
There is some evidence that the divorced started married life without their own accommodation, shared more often and moved more

frequently. There is no doubt that housing for the newly married is a priority that every government should consider.

5. *Mixed backgrounds*
There is evidence that couples of mixed religion, race, colour, social class run a higher risk of marital breakdown. Here however patterns of behaviour are changing and it is possible that in the future such mixed marriages may be less vulnerable. Nevertheless whenever the background of the couple is seriously different there is a need to ensure that the couple are suited emotionally to each other, so as to overcome any residual conflicts of social customs.

6. *Courtship*
Courtship is a good indicator of how a couple will fare in their marriage. Short courtships have been shown to be associated with marital breakdown and this is not surprising because the couple hardly know each other. Sometimes unduly prolonged courtships of many years are a sign of danger if one party or both are really afraid to commit themselves to marriage or children and they make excuses which are obviously rationalizations.

Courtships which are torn with dissent, with frequent quarrels and separations augur badly for the outcome of the marriage. Broken engagements are also warnings of personality difficulties.

Above all the man or woman who is an alcoholic, gambler or drug addict and who promises to reform after marriage should not be married. Men and women believe that their love can change the person they are in love with. Sometimes this is achieved, on other occasions it is not. It is infinitely preferable to convert the future spouse before marriage rather than afterwards.

The same applies with sexual activity. The promiscuous man or woman, or the one with a high sex drive and multiple sex relations premaritally is unlikely to change with marriage.

Finally there is evidence that a number of marriages which run into difficulties later on appear to have involved one partner who was not entirely willing to get married. It is true that memory can play false but there are recurrent authentic accounts when one partner had marked doubts and indeed was coerced into marriage. Arrangements may have been made and it would have been difficult to withdraw at a late stage. The partner may have pleaded and even threatened suicide or the marriage took place on the rebound from another disappointed relationship. One way or another there are clear recollections that they were not really in love when they got married. The pastor preparing couples for marriage must ensure that these reservations are not ignored at the courtship phase and indeed that the couple are asked about their real and free consent in their decision.

7. *Parental Opposition*
When one or both sets of parents are persistent in their opposition then the marriage starts with a serious handicap, for the newly married need the support of their parents. Such an opposition should be considered seriously and if it is to be ignored then the objections of the parents should be carefully evaluated. Since the couple themselves are unlikely to be in a position to do this the pastor concerned should make sure that such opposition does not exist, or if it does that they try to overcome it.

It is not maintained that the knowledge of these social factors will eliminate marital breakdown, but if these research findings were made widely known, became part of the education system and an essential part of preparation for marriage, a good deal could be achieved in the process of reducing breakdown. Further help could be given during the various phases of marriage.

First phase of marriage

This phase includes the first five years and as already noted these are crucial years for the survival of the marriage. There is evidence that during these years some 30 to 40 per cent of all breakdown occurs. Furthermore the problems initiated during this phase have an important impact on the outcome of the marriage many years later. Perhaps one general point that can be made about these years is that the wife is often well ahead in sensing problems. If all husbands could be persuaded to treat the serious complaints of their wives with the care they deserve, then in one socio/psychological stroke another dimension of preventive work could begin. Wives have a sensitivity and emotional awareness which by and large their husbands do not possess and, painful as it may be for the husband to face and realize this, it is an admission that may save the marriage.

It is important next to look at the social, emotional, physical, intellectual, and spiritual dimensions of this phase.

SOCIAL DIMENSION

1. *Parents*

One persistent problem is the inability of one or both spouses to extricate themselves from the influence of their parents when the latter cross the line between support and intrusion. Spouses are caught between their loyalty to their partner and to their parent. Nevertheless there is no doubt where the priority lies; it is with the spouse. At the psychological level the over-attached spouse is afraid to incur the displeasure of their parent. This displeasure must be incurred even if it elicits a period of withdrawal, emotional accusations and blackmail from the parent. During this period the other spouse must give support to their partner who may find this detachment emotionally difficult and be filled with remorse and guilt. The fact remains that a firm approach invariably succeeds. Parents need their children at this stage in their life far more than their children need them. Once the power battle has been waged parents can learn that they are still cared about and loved if their son/daughter rings once a week instead of daily, calls irregularly and is not expected to put off their social life for the parent's sake. All this may appear harsh, but marriages are wrecked on these grounds and the right relation with parents needs to be established from the very start of the marriage.

2. *Friends*

The same applies to friends but the problem is less acute. Here one partner may become exceedingly jealous of a particular friend of their spouse. In these circumstances, the friend may be given up for the sake of peace but this will not solve the problem and soon another friend will become the object of suspicion. Such a friend will be accused of putting undesirable ideas in the mind of the spouse and leading them astray. When the criticisms of a friend have been evaluated and found wanting, it is essential to get the matter clear from the very beginning. If one expression of jealousy is tolerated, then others follow. It is vital for the partner to be confronted with the jealous feelings otherwise the circle of friends will be gradually reduced and only those approved will be tolerated. This is the beginning of controlling the life of the partner which will be gradually resented, laying the foundations for serious problems later on as the organized spouse seeks freedom and rebels against their authoritarian partner.

3. *Money*

Money features very often in marital problems and there are three issues. The first is the meanness of the husband or the incompetence of the wife or both. The second is the misuse of money in gambling, drinking or pointless impulsive buying. The third is the conversion of money into an emotional attribute of love.

If a husband is really mean, that is, persistently gives his wife less than she needs and in a manner which humiliates her, then the sooner he is confronted with this reality the better. As with parents and friends, so with money, if the reality is not faced early in marriage, it will lay the foundations for resentment and anger later on. Better a bitter quarrel at the start of the marriage than the steady accumulation of anger and the loss of trust and respect. A wife faced with this situation simply asks for what she knows to be the necessary sum or refuses to housekeep. There are no half-way possibilities in fundamentals, of which money is one. Similarly a wife who is incompetent must learn as fast as possible to cope effectively, and for this she may need her husband's assistance.

Money wasted in gambling and drinking is an insidious destructive element, and again this must be cleared up from the very start of the marriage and, as already remarked, preferably from the time of the courtship. It is usually the husband who gambles and drinks excessively, rarely the wife. If neither request nor pleading is effective, the spouse may have to leave home until their partner gives up the practice.

Money is an important symbol of love in marriage. A couple should share their financial position with each other. It is unbelievable how many wives do not know what their husbands earn. Husbands make excuses that their wives do not understand financial matters and some wives are only too happy to go along with this explanation. However the bomb explodes when the wife discovers that her husband is in some financial mess or has made all sorts of arrangements with their money of which she may not approve. Sadly it is at divorce proceedings that financial details have to emerge and then bitterness and frustration may cloud the issue even further. It is a useful rule for both spouses to know exactly their financial situation.

4. *Domestic arrangements*

Despite the increased involvement of husbands in household chores wives still find themselves doing the majority of housework, the cooking and the cleaning.

A genuine sharing of responsibilities has yet to be attained even if there is a movement in that direction. Wives often accept this discrimination with a fatalistic resilience. Some women refuse to accept this position and insist on the husband taking a larger share of housekeeping. It is important to make sure that whatever is agreed is adhered to. Husbands make promises which they do not fulfil, and it is the sense of being let down that hurts the wife. It is important that the husband does what he promises, however little it may be, and at times of illness or other emergency to do everything to the best of his ability. When children arrive the husband is normally expected to do much more. Changing nappies, feeding the baby, taking turns to cope in the middle of the night are all an essential part of sharing and caring.

5. *Leisure*

If courtship has been satisfactory, the newly married have leisure interests in common as well as individual predilections. What matters is that one spouse should not gradually eliminate the leisure activities of the other and organize them solely into their own orbit of interests. Even worse is the spouse who has no leisure interests, finds social activities unacceptable and gradually imprisons their partner into solitary confinement at home with no one else other than themselves. All these positions should be resisted, for they build bitterness and frustrations which explode later on.

Some readers may find the suggestions of resolute and firm opposition to a partner difficult to reconcile with the principle of not interfering or coercing the partner with change. Clearly partners must respect each other's personalities which usually enrich one another. They also usually accept a whole range of idiosyncracies which may be irritating but not seriously detracting from the relationship. However whenever one spouse finds himself/herself treated in a manner seriously unacceptable to themselves, then to acquiesce out of fear is simply to store up an anger which will explode when fear disappears. It is much better to tackle the important differences right at the very start of marriage than to let them erode the compatibility of the relationship.

EMOTIONAL DIMENSION

1. *Dependence*

Spouses do in fact depend on each other emotionally. They need security, care, affection, love. They need affirmation and reassurance. They need hope, consolation, forgiveness and comfort. All this is mutual. Couples complement each other in their needs. Initiative and change balances passivity and steadiness; risk-taking is countered with caution; logic with feelings; excess with moderation; decisiveness with hesitation; confidence with doubt; patience with impatience. Furthermore these roles can be reversed temporarily or fluctuate as shared qualities in appropriate circumstances.

But dependence can take a different form. This happens when one spouse continues to treat the other as a figure of authority, wisdom, initiative and dominance. They like to be told what to do, what to choose, where to go, what to read; they easily accept responsibility for whatever goes wrong and generally act as a dependent child. This form of dependence is extremely dangerous. It means that sooner or later such a person will begin to mature and rebel against their spouse as they would do against a parent, and this rebellion costs millions of marriages.

When one spouse sees themselves behaving in this manner they need to take stock of the situation. It is a situation fraught with difficulties because they enjoy this marital pattern. They enjoy being looked after, and for some years they simply do not grow up. But as late developers they will grow up emotionally and then may find that all that pleased them is repudiated with a vehemence that takes even them by surprise. So the sooner they realize their dependence, and discuss it with their spouse, the sooner they will take the first steps of independence with the help of their spouse who will then be experienced as a facilitator rather than as an oppressor. Similarly the dominant spouse may find it most ingratiating to be treated with the deference they receive, but if they are alert to the situation they will encourage the autonomy of their partner at the speediest possible pace without arousing undue anxiety.

2. *Self-Esteem*

One of the essential features of contemporary marriage is the need of spouses to be held in esteem by their partner, to feel they matter and in this way to retain their own self-esteem. And yet a number of marriages live on an emotional see-saw. When the self-esteem of one is down through criticism, then, relatively speaking, the other spouse feels up having established their temporary superiority. This is short-lived and soon the position is reversed. What couples want from one another is both honest criticism and, even more, appropriate and recurrent appreciation. If a spouse cannot affirm by words and actions, then the sooner this is faced the better. Modern marriage needs love and one powerful expression of this love is affirmative appreciation.

Couples come to marriage counsellors complaining bitterly that they no longer feel loved. From the very beginning of the marriage their spouse has failed to give them any sign that they are lovable. They may have had an affair in which they felt wanted and appreciated. They are angry with their spouse who denies them this salutation. Is it not better to end the marriage now? They are sometimes astonished to find that their spouse does love them and can say so in the presence of the marriage counsellor. Couples cannot however live in the pockets of marriage cousellors. They need to learn to recognize each other lovingly, and the early years are crucial in overcoming such a handicap. Couples must insist on appropriate demonstrations of affection, affection which they can see and feel. If it is not forthcoming, they must not compromise, for compromise is fatal. If necessary they may leave the matrimonial home to show their spouse that they mean business.

3. *Intimacy*

During courtship couples are likely to spend a good deal of time together. It is of the very nature of this phase of relationship that togetherness should be one of its principal features. Hiding behind this intimacy lie two risks. The first is the inability of one partner to cope with aloneness. This will be disclosed later on in the marriage where balance between closeness and distance will have to be established. Each partner will wish to have some time for themselves and of course a good deal of time together. The spouse, who finds it difficult to stay alone, follows their partner from room to room and wants to be constantly close to them inside and outside the house. They cannot cope without their partner's presence, and the togetherness which was interpreted as a sign of great affection towards the partner now becomes a smothering sensation. The person who cannot cope easily with being alone is also likely to be a jealous person afraid of losing their partner. For the sake of peace the spouse may allow himself/herself to be pursued relentlessly, but such a compromise simply generates resentment. The dependent spouse must be encouraged to find their independence. They should be encouraged to do things and go to places alone for short periods until they can cope with aloneness. They need to be helped to recognize their anxiety of being alone and if necessary get specialized help to overcome it.

The second problem is the absence of intimacy. After the wedding the husband may return to his pals at the pub or club, work late and generally repudiate the closeness that was shown during the courtship. By working late the man has the excuse that he is doing this for his family even if his wife and children hardly ever see him. If closely questioned, such a spouse admits that marriage is emotionally suffocating for him. The wife should confront her husband and insist that he should spend a minimum of time at home. She should, at the same time, find out what atmosphere pleases and what detracts from companionship. If the husband fails to respond, then once again a show of strength should be exhibited. It is better to have a show-down when good will still exists than later on when patience has been exhausted.

4. *Isolation and Socializing*
Intimately related to courtship togetherness is socializing. If a couple cling to each other during their courtship and do not want to mix with others, they are not likely to change after marriage. During courtship the excuse is that they don't want anybody else to intrude in their little heaven. But such isolation should act as a warning, particularly when one partner does want to mix.

After marriage the isolated and aloof spouse will restrict their partner's socializing activities and their world will become a narrow one inhabited solely by their presence and that of close relatives, with the partner who wants to go out becoming a prisoner. If this pattern is developing there should be no collusion. The partner who wants to go out or have friends at home should proceed with these legitimate desires. The anxious spouse should be encouraged to overcome their social fears. Often such men and women are apprehensive before a social event but enjoy it when they get there.

5. *Defences*
In order to handle these various limitations couples resort to psychological mechanisms which aid and abet their distorted image of the situation.

(a) PROJECTION

In the early years of marriage there is a specific distortion which depends on the principle of projection. The projective mechanism alters their experience of the spouse. Instead of perceiving them as they are, the partner fashions them after the image of a father, mother or an idealized figure. In these circumstances they are not experiencing their spouse as they are but as they would like them to be and they relate to them on the basis of this phantasy. In some instances the partner may like to fit in to the identity fashioned for them. The husband who likes to treat his wife as a little girl, the wife who likes to treat her husband as a little boy, the husband who treats his wife as a sister and the wife who treats her husband as a brother – the partners may be pleased to oblige. Both selection and response have been at emotionally immature levels. These collusive relationships may also include sado-masochistic patterns in which the superiority and aggression of the one meets the inferiority, and desire-to-be-punished feelings of the other. There is a subtle extension between desirable complementarity and collusive phantasy. The latter of course is a highly unstable situation because sooner or later the reality of the spouse will emerge and shatter the phantasy. If one partner is being treated in a phantasy manner, they can insist that they are not a mother or father but husband or wife, and they can refuse to act in the phantasy role required by their spouse. They should insist on reality at all times.

(b) RATIONALIZATION

Projection is an unconscious mechanism whereby the choice and response is the lost, idealized or hitherto unobtainable object.* When the spouses come together they have to make sense of each other, their present and past. In order to do this they may resort to rationalization. Rationalizations are used not only in collusive marriages but in any marriage when some emotional issue or anxiety cannot be faced. The anxiety is dealt with by reducing it to a rational explanation. In this way one or both spouses may persistently refuse to deal with the emotional conflict they are facing. The spouse who feels the reality must insist on tackling the issue at a reality level. Rationalizations must be emptied of their falsehoods and the underlying anxiety, fear and guilt faced openly.

---

* 'Object' is here a technical word for 'person'.

(c) DENIAL

If rationalization fails then denial may be resorted to. If we are accused by our partner of some offensive act (frequently) or praised for some good conduct (less frequently), we may jump to our protection by denying the hurt or the motive behind it. Denial is not lying. Lying is conscious and deliberate. Denial is convinced repudiation stemming from the unconscious which often cannot accept responsibility for unpleasant events and sometimes cannot accept praise.

Between them projection, rationalization and denial distort the exchange between couples who, unless they can see their motives, are floundering in the dark. This is where a constructive third person as interpreter is of assistance.

SEXUAL PROBLEMS

Evidence has been presented in chapter 8 that sexual fulfilment and happy marriages are related to each other. It is important therefore to seek to overcome sexual difficulties which are present or arise in the first phase of marriage.

1. *Preparing for sexual intercourse*

It is rare for a couple to come to their wedding nowadays without having had sexual intercourse with each other. Nevertheless it is in the established on-going experience of marriage that the couple will have the absolute security and opportunity to teach each other what they like in sexual arousal. Given that sexual intercourse is a celebration and an act of worship, the details surrounding it are of the greatest importance. Sexual communion needs preparation, which in turn needs adequate communication between the spouses. Each has to tell the other what they enjoy in the phase of foreplay. They need to convey information about appearance, touch, stroking, caressing, kissing and the time needed to arouse both partners. Men are often in a hurry to proceed to intercourse, oblivious to the unprepared state of their wife, and the wife may be too shy or frightened to let her husband know what she desires. Good communication is thus essential, spouses should not be frightened to reveal their real sexual desires in case they are rejected. They should encourage each other to realize their desires and please each other as much as possible.

2. *Sexual Intercourse*

Sexual intercourse is the culmination of sexual arousal and here the position adopted by the couple, the duration of intercourse, the reaching of climax and the aftermath are all significant. The faking of orgasm by the wife has been an art practised by some women throughout the ages. It is not a satisfactory answer in this age of personal authenticity. If the wife does not enjoy intercourse she needs to tell her husband and between them find the reasons and correct them.

Sexual intercourse may not be proceeded with. A small number of couples cannot consummate their marriage. In this case they can seek help nowadays with good chances of success.

Premature ejaculation and primary impotence on the part of the husband and lack of sexual pleasure, orgasmic difficulties and vaginismus on the part of the wife are also likely to be helped with current methods of sexual therapy.

INTELLECTUAL AND SPIRITUAL DIMENSIONS

The essential preventive work for intellectual and spiritual incompatability begins during the courtship. This is the time when a couple need to match their education and system of values. There must be a certain amount of mutual understanding at the intellectual level so that they can make sense of each other. Similarly they need to know something about each other's values politically, aesthetically, culturally and so on. A house divided in itself cannot easily survive. Couples who neither understand nor comply with each other's values can hardly function. Hasty marriages in which bodily attraction dominates or there is need to escape from an intolerable situation are often the cause of marriages in which a couple find they have very little in common.

Second phase of marriage

Given a certain material well-being which gives people minimum standards of food, health, shelter and work, the couple during these two decades can concentrate on raising their family and facilitating the sustaining, healing and growth of each other. Breakdown during these years is at face value often a mystery. If a couple survive the first phase, why should they experience such massive difficulties which lead to the breakup of their marriage and what can be done about it? Isn't the fact that they have already been married for a number of years evidence that they have been truly married and their marriage has come to an end? Don't marriages simply die in this and the next phase?

SOCIAL DIMENSIONS

1. *Unilateral change*

Perhaps one of the commonest reasons for social change during this phase is an upward, or downward social drift. This social move upward often means that the husband has a new social milieu which may or may not suit his wife. The reason for her discomfort is a general embarrassment in the world she has to mix with now. But many women have achieved this transformation and stayed with their husbands. The key to this staying power is flexibility and adaptability. If a wife has these two requisites, she can cope with new situations without too much anxiety. But anxiety is often associated with rigidity, the refusal to move from the old and the familiar. A husband can assist and encourage his wife to meet the new situation. Above all he can show her that their new status has not minimized his love for her. In a few circumstances the exact reverse occurs as the wife makes the upward social progress. Once marriage is recognized as a dynamic process, such changes will not cause surprise and couples will be better prepared for them. The downward social drift is the opposite characteristic. Illness often plays an important part in this deterioration and psychiatric illness predominates. If the husband drifts downwards through mental illness, alcoholism or crime, his work suffers and the standards of the whole family fall. The spouse may leave and label the partner as 'no good'. The vow to stay with one's spouse for better or worse applies particularly in these circumstances. A husband needs the support of his wife to escape from a bad patch.

2. *Social Stress*

In the second decade of this phase a number of social events occur which may have a bearing on the outcome of the marriage. The children become adolescents and one parent, usually the mother, may call upon the other to discipline them. Sometimes spouses feel unsupported by their partner who is considered disloyal and unsupportive in this situation. A much earlier combined involvement with the raising of the children would give the parents a sense of mutual trust and the confidence to ride the challenge of adolescence together.

One or both of the parents of the spouses may die, and the death may bring emotional pressure on the spouse who feels the loss acutely. Such a loss can raise the level of anxiety or cause depression, and the partner may find it difficult to cope if they are unaccustomed to accept the regressed emotional needs of their partner. They may need much reassurance, loving and holding which is non-sexual love. If a couple are trained to give this support early in marriage, they can do it in this second phase when social events can plunge them into emotional distress.

The husband may also have his own special problems during this phase of marriage. At any time, but particularly in the forties, he may find himself either out of work or realize that he is not likely to be promoted further. These social shocks have their emotional counterparts and need the loving support of the wife.

None of these events are likely to precipitate a marital breakdown in a state of emotional intactness. If the couple have hitherto supported each other emotionally, they can take one or more of these stresses without too much tension. But if there has been a steady alienation from the beginning of marriage, with the couple living on the fringes of each other's lives, then these stresses may be the final events in a long chain of disappointment and emptiness. But even if the relationship is not close or secure, a couple can overcome their alienation at this stage by making a concerted effort to discover their mutual needs and respond to them.

EMOTIONAL DIMENSION

1. *Emotional growth*
The unilateral social growth of one spouse is matched in these years by unilateral emotional growth. One wife said descriptively and succinctly, 'Up to now I have been what every one else, my parents, relatives and husband wanted me to be. Now I want to be myself.' Variations on this theme provide one of the main reasons for marital breakdown in this phase, and therefore prevention is vital. Prevention is difficult because by definition such a spouse has been con-

fused in their identity and has been happy to go along with the suggestions made by others. Such close co-operation with the wishes of others is always suspect. A couple are often happy to meet each other's need, but in the process there will be disagreement and some distinctive refusal to do or be something, a refusal which is made not out of sheer cussedness but because to agree would be incompatible with the basic make-up of the partner. Thus spouses learn little by little how far they can go with each other and at what point to cease persisting. Such tension, opposition and establishing of separate identity are healthy phenomena. Danger signals should be hoisted when one partner apparently fits in with perfect malleability and flexibility to the wishes of their spouse. Such a person has not separated yet from the symbiotic dependence (the sense of oneness) with their spouse. These are the 'perfect' marriages which are run by one of the partners with the other complying. At some stage the perfect unity will crack and the ever-obliging wife or husband will begin to murmur, first softly and then loudly about their wishes. At the beginning there is a gentle flow of protest but the speed with which it can become a torrent will depend on how it is handled. If it is seen as the emergence of a person in his/her own right, then their need to be recognized and treated as such can be met. If their tiniest protest is interpreted as a selfish protestation, then the marriage may be doomed.

2. *Continuing emotional dissatisfaction*
These two decades may see the disappointments of the first phase become entrenched with no improvement. The spouse remains undemonstrative or uninvolved, cannot be trusted, has repeated affairs, is aggressive, drinks too much or does not care about the children. The husband may have a poor work record, and either partner may feel overwhelmed by the demands of marriage for which they were not prepared. These marriages do not break up but rather peter out early in the second phase. Neither partner was ready for marriage.

PHYSICAL DIMENSION

1. *Sexual dissatisfaction*
The same applies to sexual dissatisfaction. The problems of the first phase such as poor sexual drive, male and female difficulties, impotence and non-consummation remain. When sexual and emo-

tional difficulties combine there is very little of the relationship left. The sexual difficulties of limited sexual desire, impotence and premature ejaculation can all be treated nowadays, and if they persist help should be sought so that a sense of despair does not develop.

2. *Post-puerperal loss of sexual desire*

A woman may have normal desire and frequent sexual intercourse before having a baby and no desire afterwards. This loss of desire is a complicated phenomenon with contradictory explanations. If such a loss persists for more than a few months, a couple should seek help from their doctor. Persistent loss of sexual desire for years after childbirth is often recounted in marital problems and if this single issue could be eliminated a good deal of marital breakdown would also disappear.

3. *Infidelity*

The incidence of infidelity is high during these years. One or both spouses may be involved in single or multiple incidents. In the case of repeated episodes the spouse may simply tolerate it no longer. Up till now their confidence may have been low and they may have stuck to their spouse because they could not trust themselves to find anyone else. Now their image of themselves begins to change and they feel they do not have to put up with this intolerable situation. But every act of infidelity, from the very beginning, needs understanding and not simple toleration. It is vital that a spouse prone to such behaviour knows that repetition will have serious consequences which should deter this pattern of behaviour.

Occasionally a single act of infidelity during this phase may bring the marriage to a halt. This depends on the background of the marriage which usually has been deteriorating emotionally, sexually and socially for some time.

INTELLECTUAL AND SPIRITUAL DIMENSIONS

During this phase of marriage dependence on authority usually subsides and this means also a change in the relationship with God and the establishment of different values. In general these values are a move from external criteria of authenticity, that is to say, from respecting the social and moral mores of society to a more sophisticated trust in one's own resources of establishing what is right and what is wrong. This change may lead a person away from practising their faith by ceasing to go to church. The change in faith and value systems needs to be tested by the partner in depth, in order to distinguish a deepening rather than a superficial drift away from responsibility.

Third phase of marriage

This last phase occurs between fifty until the death of one partner. During this phase risk of breakdown of marriage continues, and some steps can be taken to prevent this.

SOCIAL DIMENSION

Perhaps the single most important event during this phase is the departure of the children, about which more will be said below. Life careers of husbands terminate at this stage and marital breakdown may occur as a consequence. Some senior officials relate to their wives on the basis of these ladies having been social adjuncts to their careers; when their careers terminate the couple find they may have little in common. Thus there is always the need to cultivate intimate as well as social bonds between spouses so that when one is no longer needed the other may maintain the relationship.

EMOTIONAL DIMENSION

1. *Dependency*

There are some marriages that breakdown in this third phase. When asked the reasons one or both partners will explain the event on the basis of boredom or the absence of any unitive element. Close examination reveals that one reason for this alienation is the continuation of the movement from dependence to independence. There are men and women who reach their emotional adolescence in their fifties. They find that they have just reached a stage of defining their own identity, who they are and what they wish to experience. Not surprisingly in some instances it is their spouse they wish to repudiate, with whom they now find little in common. These are men and women who have often related to their spouses as dependent people with little or no autonomous life or pleasure.

The prevention of this sad phenomenon, for it is sad to separate after twenty to thirty years of marriage, depends on the facilitation of earlier maturation by the dominant spouse who may find subjection to their wishes highly attractive but needs to remember that at some stage there may be pronounced revolt.

2. *Lack of relationship*

The departure of children may become the signal for one spouse also to depart. Again a long-standing marriage breaks up, but the reason here is different. When this couple examine their relationship closely, they find that, despite the fact that they have lived, eaten, slept, made love, in what has typically appeared to be a marriage, they have not lived through each other but rather through their children or work. Their emotional lives have been entirely involved with others rather than with each other, and so when their children have left, they look at each other and they find they are strangers. They have nothing to hold them together except memories. They mean little to each other except, at the best, being good friends. That of course does not mean that there is no major upheaval in their personal lives when they separate.

Clearly such painful upheaval needs careful attention to the quality of the relationship throughout the marriage. Mothers may become over-concerned with their children and fathers with their work. In this way the two drift apart. Despite the presence of children, a couple need to maintain their conjugal life with its own tempo of social, emotional and sexual life. If this is insisted upon, the departure of children does not leave a vacuum behind.

SEXUAL DIMENSION

During this phase an increasing number of husbands will gradually cease to be potent but on the whole this does not affect the stability of marriage. If the impotence cannot be reversed then understanding its physical nature and compensating with affection will help a great deal.

INTELLECTUAL AND SPIRITUAL DIMENSIONS

In this phase of marriage there is a gradual resolution of the conflicting elements in the personality. Men and women, in particular the former, are said to mellow and this means that there is a gradual integration of conscious and unconscious, logic and feelings, anger and toleration, masculine and feminine, and of other complementary qualities. Such integration transforms priorities, values, opinions, objectives and motivations. The spouses may find themselves drifting apart as their sense of the meaningful no longer coincides. If there are regard, respect and love for each other, such differences can be accommodated, but there is need to maintain those aspects of the relationship which act as the supporting framework for the internal differences in priorities.

Warning signals at any time

The comments made so far in this chapter on prevention have been largely devoted to specific issues and patterns which research and clinical experience have shown to be important. There are three additional behaviour patterns which are of considerable significance, lack of communication, quarrelling and apathy.

COMMUNICATION

In the traditional type of marriage communication was not necessary beyond negotiating the daily necessities of life. As for love and affection, some couples established warm and close rapport but such an intimacy was not a required part of the relationship. Increasingly it is becoming so. This does not mean that there are not many marriages where communication is poor, but it does mean that, when such poverty is unacceptable, it is recognized by society as a legitimate cause for complaint and if necessary as grounds for divorce.

Communication can be verbal, physical, social, emotional, intellectual or spiritual. Husbands and wives talk and listen, touch and respond, make love, socialize and act as a group, express and receive affection, exchange ideas and give and receive spiritual acknowledgement of each other. There are few couples who are successful in all these dimensions, nor is this necessary. What is important is that a couple feel and know that they trust and can reach each other in whatever combination suits them best. Temporary breaks in communication occur in all marriages.

It is a total lack of communication which persists for weeks, months and years that is a warning that there is something seriously wrong with the relationship. Such persistent lack of communication must not be allowed to continue, for in the end there is no relationship to resume. Communication must be re-established and the hurt and anger, rejection and fear, laid bare so that spouses know what has gone wrong.

QUARRELLING

Every couple quarrels. If they did not then the reality of their happiness would be suspect. There are bound to be differences, neglects, conflicts, acts of omission and commission that hurt and misunderstandings which lead to quarrels. It does not really matter whether there are few or many quarrels. Personalities differ. There are volatile extroverts who pick a quarrel at the drop of a hat, but the fury does not last, evaporating in seconds or minutes. No ill will is maintained and the quarrel finishes as abruptly as it began. There are couples who rarely quarrel, but when they do it is a serious matter and takes times to heal.

There are two warning signals that something serious is present in the relationship. The first is that quarrels begin to escalate, are repetitive and the issues remain unresolved. The second is the gradual or abrupt cessation of quarrelling with the issues remaining unresolved. In both instances one or more important issues remain unresolved and it is bound to emerge in some further form, possibly in the breakup of marriage.

APATHY

The cessation of quarrelling is a form of apathy which may become generalized and lead to the couple beginning to lose interest in each other. In the presence of strong feelings, even of anger, there is active involvement of the spouses. When emotions and feelings begin to die this is followed by decrease of interest in what happens to the relationship. Nothing is argued about because nothing matters. There is a gradual decline in interaction to the point where affection is reduced to politeness, sex ceases, social interaction becomes co-existence and the flavour of the relationship is lost, becoming instead a hazy friendly or indifferent notional presence. Such presence may be the prelude to termination, and therefore apathy joins quarrelling and communication as three important warning signals of serious danger to the marital relationship.

The first act

Marriage has been described in this book as the second act of a two-act play. The first act is the relationship between child and parents. It is during childhood that the child learns the essentials of trust without which intimate relationships cannot be forged or sustained. Every effort made by the parent to act in a reliable, available and predictable manner heightens the child's experience of trust, trust in itself and in others.

In the framework of trust the young person learns to receive and return love, to give and to accept, another essential component of the marital relationship. Both giving and receiving are important. There are people who can only receive and these are labelled as immature adults, narcissistic in nature or in plain terms selfish. They have not outgrown their need to take in and be looked after. There are others who can only give and cannot receive because they don't feel they deserve it. The young person needs to be helped to both accept and register love and to give generously to others, a combination which ensures the continuity of love in marriage.

Intimately connected with giving and receiving love is the experience of self-esteem or of feeling worthwhile and lovable. Parents have a unique opportunity to make their children feel lovable. They can do this by affirmation, and praise and by the ability to make the emerging person feel that they posses their bodies, feelings and mind and what they own is good unconditionally. They need to feel that they are loved not for what they have done or achieved but because they exist. This acceptance of self and others, because they are and not because of what they are worth to us, is a necessary prelude to treating people as persons and not as objects. Love belongs to personhood and much of the yearning in contemporary marriage is to be treated as a person.

The ability of parents, relatives and teachers to facilitate the growth of people who feel trustworthy and can trust others, who are lovable and can love others, are self-accepting and can accept others unconditionally, augurs well for the second act of love in marriage. Of course all these qualities are not entirely dependent on nurture; they also reflect nature and the ability to respond to parental intiatives, but the response needs the initiative.

Commitment

A great deal has been said in this chapter on prevention based on research and clinical findings and in this way the impression may have been given that such care is enough to prevent marital breakdown. This is not true. None of these measures are going to save a marriage unless there is the commitment to indissolubility. I believe that permanency belongs to the nature of marriage and the whole approach of this book is to show how the permanent nature of marriage, seen in social, physical, emotional and intellectual terms, has an infrastructure in the formation of a human attachment or bond. But this bond is fragile and the whole of the Judaeo-Christian tradition has shown that this vulnerability needs God's grace to overcome it. The sacrament of marriage is the meeting point where the natural meets the divine and is thoroughly penetrated by the latter. Marriage is a secular reality taken up in the divine order and transformed by it. Commitment through faith needs the natural knowledge collated by science, and science needs the motivation of the divine order of things. It is the resultant forces that give life to marriage. Commitment to permanency is part of the motivation that only God can and does supply in this sacrament.

Summary

Prevention of marital breakdown is a matter of following the various phases of marriage and attending in great detail to the social, physical, emotional, intellectual and spiritual needs. A combination of attention to these details coupled with the commitment through faith is the best safeguard for marriage.

PART V

The Christian Dimension

CHAPTER 16

Pastoral Care

In the previous chapter the dual needs for the support of marriage were stressed, namely an ever deepening understanding of the way it is experienced through the findings of research coupled with the motivation to maintain it that springs from faith. In a sense this is the uniqueness of Christian marriage, namely the interaction between nature and faith, and the next two chapters will outline how the commitment of faith can be nurtured over the cycles of marriage.

In the past the pastoral care for marriage and the family consisted in a brief preparation for the wedding and the wedding ceremony. The couple were then virtually forgotten until the baptism of their first child. The pastoral concern continued to be directed primarily towards the child with entry to a Catholic school, first confession and communion followed by confirmation. Throughout this time the needs of the couple as a married pair were completely ignored. When we compare this to the preparation and support given to the sacrament of the priesthood, we can see that marriage, which involves 95 per cent of the community, has been profoundly neglected. The historical reason for this has been the conceptualization of the sacrament as an entity which was complete in the exchange of rights over each other's bodies followed by sexual consummation. Clearly this understanding of marriage was devoid of its central characteristic, that of an unfolding relationship. Once this is fully realized then pastoral care extends widely before and after marriage.

Care before marriage

In so far as marriage is the second significant relationship in people's lives, then an essential part of pastoral care is the support that is given to spouses as parents so that their children emerge from childhood with the capacity to form stable, loving relationships. A vital element of pastoral care is the teaching and encouragement of parents to help them give their children an understanding of the meaning of love in personal relationships. The home and school share this responsibility.

HOME

No one doubts the influence of parents on the education of love for their children. It is in the home that children experience their first relationship of love. Every child forms a bond early in the first year of life and within that bond it learns to feel acknowledged, wanted and appreciated. These feelings are conveyed physically, emotionally, socially and intellectually. Pastoral care is needed to assist parents to see that giving their children an affirmative experience of feeling lovable is acting as God does with his people. He loves them first in order for them to learn the meaning of love as an intrinsic part of themselves, facilitating in turn their donation of themselves to others in love. St John put this idea theologically when he writes in his first epistle: 'We are to love, then, because he loved us first' (John 4:19). Just as all of us receive the gifts of loving because God first loved us, so children receive the capacity to love through their experience of their parents.

At the heart of loving lies our capacity to acknowledge and understand the needs of others correctly and to respond to them appropriately. Our parents did precisely this from the time when we could not speak but were thoroughly understood to the period when we could express our needs in the most explicit way.

Just as Jesus Christ felt the trust of his Father which made him trustworthy, so the trust of our parents make us feel trustworthy. Springing from this source of trust we can evaluate our behaviour towards others. They may make us cross, they can arouse hostility and anger in us, but ultimately our love must be greater than our anger. Jesus was also angry but his love was greater than his anger. In this way parents can bring to the fore the close association between the normal development of their children and the balance between the affirmative and destructive forces in them, and can help them to see that Christian life centres on living like Jesus Christ who managed to overcome hostility with love, love which ultimately cost his life.

The central pastoral task during the early years is to show to parents that their role as instructors is much more than a pedagogic exercise of teaching their children the facts of life. Much more important is endowing them with a capacity to possess themselves and to be aware of the balance between hate, anger and love. The development of love conquering jealousy, envy, hate, revenge, destruction, is basing the development of their children on the model of Jesus Christ.

The pastoral care of these early years is to help parents see that their efforts in bringing up their children are closely related to living a deep Christian life, in which the results of their own growth lay the foundation of their child's personality, a personality approaching that of Christ.

There are now innumerable books and pamphlets helping parents to convey accurately the information which the child needs for a full awareness of his/her personal development. Each child varies in its make-up and its development will form an intuitive partnership between parent and child. The role of the pastor is to make it possible for the parent to see that in facilitating the growth of their child they are not only carrying out what belongs to their natural responsibility as parents but are also acting simultaneously as God's agents in inspiring a Christ-like dimension in this growth.

SCHOOL

The same applies to the school but with a difference. The community of the school introduces the child to the wider world in which intimacy is replaced by competition and achievement. At home each child is loved unconditionally because it has a being of its own. At school the child is acknowledged as a social being in a setting where achievement is part of its value system. The child learns here something of its worth as a doer whereas at home its principal value is its reality as a person with whom a relationship of love has been established. These attributes are not fixed or rigid. The home gradually acknowledges achievement and the school personal worth, but the two environments provide different emphases. They complement each other in the Christian order. God loves us unconditionally because we exist but he also loves our efforts to be Christ-like. These two dimensions have important repercussions later on in marriage. Couples have unconditional meaning for each other as objects of their mutual love, and this love fluctuates with the quality of the actual concrete achievement of the relationship.

The school is a place for growth of skills and knowledge, it is also the place for the more intimate instruction in personal relationships. It cannot replace the home because it is in the latter that the growing person learns the actual meaning of loving as it is seen and experienced. What the school can do is to widen the scope of this experience by discussing, debating and encouraging a development of values. This is the time, particularly at adolescence, when young people want to debate contraception, masturbation, divorce, premarital sex, abortion and other such charged subjects. A discussion of the values attached to these practices are part of the adolescent's needs in understanding personal relationships.

But the adolescent is not only trying to understand but is actually involved in exploratory relationships with the other sex. This is the time when both home and school need to combine to help the young person understand the integrity of authentic human relationships. In particular what needs to be imparted is that sex is a gift given not as a means of exploring relationships but rather as an expression of sealing a commitment.

A warning is needed at this point. It is often felt that instruction in human relationship is something which concerns sex alone and is appropriate at the time of adolescence. As already indicated this is not true. The child has a dozen years of being thoroughly immersed in personal loving which is not genital in expression. During these years the young person learns to achnowledge and be acknowledged, give and receive, appreciate and be appreciated and express affection physically, emotionally and verbally. These prepubertal characteristics of love need to be fused with its genital expression in sex. This is indeed the greatest challenge to love. In particular love requires a fusion of the genital and the affective, and pastoral care at this stage of development is crucial in achieving this. Chastity is concerned with the proper expression of this fusion. If sex is used in isolation, it ceases to be fully human and if the loving encounter ignores the sexual dimension it is also distorted.

COURTSHIP

Traditionally the time after school has been a pastoral concern in which young people have been warned to remain chaste, which in practice has meant to avoid having sexual intercourse. So long as sexual intercourse ran the risk of leading to pregnancy there was an in-built deterrent which combined with spiritual admonition. A large part of the deterrence was fear, and a small part was the conviction that intercourse belonged to marriage. The reason for not avoiding intercourse before marriage was the experience of people in love that they wanted intercourse to complete what they felt for each other.

With the advent of widespread birth control the fear of pregnancy has diminished and this negative reason for avoiding sex largely removed. In orthodox circles the blame is put on the advent of birth control. I think it is more appropriate to realize that the grounds for confining intercourse within marriage were not properly given. The reason for having intercourse within marriage is not that something illicit is made licit but rather that marriage contains the proper conditions for doing justice to sexual intercourse.

If sexual intercourse is seen as an extremely positive and affirmative activity which contributes to sustaining, healing and growth; to continuity, reliability and predictability; and to all its individual characteristics as mentioned in chapter 8, then it needs a relationship we call marriage to give it full scope. Sexual intercourse is impoverished prior to marriage because its full potential does not have a chance to express itself.

Readers may say that although the explanation may be different, the person is still expected to remain continent prior to marriage and this is impossible, that it is impossible because there is a sexual urge in both sexes, but particularly in the man which needs release.

Nobody would deny the strength of this sexual urge which leads to spontaneous emissions and masturbation. The urge is there and these are the ways that the physical needs can be relieved. But, as stated, the central human challenge is to combine genitality with love, and the release of sexual tension alone may be a necessary but incomplete expression of human integrity. So sacrifice and effort is certainly needed. My contention is that people will make both when they see clearly the reason for this.

The reason for confining sexual intercourse to a relationship of exclusive and permanent commitment is that its enormous potential can find there authentic expression. Sacrifice is needed to exploit its rich meaning and this is infinitely more understandable. Traditionally something illicit and wrong becomes licit and right within marriage. That did not and does not correspond to human experience, and therefore it does not arouse the proper motivation for

effort and sacrifice. Sex is expressed as something rich and rewarding, and so it is, and in the explanation offered here its withholding
is for a good and rich reason, namely to do justice to its enormous
potential.

Sex in the service of relationship, which is the key to this interpretation, makes human sense. It does not make continence any
easier, it calls for no less effort and sacrifice, but it touches the part
of the human person which can respond with an affirmative
rejoinder.

What about the other traditional interpretation, namely that sex
is for children and children belong to marriage? There is a great
deal of truth in this proposition but the truth is blunted by the
advent of widespread birth regulation of the type acceptable to the
Roman Catholic Church or non-acceptable alternatives. But that is
precisely one of the reasons for condemning birth control, that it
severs the link between procreation and coitus and therefore detracts
from the fullness of the act. This is persuasive until it is realized
that this is not how couples experience intercourse. Each and every
sexual act is approached as a personal encounter in which bodies,
minds and feelings unite. This is its basic experience. The fact that
a sperm and ovum may fuse is not at all a direct part of the
experience. It is a biological consequence which proceeds independently of the existential experience of the couple. That is why the
so-called evil of contraception is so difficult to grasp. For the majority of people, intercourse which is not intended for procreation
is seen as a completion of the evident experience; it is a reality of
loving carried to its ultimate conclusion.

When sex however is seen at the service of relationship, the
presence or absence of birth control is irrelevant. To use sex prior
to its proper rich expression is a violation of the human encounter
and this argument makes infinitely more sense. Refraining from
intercourse is no longer to avoid conception, which is not an intrinsic
part of the experience of the couple, but a subscription to the full
meaning of sex in human relationship.

So pastoral concern at this period is for the development of the
meaning of relationship. Both from the natural and Christian point
of view the pastoral emphasis needs to be on relationship, covenant,
faithfulness, commitment. In other words people must not be used
and exploited as stepping stones in the progress of growth. When
sex loses its significance as a service to relationship, it becomes an
exploitive instrument in which people are sacrificed on the altar of

simple sexual satisfaction which impoverishes and really distorts its meaning.

Courtship is a time to discover the characteristics of another. These characteristics are social, emotional, intellectual, physical and spiritual. Are we at peace in the presence of our friend? Do we find their attitude to life similar to our own? Do we feel understood? Can we make sense of each other emotionally? Is there enough communication? Enough demonstration of affection? Is there joint responsibility about decisions? Is blame shared or responsibility avoided? These and similar issues are vital for discovering whether the partnership can become a permanent one. Pastoral care needs to support these journeys of discovery between young people and ensure that short cuts are not taken.

ENGAGEMENT

When a couple find that the answers to the above questions are positive they move closer to one another and begin the preparations for a final commitment to marriage. They are unlikely to go through the list and check each question but they will experience a sense of convergence towards each other which will tell them intuitively that they want to be together for good.

Increasingly the couples who are engaged or who are becoming committed to each other are given an opportunity to attend courses which have practical emotional and sexual training.

It used to be thought in the past that such a course was sufficient to see a couple through their married life. Clearly this is not so. Such a course can only anticipate events and their grasp is often intellectual. Facts are seized mentally. There are a number of facts such as buying a house, setting it up, learning about birth regulation which are useful to learn in advance, but the day-to-day living with all its subtle nuances can only be learned in practice later on.

Catholic organizations throughout the world have now got various courses for engaged couples, and the details vary from course to course. These courses are useful provided they are seen in the context of an on-going programme of support before and after marriage.

WEDDING

The actual wedding remains the solemn occasion where a couple give their personal undertakings to each other and essentially surrender the rights over their bodies to each other for life. The actual words of the ceremony vary and the exchange of rights is expressed in terms of the traditional ends of marriage namely children, mutual love and faithfulness and the sacrament. The sacrament is in fact conferred by the couple to each other, and the presence of the priest, witnesses and congregation is part of the public element of the ceremony in the sense that marriage has both a private and a public dimension.

Traditionally the Church has been concerned that the wedding involves two persons who are free to marry and have the right intentions and that the ceremony is carried out in a proper manner. Up to recent times these canonically legal requirements have been overwhelmingly important and the sermon preached was dominated by the 'goods' or 'ends' of marriage.

But in fact the wedding is the beginning of an unfolding relationship that may last fifty years or more, and the essence of the marriage is situated in this covenant between the couple. The sermon needs to stress both the length and depth of this encounter in terms of sustaining, healing and growth within a framework of reliable permanency. These human events need to be put in the context of the covenant relationship between God and his people in the Old Testament and Christ and the Church in the New Testament. In other words, here as elsewhere, the human elements of marriage have to be transformed in the God–man, Christ–Church symbolism. But the encounter between husband and wife is more than a sign and a symbol; in the words of one theologian, 'The love and faithfulness that Christian husbands and wives have for each other, then, are not simply the sign and symbol of the love of God– they are the effective sign, the fulfilled symbol and the real epiphany of the love of God that has appeared in Jesus Christ.'[1]

But it is not sufficient to express pastoral care in these terms alone, the priest needs to spell out the various possibilities of support for the couple.

Pastoral care after marriage

It has become increasingly clear that pastoral care is needed after marriage, indeed for the whole duration of its life. Every priest and

married couple need to be acquainted, at least in outline, with the
marriage cycle outlined in this book so that they can make sense of
the events that are negotiated by the married.

PARISH SUPPORT
I was asked once, what gift would I give to a newly married couple
as their wedding present. I replied that I would give them my
telephone number and put it to them that they could contact me if
I could be of any assistance to their marriage. What I meant by
this is the need for the immediate community to become available
to the newly married couple. In our society, social isolation is a
significant phenomenon. The newly married may have access to
friends and relatives, but they may not and they may need help
which is not available. They may in fact want to talk to a compara-
tive stranger, provided that there is present the trust and bond that
belongs to fellow Christians. Just as the newly born baby at baptism
has a godfather and a godmother, so the newly married couple may
wish to have a couple who offer to be available to them when
needed. Such a couple need in no way be trained or be specialists
in marriage. They need simply to be caring and prepared to listen
when either of the couple wish to talk to them, about trivial or
major matters. So much marital distress and even breakdown occurs
because defects in the relationship arise which cannot be ventilated
and put into perspective.

The availability of existing couples to the newly married is one
way by which pastoral care can be extended to them. It goes without
saying that such caring needs discretion, confidentiality and a great
deal of loving concern. But all this exists in parishes—it is a matter
of realizing existing potential.

As already stated, the availability of one couple to another does
not imply any special training for this. The role of specialized
marriage cousellors is an entirely different matter. They offer expert
help when a marital relationship runs into considerable difficulties.
The sponsoring couples are there to provide whatever help they can
emanating from their concern and experience.

GROUPS
The meeting of couples in groups is a further step in the direction
of mutual help. Groups are not everybody's first choice but they

can be of enormous assistance. Married couples can form themselves
into groups which represent the married state they have reached
and then can become the means of pooling, sharing, exchanging
experiences as well as deepening their faith in the meaning of
marriage. Most people, and the married are no exception, believe
that their experiences are unique. When they face difficulties it is
very hard for them to appreciate that others have had similar
happenings and have negotiated them. Groups can help to break
down barriers and give mutual support. This support can be practical, social, emotional, physical, spiritual. Couples can help each
other with baby-sitting, at times of ill-health and whenever needs
arise.

As the children arrive, their parents can share their needs and
anxieties in bringing them up, facilitating the growth of their personalities and feeling secure that they are discharging their duties
as parents well. In particular parents need to help each other in
instructing their children in matters of faith and sex. Both these
topics raise difficulties and the sharing of experience is helpful.

Above all a group is a mutually supportive entity. All couples
experience difficulties and challenges, and a frank and authentic
openness reinforces the motivation to love in the midst of recurrent
tribulations. Formal groups are sometimes difficult to organize. But
there are other situations of informal group gatherings. One of them
is the time in the afternoon when mothers and sometimes fathers
come to pick up their young children from school. This is an occasion that can be structured to meet the married needs of the
participants. House masses are becoming a regular event in the life
of parishes. This is an occasion when the married can come together
and preaching take place on topics dealing with marital
relationship.

FIRST CHILD

The advent of the first child is vital for the family. In the past the
main contribution of the Church was its baptism. We now realize
what an upheaval in the marriage is caused by the arrival of the
first baby. In particular the mother, who often gives up work, may
feel intensely the isolation of her new situation and need support.
She may become temporarily depressed and need help from others.
The range of possibilities in helping in this situation is endless.

MARRIAGE CYCLE

Although the first few years are vital in the life of a marriage and are intimately related to its outcome, the marital relationship continues over many phases in the marriage cycle. These various phases, already discussed in the book, demand different types of groups, meetings and exchanges. Parents may become involved in parent-teachers associations and form their mutual help relationships from this angle.

ROLE OF PRIEST

The pastoral care of the married is not a responsibility to be discharged by the priest alone. He is there to act as a facilitator to bring couples together and then let them proceed under their own steam. He provides continuity, which is vital, and also animates the community spiritually. Masses and other liturgical events can be initiated by him which constantly show his people how their everyday married experience is their encounter with God. This is his special task and for this he needs to be prepared with a reasonable understanding of the cycle of married life and equipped with a scriptural background to match the two. The continuous liturgy for the married will be dealt with in the next chapter.

Summary

The pastoral care for marriage is a process that involves the preparation of people through the whole period prior to marriage and specifically after marriage. The objective is to help the married see that their daily life is an encounter with Christ which is realized in the minute-to-minute exchange between themselves and between themselves and their children.

References (Chapter 16)

1. Kasper, W., *Theology of Christian Marriage*, p.35 Burns and Oates, 1980.

CHAPTER 17

Liturgy for Marriage

(In order to aviod making this chapter too long some familiar passages or those that have appeared elsewhere in the book are not printed in full.)

The previous chapter was concerned with the ways and means by which the couple can be helped pastorally. Such an approach presupposes that the everyday experience of the couple is at the heart of their marriage and this very same reality is transformed or taken up into the divine dimension. In the Christian community it is important that the couple understand, feel and live this reality in the Lord. This means that the married should be able to see that their life comes from God and is offered back to him.

The overwhelming majority of married Christians cannot relate their life to events in the scriptures except on the occasions when a profound moral law is at stake, like divorce. In this way, the couple only become aware of God's word when its violation is at stake. It is not appreciated that 99 per cent of their life is not entangled with violations of law but with a positive, affirmative experience of living and trying to love. The scriptures abound with teachings and events which are concerned with married life and one way of assisting the married is to show them that their experience is encompassed by the word of God which in the Old and the New Testaments shows that marriage is the means of salvation for the overwhelming majority of human beings. Couples need to be helped to see that their experience is truly in the Lord and furthermore that they can offer back their married life to God in liturgy. By liturgy we are to understand the worship offered to God by the Church, in this case by the married. We need to introduce in Christian life a two-way exchange whereby the married see that their life is God's way of salvation for them and that in turn they can offer this life back to God as an act of thanksgiving and also as a request for constant help to maintain its authenticity always in the Lord.

At the present moment the liturgy of marriage is primarily confined to the wedding and the accompanying mass. This is the time when the couple make their vows and the renewal of vows is another event which occurs on special occasions. There is however, no extensive liturgy by which the daily events of the married in the different phases of marriage are captured in a liturgical cycle of marriage.

Liturgical cycle for marriage

What is proposed in this chapter is the possibility of an annual liturgical cycle of marriage which is related to its life cycle. Courtship, the early years, middle and late years can be used as the basis for liturgical expression annually, and the married can see their life depicted in the scriptures and have an opportunity to offer back their particular experience to God. The possibilities for such an exercise are endless and I do not pretend for one moment that the cycle offered here is the last word on the subject. It is possible however to use four Sundays of the year or, if that is not considered appropriate at the moment, to use four days in the year when the married are invited to listen and respond from their own experience to the word of God about marriage in its various phases. These four occasions can coincide with Advent, Lent, Pentecost and the conclusion of the Church's year or at other times. The important point is to build up gradually an annual cycle of liturgy which focuses on the married state. In the Roman Catholic tradition it is customary nowadays to have four readings at mass, and so four readings will be chosen for each phase. The pieces chosen here can be supplemented by other texts in the book or indeed other passages.

COURTSHIP
In Western society the period of courtship has become a source of controversy because young people choose in certain circumstances to have sexual intercourse prior to marriage and a small number prefer to live together for a while instead of getting formally married.

There is no doubt that these issues are important, but it is even more important to appreciate that courtship is a time when physical attraction plays a prominent role in a positive way. Christianity has a tradition of acknowledging the importance of the body but being afraid of it. Our times are concerned to show that there is a beauty and joy in the body which is immensely human and which is a source of rejoicing. Lovers all over the world rejoice in their bodily features and mutual attraction and the scriptures attest positively to this.

Passages from the Song of Songs in the Old Testament celebrate the attraction, the love which we would call romantic, and fidelity between a man and a woman. Here is the way the Bridegroom describes the bride:

> How beautiful you are, my love,
> how beautiful you are!
> Your eyes, behind your veil,
> are doves;
> your hair is like a flock of goats
> frisking down the slopes of Gilead.
> Your teeth are like a flock of shorn ewes
> as they come up from the washing.
> Each one has its twin,
> not one unpaired with another.
> Your lips are a scarlet thread
> and your words enchanting.
> Your cheeks, behind your veil,
> are halves of pomegranate.
> Your neck is the tower of David
> built as a fortress,
> hung round with a thousand bucklers
> and each the shield of a hero.
> Your two breasts are two fawns,
> twins of a gazelle,
> That feed among the lilies.(Song of Sol. 4:1-5)

Another passage that can be used to describe the bridegroom's joy is the following:

> How beautiful are your feet in their sandals,
> O prince's daughter!
> The curve of your thighs is like the curve of a necklace,

work of a master hand.
Your navel is a bowl well rounded
with no lack of wine,
your belly a heap of wheat
surrounded with lilies.
Your two breasts are two fawns,
twins of a gazelle.
Your neck is an ivory tower.
Your eyes, the pools of Heshbon,
by the gate of Bath-rabbim.
Your nose, the Tower of Lebanon
sentinel facing Damascus.
Your head is held high like Carmel,
and its plaits are as dark as purple;
a king is held captive in your tresses.
How beautiful you are, how charming,
my love, my delight! (Song of Sol. 7:2-7)

There are further passages when the bride answers in turn with her proclamation of loving appreciation of her bridegroom. It is rare in the scriptures to find so much spontaneity, openness and freedom of expression put into the mouth of a woman, and it shows that ancient woman had on occasions the opportunity to acclaim her sexuality in terms no less pronounced than her contemporary sister.

The Bride
My Beloved is fresh and ruddy,
to be known among ten thousand.
His head is golden, purest gold,
his locks are palm fronds
and black as the raven.
His eyes are doves
at a pool of water
bathed in milk
at rest on a pool.
His cheeks are beds of spices,
banks sweetly scented.
His lips are lilies
distilling pure myrrh.
His hands are golden, rounded,
set with jewels of Tarshish.
His belly a block of ivory

covered with sapphires.
His legs are alabaster columns
set in sockets of pure gold.
His appearance is that of Lebanon,
unrivalled as the cedars.
His conversation is sweetness itself,
his is altogether lovable.
Such is my Beloved, such is my friend
O daughters of Jerusalem. (Song of Sol. 5:10-16)

Finally, in another passage, the man expresses in most powerful poetical language his eternal faithfulness. He asks the Bride to set him like a seal on her heart. All lovers long that the love they experience during the courtship will continue for ever and become a permanent part of each other.

The Bridegroom
I awakened you under the apple tree,
there where your mother conceived you,
there where she who gave birth to you conceived you.
Set me like a seal on your heart,
like a seal on your arm.
For love is strong as Death,
jealously as relentless as Sheol.
The flash of it is a flash of fire,
a flame of Yahweh himself.
Love no flood can quench,
no torrents drown. (Song of Sol. 8:5-7)

Psalm
In that concluding passage from the Song of Solomon the man invokes the strength of love which he describes as 'a flame of Yahweh himself'. Love, faithfulness and God are intimately related, indeed God is the source of all faithfulness, and if love is to remain strong, it needs faithfulness to nurture it. Psalm 89 is a hymn and a prayer to God's faithfulness.

I will celebrate your love for ever, Yahweh,
age after age my words shall proclaim your faithfulness;
for I claim that love is built to last for ever
and your faithfulness founded firmly in the heavens.

'I have made a covenant with my Chosen,
I have given my servant David my sworn word:

I have founded your dynasty to last for ever,
I have build you a throne to outlast all time.'

Yahweh, the assembly of holy ones in heaven
applaud the marvel of your faithfulness.
Who in the skies can compare with Yahweh?
Which of the heaven-born can rival him?

God, dreaded in the assembly of holy ones,
great and terrible to all around him,
Yahweh, God of Sabaoth, who is like you?
mighty Yahweh, clothed in your faithfulness! (Ps. 89:1-8)

The response to this psalm is, 'Yahweh, the assembly of holy ones in heaven applaud the marvel of your faithfulness'.

Epistle
During courtship sexual intercourse becomes a vital issue. The Christian tradition, following the Jewish one of the Old Testament, places sexual intercourse securely in a relationship which is both a commitment of love and a permanent enduring entity nurtured by fidelity. Transient sex, in which bodies meet for pleasure without a personal encounter of enduring love, is not part of God's revelation. St Paul brings this out in his letter to the Corinthians. The Corinthians believed that everything was permitted to them including intercourse with prostitutes. But Paul reminds them that sexual intercourse is a bodily union and the body saved by Christ is his; it is the temple of the Holy Spirit and therefore its availability to others can only be in the context of an enduring love. Relationships short of that deprive the body of its full meaning and significance, and in this book it has been shown that the capacity of sex to serve a relationship is indeed most extensive. Anything which makes the sexual act fall deliberately short of its potential damages love and is incompatible with Christ who lives in the body as much as in the whole person.

For me there are no forbidden things; maybe, but not everything does good. I agree there are no forbidden things for me, but I am not going to let anything dominate me. Food is only meant for the stomach, and the stomach for food; yes, and God is going to do away with both of them. But the body – this is not meant for fornication; it is for the Lord, and the Lord for the body.

God, who raised the Lord from the dead, will by his power raise us up too.

You know, surely, that your bodies are members making up the body of Christ; do you think I can take parts of Christ's body and join them to the body of a prostitute? Never! As you know, a man who goes with a prostitute is one body with her, since the *two*, as it is said, *become one flesh*. But anyone who is joined to the Lord is one spirit with him.

Keep away from fornication. All other sins are committed outside the body; but to fornicate is to sin against your own body. Your body, you know, is the Temple of the Holy Spirit, who is in you since you received him from God. You are not your own property; you have been bought and paid for. That is why you should use your body for the glory of God. (1 Cor. 6:12-20)

Gospel
Courtship is a time of joyous anticipation of a relationship. But what kind of relationship? Temporary or permanent? Although divorce was permitted in the Old Testament it was not something that Yahweh was pleased with but it remained a possibility and Christ was tested on this possibility.

> Some Pharisees approached him, and to test him they said, 'Is it against the Law for a man to divorce his wife on any pretext whatever?' He answered, 'Have you not read that the creator from the beginning made them male and female and that he said: This is why a man must leave father and mother, and cling to his wife, and the two become one body? They are no longer two, therefore, but one body. So then, what God has united, man must not divide.'
>
> They said to him, 'Then why did Moses command that a writ of dismissal should be given in cases of divorce?' 'It was because you were so unteachable,' he said, 'that Moses allowed you to divorce your wives, but it was not like this from the beginning. Now I say this to you: the man who divorces his wife – I am not speaking of fornication – and marries another, is guilty of adultery.'(Matt. 19:3-9)

This is one of the clearest teachings of Christ, and courtship is a time to test as far as it is possible whether the relationship is likely to endure for some forty to fifty years. Not only is compatibility important but this is the time to test the motivation of the commitment to marriage. Are the couple really free socially and emotionally to make the commitment or are they being pushed by pressures which they find difficult to resist?

Courtship is a time of joyous anticipation of an enduring relationship of love, but it is also an appropriate time to consider in depth whether the couple have the resources and the will to enter into a permanent commitment. In the petitions of the mass the appropriate requests for strength and encouragement can be made for this period.

EARLY YEARS OF MARRIAGE (FIRST PHASE)

In the Western tradition of Christianity marriage begins when a couple exchange vows of giving and receiving each other as whole persons and consummating this exchange sexually. Vatican II declared, 'The intimate partnership of married life and love has been established by the Creator and qualified by his laws. It is rooted in the conjugal covenant of irrevocable personal consent. Hence, by that human act whereby spouses mutually bestow and accept each other, a relationship arises which by divine will and in the eyes of society too is a lasting one.'[1]

In this statement the Church is concerned to describe the beginning of what is to be a permanent relationship. We know however that couples experience their marriage stage by stage, having to overcome the particular challenges of each phase. The first phase, as described in this book, covers the first five years which are crucial to marriage. Some 30 to 40 per cent of all marital breakdown occurs during this period, and the problems which are initiated in this phase may lead to breakdown in later years. So when marriage is seen as an unfolding relationship these early years are vital. The scriptures abound with material applicable to these early years. What is marriage for? What is the significance of these early years? What is the meaning of sexual intercourse? These are some of the issues that can be handled on this occasion. The couple can listen to relevant messages in the scriptures, and in the course of the mass with its petitions reflect and offer back their own experience.

Old Testament

There are two accounts of creation. In fact the second is the earlier of the two and is the one that specifies the relationship aspect of marriage most clearly. (Gen. 2:18-23)

Clearly man and woman were meant by God to relate to each other. Their make-up had marked affinity which complemented each other. The contemporary seeking by women of equality of dignity between the sexes has nothing to be afraid of from the scriptures. In this passage the essential being of woman is clearly similar to man.

Another point which this passage brings out is the need for the couple to leave their parents in order to get married. This feature has modern applications. Couples need to feel free from the authority of parents when they marry and to turn to each other as the principal person in their life. When parents interfere or when young people cannot separate from their parents, then the relationship between the husband and wife is not operating effectively and the marriage has not really commenced.

The third point to note again is the totally unashamed nature of sexual intercourse. It is true that this is a description before the fall but Christ's reconciliation of fallen humanity to God the Father has restored all things to their pristine possibility. The fall is a reality and sex has suffered in common with all humanity. But marriage, lived in the life of grace, restores the possibility of the beauty, joy and love of the design for man by God. In the intimacy of their married life couples face each other naked. This is not only physical nakedness but social and psychological as well. The couple get to know the depths of each other, and their love is always pursuing an aspiration of total, accurate, and appropriate response.

The first description of creation is in fact the later of the two. There are similarities with the second description, but also differences. Given that the earlier passage emphasized relationship, the later stresses procreation. (Gen. 1:26-8)

In this second passage man's likeness to God is stated unequivocally. Man and woman are created in his image and therefore once again the scriptures attest to the equality of status and dignity between the sexes although they have different functions. But this passage with its emphasis on 'him' and 'them' shows clearly that we can only understand humanity in terms of man and woman. This division of the sexes is fundamental and, although we cannot comprehend the mystery about the nature of God to which it is referring, we can say with safety that both sexes find a presence in God which is real. We can also say that their sexual union is inseparable from their nature and its character is not only good but very good. Finally an essential part of its goodness is its life-giving quality. But as we know only too well this life-giving quality is only on rare occasions procreative, for the rest it is a communion of love. And love is the key to God's nature, the essential quality of the relationship between the sexes and their sexual union.

Thus these two passages establish the two fundamental aspects of the man–woman encounter, namely relationship in all its aspects and creativity. The Old Testament gives us other insights about this relationship. For example, one of the criticisms of the Christian tradition is that sexual intercourse which is illicit prior to marriage becomes licit afterwards. When sexual intercourse is seen in crude terms of permissible and not permissible, Christianity appears a legalistic religion without feeling or understanding of the nature of sex. It appears to be concerned only with what is right and wrong without reference to the personal quality of sex. There is much truth in this criticism, but this approach does not reflect the insights of the scriptures, and the story of Tobias is a good example to illustrate the opposite approach.

We are told something of Tobias' bride-to-be and her problem:

> You must know that she had been given in marriage seven times, and that Asmodeus, that worst of demons, had killed her bridegrooms one after another before ever they had slept with her as man and wife (Tobit 3:8). (The Vulgate version of this is that the seven husbands had died at their first going 'in unto her'.)

There is really no satisfactory explanation of what happened to Sarah and her seven husbands. A possible interpretation, mere conjecture on my part, is Sarah's inability to consummate her marriage, which modern insights would understand as her anxious response to sexual intercourse. In any case she was in great distress with her failure, a distress which made her contemplate suicide.

> That day, she grieved, she sobbed and went up to her father's room intending to hang herself. But then she thought, "Suppose they blamed my father!" They will say, 'You had an only daughter whom you loved, and now she has hanged herself for grief.' I cannot cause my father a sorrow which would bring down his old age to the dwelling of the dead. I should do better not to hang myself, but to beg the Lord to let me die and not to live to hear any more insults." (Tobit 3:10)

The word insult may indeed refer to her inability to have sexual intercourse.

But Tobias fell in love with her and, hearing the disaster that befell her previous spouses, nevertheless decided to marry her. On their wedding night he and Sarah prayed together before consummating their union in what has become one of the classical nuptial prayers. The two began to pray:

'You are blessed, O God of our fathers;
blessed, too, is your name,
for ever and ever.
Let the heavens bless you
and all things you have made
for evermore.
It was you who created Adam,
you who created Eve his wife
to be his help and support;
and from these two the human race was born.
It was you who said,
'It is not good that the man should be alone;
let us make him a helpmate like himself.'
And so I do not take my sister
for any lustful motive;
I do it in singleness of heart.
Be kind enough to have pity on her and on me
and bring us to old age together.' (Tobit 8: 5-7)

That is exactly what happened – and, following the hypothesis offered here, it was precisely Tobias' gentleness and tenderness which overcame Sarah's difficulties in allowing the consummation of her marriage.

It is important nevertheless to explore further the statement that he did not intend to have intercourse with any lustful motive. In the simple black and white situation of what is licit, coitus is permitted after marriage. But there is intercourse and intercourse. In this story Tobias makes it clear that he is concerned about his wife prior to his sexual pleasure. His motive springs from his heart, and the heart is intimately related to love.

Love in intercourse requires not only that a couple be ready to have sex when asked by their partner, it means much more than that. It means that the person who initiates the request should ensure that he or she does not ask for it if their spouse is clearly indisposed. Such a sacrifice is part of marital love, and every couple who care are aware of each other's readiness. It is often advanced by the polemical advocates of the infertile period that such a method introduces a deliberate sacrifice in the life of the couple. But the fact is that sacrifice is present all the time when one partner wants sex and the other does not. The case for additional sacrifice has to be made more explicit and this remains to be done.

Given that intercourse is to be pursued, the person who initiates it has to ensure that their partner is suitably prepared to respond, that care is taken that orgasm is achieved by both and that the exchange is lifted to an exchange of care and love which goes beyond attaining orgasm for one person without proper and due concern for the other. A lustful motive remains in marriage what it is in all circumstances, namely sex which is preoccupied with unilateral pleasure without loving concern for the partner. Sex in the early years of marriage is a powerful means to convey pleasure, joy and mutual concern and regard.

But sex is only one part of the life of the newly married. They need to have adequate time to understand, share and create their common life. So often the man gets married and then proceeds to live as if he was a bachelor, giving his time to all and sundry, i.e. work and friends other than his wife and sometimes the wife continues to spend more time with her relatives than her husband.

The Old Testament gives expression to this need of spouses to have time for each other: 'If a man is newly married, he shall not join the army nor is he to be pestered at home; he shall be left at home free of all obligations for one year to bring joy to the wife he has taken' (Deut. 24:5). I cannot imagine for one moment modern armies or industry giving such a concession. But the need to spend time together to forge a new life is made absolutely clear.

Psalm
Tobias like everyone else turns to God to find the enduring ground of love. God is love and from that love springs the love of the spouses. It is the early years of marriage that have to give witness to this love, and Psalm 103 expresses this with great insight. The answer to the psalm is, 'Bless Yahweh, my soul'.

> Bless Yahweh, my soul,
> bless his holy name, all that is in me!
> Bless Yahweh, my soul,
> and remember all his kindnesses . . .

Yahweh is tender and compassionate,
slow to anger, most loving;
his indignation does not last for ever,
his resentment exists a short time only;
he never treats us, never punishes us,
as our guilt and our sins deserve . . . .
Man lasts no longer than grass,
no longer than a wild flower he lives,
one gust of wind, and he is gone,
never to be seen there again;

Yet Yahweh's love for those who hear him
lasts from all eternity and for ever,
like his goodness to their children's children,
as long as they keep his covenant
and remember to obey his precepts. (Ps. 103:1-2, 8-10, 15-18)

Epistle

A couple open their married life with a high commitment to love one another physically and emotionally. St Paul has wise words to say about both. He prefers celibacy, this he makes amply clear. But he is totally realistic about sex. Sex which has no means of being expressed in a loving relationship is going to find alternatives, and Paul in no way wishes to encourage fornication. So a loving relationship in marriage is appropriate, and within it sex has an important part to play. Some would say that despite these positive views Paul is rather reluctant in his admission of the married state. Such reluctance as there is has to be seen against the background in which Paul expected the Second Coming soon. Time was growing short in relation to the Second Coming and he wished everyone to be ready to meet it. Although he has no objection to marriage or sex, he is aware of a greater prespective, hence his hesitancy to give overwhelming encouragement to anything which diverts attention from eternal objectives, but within these limitations he is positive about both marriage and about sex.

In the first epistle to the Corinthians Paul is answering questions from them about sex and marriage (1 Cor. 7:1-7). It should be noticed that Paul sees celibacy as a gift and equally so the married state; he does not attempt to give priority to one over the other.

But ultimately Paul goes well beyond these practicalities into a supreme vision of marriage. God has revealed himself fully in Jesus

Christ. In turn the Lord becomes head with the Church as his bride. Just as Christ relates intimately to the Church, so husband and wife relate intimately to each other. This epiphany of God in Christ, continues with the presence of Christ in the married couple. Paul sees a connection between God revealing himself fully in Christ, Christ joining himself fully to the Church and marriage being the domestic church where Christ presides in the relationship of the spouses, the whole sequence of relationships being held together by love. All this is to be found in the grand vision of Paul in Ephesians 5:21-32 quoted in chapter 1. One further interpretation of this famous passage is that just as Christ and his Church are united physically in the head–body relationship, so the couple are united physically principally through sexual intercourse. But the relationship between Christ and the Church, bodily though it is, is much more than that. The whole divine being is inextricably related to the Church, and so spouses are related to each other deeply not only physically but socially, emotionally, intellectually. In all these dimensions however there is a physical infrastructure. Social actions need bodies and so do emotional and intellectual exchanges.

Gospel

The most fitting incident from the gospels is Christ's presence in Cana, the occasion of his first miracle.

> Three days later there was a wedding at Cana in Galilee. The mother of Jesus was there, and Jesus and his disciples had also been invited. When they ran out of wine, since the wine provided for the wedding was all finished, the mother of Jesus said to Him, 'They have no wine.' Jesus said, 'Woman, why turn to me? My hour has not come yet.' His mother said to the servants, 'Do whatever he tells you.' There were six stone water jars standing there, meant for the ablutions that are customary among the Jews: each could hold twenty or thirty gallons. Jesus said to the servants, 'Fill the jars with water,' and they filled them to the brim. 'Draw some out now,' he told them, 'and take it to the steward.' They did this; the steward tasted the water, and it had turned into wine. Having no idea where it came from – only the servants who had drawn the water knew – the steward called the bridegroom and said, 'People generally serve the best wine first, and keep the cheaper sort till the guests have had plenty to drink; but you have kept the best wine till now.'

This was the first of the signs given by Jesus: it was given in
Cana in Galilee. (John 2:1-11)

THE MIDDLE YEARS (SECOND PHASE)

The middle years of marriage are concerned with the arrival and
development of the children. The arrival of children is often delayed
nowadays to this phase. These are also the years when the first
wave of exhilaration in marriage gives way to disappointment, to
marital conflict, infidelity, and moments of despair and doubt about
the wisdom of carrying on. All this is captured once again by various
passages in the scriptures.

Old Testament
There are innumerable sections extolling the joys of having children,
particularly if they are sons.

> Sons are a bounty from Yahweh,
> he rewards with descendants,
> like the arrows in a hero's hand
> are the sons you father when young.
> Happy the man who has filled his quiver
> with arrows of this sort;
> in dispute with his enemies at the gate,
> he will not be worsted! (Ps. 127:3-5)

Sterility on the other hand was a mark of considerable disgrace.
Rachel screams at her husband Jacob, 'Give me children or I shall
die.' This made Jacob angry with her and he retorts, 'Am I in
God's place? It is he who has refused your motherhood.'(Gen.
30:1-2)

Children however grow up and indeed during these middle years
parents are likely to experience the usual range of problems with
them. On the one hand children want to realize their independence,
on the other parents want to ensure that they are capable of looking
after themselves before they take control of their lives. This tension
will be depicted in passages of the epistles and the gospels.

In the meantime the life of the couple goes on. During these years
there will be conflict, and the Old Testament illustrates this. Conflict almost invariably results from the contributions of both spouses.
The andro-centricity of the Old Testament is heavily biased towards
men, and the examples are, as might be expected, from disgruntled

men. Women could get angry when it came to childbearing but men had the advantage over marital tension. Nowadays both men and women have the right to grumble and complain, but in the examples that follow it is women who are indicted. Nevertheless this indictment shows that, however subordinate women may have been in their public status, they could certainly make themselves felt at home.

Any wound rather than a wound of the heart!
Any spite rather than the spite of a woman!
Any evil rather than an evil caused by an enemy!
Any vengeance rather than the vengeance of a foe!
There is no poison worse than the poison of a snake,
there is no fury worse than the fury of an enemy.
I would sooner keep house with a lion or a dragon
than keep house with a spiteful woman. (Ecclus. 25:13-16)

This tirade continues in the following verses and ends with supreme arrogance in which the man is advised to get rid of her and indeed a great deal of tension in the Old Testament was caused through the husband's ability to get rid of his wife, something which Jesus Christ put a decisive end to.

Do not let water find a leak,
do not allow a spiteful woman free reign for her tongue.
If she will not do as you tell her,
get rid of her. (Ecclus. 25:25-26)

But there is also deep appreciation of what is considered to be a good and attractive wife.

Happy the husband of a really good wife;
the number of his days will be doubled.
A perfect wife is the joy of her husband,
he will live out the years of his life in peace.
A good wife is the best of portions,
reserved for those who fear the Lord;
rich or poor, they will be glad of heart,
cheerful of face, whatever the season. (Ecclus. 26:1-4)

The grace of a wife will charm her husband,
her accomplishments will make him the stronger.
A silent wife is a gift from the Lord,
no price can be put on a well-trained character.

A modest wife is a boon twice over,
a chaste character cannot be weighed on scales.
Like the sun rising over the mountains of the Lord
is the beauty of a good wife in a well-kept house.
Like the lamp shining on the sacred lamp-stand
is a beautiful face on a well-proportioned body.
Like golden pillars on a silver base
are shapely legs on firm-set heels. (Ecclus. 26:13-18)

These passages are somewhat contradictory. The husband wants a silent wife. Nowadays wives are not expected to be silent but to contribute their share to the relationship. Nevertheless the writer continues to acknowledge physical beauty. This is a point that needs to be brought out during these years of marriage. The children are important, but their welfare depends on the stability and happiness of the parents and that in fact demands that couples should continue to appreciate each other in every dimension including the physical.

Psalm
The struggle to maintain love in these years is demanding. Spouses change, their development sometimes alienates them from each other, their commitment becomes diluted as a result of disappointment and failure. The people of God in Israel were constantly aware of their inability to love fully and keep the law as required. They were constantly turning to Yahweh their God for support in time of danger, indeed at all times. An awareness of God and his complete and fulfilled love and faithfulness is needed as a constant reminder to persevere in loving one's spouse and children through some twenty years, which is the duration of these middle years. Spouses lose their way and they need God's help to find the right approach again.

In Psalm 107, which describes human loss of direction, God is invoked to chart the way afresh. The response to the psalm is 'Give thanks to Yahweh for he is good.'

Give thanks to Yahweh, for he is good,
his love is everlasting:
let these be the words of Yahweh's redeemed,
those he has redeemed from the oppressor's clutches,
by bringing them home from foreign countries,
from east to west, from north and south.

Some had lost their way in the wilds and the desert,

not knowing how to reach an inhabited town;
they were hungry and desperately thirsty
their courage was running low.

Then they called to Yahweh in their trouble
and he rescued them from their sufferings,
guiding them by a route leading
direct to an inhabited town.

Let these thank Yahweh for his love,
for his marvels on behalf of men;
satisfying the hungry,
he fills the starving with good things. (Ps. 107:1-9)

Epistle
Paul does not focus on procreation and marriage. Given his Jewish background he takes this for granted. But he is aware of tension between parents and children and gives sound advice in this passage:

> Children, be obedient to your parents in the Lord – that is your duty. The first commandment that has a promise attached to it is: Honour your father and mother, and the promise is: and you will prosper and have a long life in the Lord. And parents, never drive your children to resentment but in bringing them up correct them and guide them as the Lord does. (Eph. 6:1-4)

Paul is constantly preaching the importance of love. Couples are continuously trying to make sense of loving each other. In the following famous passage Paul describes the qualities of love, and its contents need to be known and meditated upon by all couples.

> Love is always patient and kind; it is never jealous; love is never boastful or conceited; it is never rude or selfish; it does not take offence, and is not resentful. Love takes no pleasure in other people's sins but delights in the truth; it is always ready to excuse, to trust, to hope and to endure whatever comes. (1 Cor. 13:4-7)

These few sentences hold the key to all love expressed in relationship but are specifically applicable to the married who have to handle all their exchanges in love. The concepts expressed by Paul are ideal and rarely attained in all respects. But they remain goals, objectives, standards by which the couple can assess their progress towards God's way of loving. During these middle years couples will have occasions to reassess repeatedly their love which is always coming under pressure. At this time sustaining, healing and growth can occur only when love is approaching this ideal, even if it is never reached.

Another famous passage on love is a substantial part of the fourth chapter of John's first epistle and this can be used as an alternative (1 John 4:7-21).

Gospel
Mary's unique position in Christianity is founded as much on the fact that she bore Christ as on her utter and complete trust in God. This penetrating, totally enveloping faith must have received its greatest challenge when the angel Gabriel made his announcement to her. (Luke 1:34-5)

Our Lady is undoubtedly blessed, but the same gospel which gives Elizabeth's vivid description of the movement of her baby in the womb, an experience which all pregnant women can identify with, also gives an episode which all contemporary parents would instantly recognize. The growth of children towards maturity is a process of gradual autonomy, with a tension between parents and children as to how much independence should be assumed, and how soon, by the child. Our Lady had similar problems. (Luke 2:41-50)

Whatever conflict there might have been between Jesus and his parents, there is no doubt that the state of childhood with its intensity, simplicity and trust is fundamentally important, and the kingdom of heaven cannot be revealed without retaining these features in adult life. (Luke 18:15-17)

Husbands and children need caring for, which leaves the wife little time for prayer and contemplation. Increasingly men help their wives in the home, but we have a long way to go before this sharing is complete. In the meantime there is always a tension in a wife, or indeed any woman, on whom the major burden of housekeeping falls, between being busy with the house and doing what she wants to do. In the very human episode of Mary and Martha, Martha was busy, indeed she was 'distracted with all the serving', whilst Mary sat and listened to Christ speaking. Everyone can picture similar situations where one member of the household feels that he or she is doing more than their share of housework and complains. Our Lord's reply was caring and sympathetic but he adjudicated in favour of her sister Mary. Our Lord is in fact saying here as elsewhere that we need to have our priorities right, to give time for God so that our human affairs are infused with God's presence. (Luke 10:38-42)

THE LATER YEARS (THIRD PHASE)

The third phase in marriage, which begins with the departure of children and continues until the death of one spouse, can span some twenty or more years. In this fourth and last occasion of the annual cycle, the scriptures give us insights about perennial issues like happiness in marriage, infidelity and the need for forgiveness and perseverance, also an outline of life after death in which marriage as such will not exist.

Old Testament
In this phase there is nowadays happiness but also marked sorrow as marriages experience infidelity. Infidelity is not confined to these years but during this phase, men and women, freed from the responsibility of child caring, have the time and energy to rediscover themselves. This is often done within the marriage but sometimes outside. The texts I have chosen tell of the ecstasy and the agony of married life.

Here is one extract that encourages fidelity in a joyous relationship:

Find joy with the wife you married in your youth,
fair as a hind, graceful as a fawn.
Let hers be the company you keep,
hers the breasts that ever fill you with delight,
hers the love that ever holds you captive. (Prov. 5:19)

And it is to Proverbs we turn for the description of the perfect wife and, through this, an image of marriage that has prevailed for some three thousand years.

A perfect wife – who can find her?
She is far beyond the price of pearls.
Her husband's heart has confidence in her,
from her he will derive no little profit.
Advantage and not hurt she brings him
all the days of her life.
She is always busy with wool and flax,

she does her work with eager hands.
She is like a merchant vessel
bringing her food from far away.
She gets up while it is still dark
giving her household their food,
giving orders to her serving girls.

The proverb continues with all her accomplishments and ends:

Charm is deceitful and beauty empty;
the woman who is wise is the one to praise.
Give her a share in what her hands have worked for,
and let her work tell her praises at the city gates. (Prov. 31:10-
15, 29-31)

The details remain true for many parts of the world, but increasingly less for the advanced industrial societies. Even here a wife looks after her home and acts as a source of material security and an affectionate catalyst.

But there are marriages which are torn apart by infidelity and adultery, and the family suffers agonies of distress. One such marriage is vividly protrayed and gives an answer to the modern propensity for divorce. There is no limit to reconciliation and forgiveness, and Hosea shows this. The story of the prophet Hosea is a moving account of one man's determination to preserve his marriage in the face of complete marital breakdown. Hosea marries a woman who is a whore and who, even after marriage, persists in her unfaithfulness. The symbolism is a continuation of the husband–wife relationship as shown in the commitment of God Yahweh to his people Israel who behave unfaithfully. Despite total breakdown and even divorce, there is a relentless pursuit by the husband to recover the love of his wife. For anyone who has listened to angry exchanges between spouses or the poisoning of the image of one parent by the other in the eyes of the children, the words of Hosea ring with a piercing veracity as they cross the centuries of time.

Denounce your mother, denounce her,
for she is not my wife
nor am I her husband
Let her rid her face of her whoring,
and her breasts of her adultery,
or else I will strip her naked,
expose her as on the day she was born. (Hos. 2:4-5)

If we changed the content we would have a characteristic angry argument of what others can provide which the husband neglects to offer and his furious retort:

'I am going to court my lovers' she said
'who give me my bread and water,
my work, my flax, my oil and my drink.'
She would not acknowledge, not she,
that I was the one who was giving her
the corn, the wine, the oil,
and who freely gave her that silver and gold
of which they have made Baals. (Hos. 2:7-10)

I mean to make her pay for all the days
when she burnt offerings to the Baals
and decked herself with rings and neckleaces
to court her lovers,
forgetting me.
It is Yahweh who is speaking. (Hos. 2:15)

After this angry outburst, after this outpouring of hurt feelings, there follows a reconciliation. He wants her love and is prepared to forgive and start afresh.

Then she will say, 'I will go back to my first husband,
I was happier than I am today.' (Hos 2:9)

The projected return fills her husband with joy which he celebrates rapturously.

Psalm
In the midst of marital tension, marital breakdown, desertion, divorce, the person who loves and feels betrayed by their partner feels that God has abandoned them also. Psalm 6 and other psalms put this agony of feeling deserted by God into words. The response to the psalm is 'Pity me, Yahweh, I have no strength left.'

Yahweh, do not punish me in your rage,
or reprove me in the heat of anger.
Pity me, Yahweh, I have no strength left,
heal me, my bones are in torment,
my soul is in utter torment
Yahweh, how long will you be?

Come back, Yahweh, rescue my soul,

save me, if you love me:
for in death there is no remembrance of you:
who can sing your praises in Sheol?

I am worn out with groaning,
every night I drench my pillow
and soak my bed with tears;
my eye is wasted with grief,
I have grown old with enemies all round me.

Away from me, all you evil men:
For Yahweh has heard the sound of my weeping;
Yahweh has heard my petition
Yahweh will accept my prayer.
Let all my enemies, discredited, in utter torment,
fall back in sudden confusion. (Ps. 6:1-10)

Epistle

Perhaps no epistle says so much about love as the first epistle of St
John. In the following passage John reminds us again that we are
to love one another, in this case spouses are to love one another
after their children have left them, because Christ loved us first.

This has taught us love —
that he gave up his life for us;
and we, too, ought to give up our lives for our brothers.
If man who was rich enough in this world's goods
saw that one of his brothers was in need,
but closed his heart to him,
how could the love of God be living in him?
My children,
Our love is not to be just words or mere talk,
but something real and active;
only by this can we be certain
that we are children of the truth. (1 John, 3:16-19)

Gospel

On this the concluding day of the marital year, conflict and reconciliation, which are one of the marks of an enduring marriage,
find their greatest echo in Christ's response to the woman taken in
adultery. The Jews knew that the punishment for adultery was
stoning to death and they wanted to put Christ to the test. His
response is a highlight of compassion and forgiveness. In exhorting

the woman to sin no more, he calls on her to become more fully human. (John 8:1-11)

But although marriage is a human reality taken up in the Lord, it is not a state that will continue after death. It is one form of loving, and it is this loving in relationship which links this world with the next.

> That day some Sadducees – who deny that there is a resurrection – approached him and they put this question to him. 'Master, Moses said that if a man dies childless, his brother is to marry the widow, his sister-in-law, to raise children for his brother. Now we had a case involving seven brothers; the first married and then died without children, leaving his wife to his brother; the same thing happened with the second and so on to the seventh, and then last of all the woman herself died. Now at the resurrection to which of those seven will she be wife, since she had been married to them all?' Jesus answered them, 'You are wrong, because you understand neither the scriptures nor the power of God. For at the resurrection men and women do not marry; no, they are like the angels in heaven.' (Mat. 22: 23-31)

Summary

In this chapter suggestions are made for an annual liturgical cycle divided into four occasions dealing with the successive phases of married life. Suitable material has been chosen for such a cycle although there is ample room for alternative texts to be used or indeed for another cycle to be chosen. The important points are that it should be an annual cycle, covering the relationship of marriage from beginning to end, that it should offer an opportunity for the married to hear the word of God relating to their marital experience, and that they in turn should offer back their marriage to God. The texts illustrate kinds of situations but the person in charge of the service has to relate such fundamentals to the reality of contemporary experience.

Reference (Chapter 17)

1. *Gaudium et Spes*, Par. II ch. 1, section 48.

CHAPTER 18

The Christian Dimension

The sacrament of marriage

All Christians are aware that there is something sacred about marriage. Christ has taught us that there will be no marriage in the next life and so marriage cannot be the ultimate objective of salvation. But it is the penultimate one. It is the state in which 95 per cent of people will find God in their life. It is the 'grammar that God uses to express his love and faithfulness'.[1] Roman Catholics go further and believe it is a sacrament.

Roman Catholics grow up with the notion of sacraments but their meaning is not always clear. The sacraments feature so often in their lives that they come to accept their spiritual significance without truly understanding their meaning. This is particularly so in the case of marriage. Almost everybody gets married, Christian and non-Christian alike, and it is difficult to see how such a common and universal experience becomes a means of salvation for Christians. There is difficulty in relating the secular reality to the divine dimension.

SACRAMENT

First then something needs to be said about the meaning of sacraments in general. At the heart of Christianity is the basic belief that God has created and accepted mankind and wishes to form a relationship of love between himself and human beings. This is the purpose of creation and the covenant that God has made with man. God who is love wishes to open himself and share his life with us. The fall was man's reply. This was a refusal to respond to the invitation. God however perseveres and wishes to reconcile himself to rejecting humanity. He does this by sending his only son Jesus

Christ. In the incarnation God the Father invites fallen humanity
once again, this time through Christ. God now sends his invitation
through the humanity of Jesus Christ who responds affirmatively to
it in the name of all humanity. This affirmation takes him to death
and resurrection, and saved humanity now also shares in this death
and resurrection. Christ becomes humanity's saviour. He is the sign
and presence of God's love, and Christians are invited to share this
love through Christ's life. One way of doing this is in participating
in the seven vital actions instituted by Christ himself for this purpose. These seven actions which are efficacious for salvation are the
eucharist, baptism, penance, confirmation, orders, matrimony and
anointing of the sick. These are the Seven Sacraments which the
Church celebrates in its liturgy. The Church is the body and everyone of us together make up the people of God; Christ is intimately
related to it, that is to each and everyone of us. In Pauline terms
the Church is the body and Christ is the head, that is in fact the
degree of intimacy between the two. Thus for every baptized person
life has to be lived fully in its human reality and yet is constantly
transformed by the sacramental presence of Christ in whom God
has accepted everything human.

   Marriage is one of these sacraments and this means that married
life is, for the married, their daily encounter with Christ and therefore the means of their sanctification. Now the sacraments are not
all of the same dignity and are not all of the same importance for
salvation. In fact for a very long time the single state dedicated to
Christ was considered to have a superior status to marriage. This
book is dedicated to the conviction that marriage, after baptism
and the eucharist, is the most important sacrament for the Church,
because it is within marriage that 90-95 per cent of the community
finds its salvation. The establishment of this sacrament in its due
significance is a process which has started in the twentieth century
and will continue in the twenty-first. In saying this there is no
implicit devaluation of the single state. On the contrary the full
dignity of the single state will be found through understanding
marriage and marriage's full dignity found through understanding
the single state. The two are complementary to each other.

NATURE OF MARRIAGE AS SACRAMENT

The sacraments have been instituted by Christ, and the key passage
in respect to marriage is Paul's letter to the Ephesians (5:21-33). In

this text Paul is saying that God's love, which was given fully to Jesus Christ and which resides in the Church, becomes available in marriage and is expressed in the love of spouses which becomes its sign. Thus spouses become Christ-like or, in the words of Paul, 'being of the mind of Christ' (Phil. 2:5) by sharing and repeating the obedience, faithfulness, self-giving and love of Christ for his Church. Christ loves his Church, in fact every person, until the end of time and this love is captured in the sacrament of marriage and fulfilled by the love of spouses for each other.

Given the sacramental nature of marriage, the question of every married couple is where are they going to find the characteristics of this sacrament? In what aspect of marriage resides the sacrament? Prior to the second Vatican Council, emphasis was laid on the moment of mutual consent whereby spouses mutually bestow and accept each other. This was the key to the sacrament which was then completed by an act of sexual intercourse. Seen in this way the focus of the sacrament was the wedding ceremony where this mutual commitment occurred. Thereafter the married were forgotten except for their presence in the sacraments of their children, such as baptism and confirmation. Hence the poverty of the married state in its sacramental significance.

Vatican II however emphasized that through the mutual bestowal of the spouses there arises a relationship which is a lasting one. Thus the essence of the sacrament is situated in an unfolding relationship which spans the whole duration of marriage until the death of one partner.

In this unfolding relationship the spouses have to treat each other as Christ treats his Church. Four characteristics have been identified in the way Christ relates to the Church, and these same characteristics have to be present in the life-long relationship of the spouses. These are obedience, faithfulness, self-giving and love. In fact all the four features could be subsumed in the word love, but the separate features help us to understand more fully the nature of love. These features have to be interpreted in the light of contemporary understanding of marriage in Western society. In other parts of the world local anthropological and social factors will dictate the interpretations of the same features.

Our understanding of obedience springs from behaviour appropriate to us as children towards our parents and as adults towards authority and law. Christ's obedience to the Father is not one of subordinate to superior. It is rather of essential belonging and

commitment. The two are inseparable and form an absolute togetherness. Obedience is the inevitability of submitting oneself to
another out of total unity of purpose. Christ obeyed the Father
because as members of the Trinity their purpose was exactly the
same, in this case to reconcile humanity to the Trinity. Obedience
is commitment in relationship, which in the case of Christ and the
Church is absolute.

Spouses, behaving in a Christ-like manner, also owe obedience
to each other. Each acts as Christ to the other. Their mutual
obedience should not be out of fear, subordination or inequality but
because they have now become one. It is their oneness through
togetherness that demands commitment to each other. They belong
to one another. Each has bestowed their total person to the other.
Obedience is a commitment which arises from their unity. They
live for what is good in each other. They can no longer be deaf or
blind to the slightest mutual signal. They are no longer two but one
and this oneness demands a total response. Obedience is availability
redirected towards each other. An essential part of the grace within
marriage is to strengthen commitment, from which arises obedience,
which is awareness and response to the partner.

Through obedience Christ and the Church become one. Arising
from this oneness is the need for faithfulness. Once Christ made this
declaration of total commitment through the paschal mystery, one
of the consequences is faithfulness. In this book the deeper meaning
of faithfulness is to be found in continuity, reliability and predictability. Christ's relation to the Church remains continuous, reliable
and predictable. He never ceases to be in relationship and he
achieves this in a reliable and predictable manner. His reliability
is one of the hallmarks of his faithfulness. He does not vacillate nor
change his mind. He has offered himself with a singular intention
which can be relied upon in a predictable way. He is always there
to respond to the call of humanity. He does not espouse other causes
but remains faithful to the people of God through time until the
end of time.

Human faithfulness is far more difficult to achieve. Spouses can
become used to each other. They are liable to compare each other
with other married couples. Even if they remain faithful to their
spouse they may fail to take their faithfulness seriously. They remain
aware of each other superficially and their oneness is shallow. They
may fail to pursue in depth their understanding of each other and
remain faithful to only a small, external part of their partner. Their

reliability may be tenuous and fragile, their behaviour most unpredictable. Once again the grace of the sacrament, Christ's presence, is needed to reinforce the faithfulness of the spouses so that their dedication is concentrated on each other.

Obedience and faithfulness need a channel of communication. This channel is bodily, emotional, social, intellectual and spiritual mutual availability. Christ did not withold any part of himself in his commitment to the Church. He created his Church out of his total giving of himself. This giving is directed towards union. Christ and the Church are one and this demands total availability. God the Father is totally available in the Son and the Son is totally available to humanity through the Holy Spirit.

Spouses intuitively want to give and receive as much of each other as possible. This exchange leads to an availability of body, feelings, mind and spirit. In the usual course of events spouses either withhold themselves, or do not have the resources to offer much of themselves or the ability to register what is offered to them. In this way availability becomes increasingly circumscribed and it needs constant renewal of energy to realize fully the riches of their resources in mutual availability. Grace is needed constantly to make this possible.

St John tells us that God is love (1 John 4:7-8). In this case love partakes of the mystery of God and as such it is difficult to understand or appreciate fully. God the Father nevertheless communicates completely his love to the Son and the Son to the Church. What is the nature of this love? Implicit in it is obedience, faithfulness and self-giving. Through this love the Trinity sustain, heal and help humanity to grow to perfection, in fact to become as perfect as the Father. Christ is always making himself available to the Church for her sustaining, healing and growth. His presence in her midst ensures that his love acts as a continuous catalyst for its members.

Love is the means through which spouses sustain, heal and help each other to grow. It is here that human frailty is most intensely present; spouses often fail to sustain, help to heal or encourage growth. Since all this is essential for remaining human such failure is the main cause of marital breakdown. Nowhere is grace needed more than in the constant renewal of the motivation to love and to love sensitively and accurately. The finite and limited love of spouses is centred in the relationship between spouses, spouses and their children and the whole family open to the whole of the community.

MARRIAGE IN RELATION TO OTHER SACRAMENTS

Until recently much of the life of the Church was centred on the
priesthood and the hierarchy, and inevitably the unmarried state of
both tended to deflect attention away from the significance of marriage. It is now increasingly realized that the fundamental unit in
the Church is the family, the domestic Church as it has come to be
called. It is there, within the relationships of the family, that everyone learns the meaning of love and practises its meaning. It is the
experience of marriage itself as love which is capable of giving
meaning to the other sacraments.

Marriage is a life-long relationship and the concept of relationship
is the key to understanding the sacrament of baptism through which
we enter a life-long relationship with Jesus Christ. In this life-long
relationship of marriage there is a singular togetherness amongst its
members made present through availability of each other. This
availability is completed in the act of intercourse when spouses
become one in the most complete sense of the word. They receive
each other totally and during intercourse their personalities fuse in
an encounter which dissolves their individual boundaries. They get
to know each other as completely as possible because they receive
each other as fully as possible. The eucharist is a liturgical event by
which the salvific reality of Jesus is realized through the words of
consecration uttered over the bread and wine. The bread and wine
become the body and blood of Jesus Christ which, when received
at communion, unite the recipient completely with Jesus.

As for reconciliation and healing, which are the sacraments of
confession and of the sick, couples experience both repeatedly and
continuously in the course of their marital life. Conflict and reconciliation are an essential part of relationship, and healing as
considered in this book is also a crucial part of the relationship.
Both these sacraments can be understood and appreciated much
better as a result of the experience of marriage.

The sacrament of confirmation with baptism and the eucharist
are sacraments of Christian initiation which together describe the
consecration and mission of Christians. Confirmation in particular
confers the gifts of the Holy Spirit which are to sustain the whole
of Christian life. Couples need to sustain each other throughout
their married life by affirming each other afresh. This sustaining
affirmation brings them close to understanding the essential meaning of the sacrament.

Finally there is the sacrament of orders. On the surface this sacrament, with its discipline of celibacy, is the very opposite of that of marriage. But celibacy is not a universal condition of priesthood and is not its principal characteristic. The priest is consecrated to the service of God and is the spiritual catalyst of the community. He preaches the word and administers the sacraments, and his principal human feature is his availability. Couples can understand this by appreciating the qualities which contribute to availability and their efforts to sanctify each other.

The relationship of marriage to the other sacraments is open to modification and expansion as we understand the nature of marriage more thoroughly. What is indisputable is that the appreciation of other sacraments will grow as the married see in them realities which they experience in their own marriage. In this way marriage can become not only the means of salvation for the married but its experience also one of the keys of appreciating and participating in the other sacraments.

Relationship

At the heart of the Trinity is to be found life-giving relationship. Marriage which reflects this life-giving, loving relationship is now seen to be a sacrament which unfolds over a lifetime. The minute daily events which contribute to its being are all taken up and transformed into a divine reality. There is nothing so little or so big in marriage that it does not participate in the Christ-like encounter between spouses and other members of the family. Couples need to be helped to see in the most minute details of their married life the presence of God in and through Jesus Christ and the Holy Spirit.

In the past the married felt that their real salvation had to come principally through the other sacraments. They did not appreciate the principal role played in their salvation by their sacrament of marriage realized in a relationship covering their lifetime. Whilst all the sacraments contribute to salvation, and none can be excluded from the Christian life, the time is now appropriate to help the married appreciate the uniqueness of their own vocation. This is to be seen in the loving encounter between themselves, which spouses struggle to negotiate for many decades and is the origin of life for themselves and their children. It is a life of love which precedes the children and continues long after their departure.

Domestic church

On the basis of the account given, it can be seen that the family which is the basic unit of society has all the characteristics of a 'little church'. The spouses are invited to treat each other as Christ treats the Church, and within this relationship the couple are faced with experiences such as conflict and reconciliation, wounds and healing, sustaining and mutual surrender with incorporation, re-current affirmation with the creation of faith, hope and love, a sense of the priesthood of the laity, all of which are reminders of the other sacraments. Thus the family can be truly called the 'domestic church' whose daily life is its liturgy.

So often in the past this whole spiritual aspect of marriage was completely ignored. Instead, the family was encouraged to pray together in a variety of different forms, forms which sometimes echoed the life of the monastery. What needs to be appreciated is that the moment-to-moment exchange between members of a family is prayer in the sense that they are addressing Christ in each other. This does not mean that specified prayer has no place in family life. It has indeed. But what is needed is prayer which is concerned with making overt and explicit what is latent in married life. The couple need God's grace to persist in obedience which is commitment, fidelity which is integrity, self-giving which is availability and love which encompasses all in sustaining, healing and growth. We need a form of daily prayer that emphasizes the contents of married life and reveals God's help and grace in achieving love in the domestic church.

What is the purpose of this domestic church? It is the place in the universal Church where life is conceived, nourished and loved. The domestic church is the school of love for the whole Church. It is the source of love in the life of the couple and in the new life which they initiate and nurture. Without the domestic church there can be no Church for it is within it that love, which is the nature of God, is kept alive and this is the reason why marriage as a sacrament is of such importance.

Summary

Marriage is a sacrament, one of the seven recognized by the Church. It commences with a mutual taking of vows of complete surrender of the spouses to each other and continues in the ensuing life-long relationship of love. This relationship is marked by obedience, faithfulness, self-giving and love, the characteristics which are found also in the relationship of Christ and his Church. In this way marriage becomes the domestic church which is the source and guardian of love in the universal Church.

References (Chapter 18)

1. Kaspar, W., *Theology of Christian Marriage*. Burns and Oates, 1980.

CHAPTER 19

Ecumenism

Mixed marriage

When the subject of ecumenism is approached, the leading concern has been modification of the requirements by the Roman Catholic Church in connection with mixed marriages. The church where the ceremony occurs, the denomination of the officiating clergyman, and the promises required regarding the religious upbringing of the children have been the contentious issues. Slowly each one of them is being tackled and a Roman Catholic can now be married in an Anglican Church, the clergyman can be a non-Catholic and the promises regarding the upbringing of children are less strict.

These details are important since the wedding is a central and public focus of the establishment of a new sacramental relationship. However the sacrament of marriage is situated in the subsequent unfolding relationship, and marriages between Christians of different traditions share in this reality, a reality that is actualized in the daily life of the couple and in the mutual endeavour to love one another.

In the past particular emphasis was laid on the conversion of the non-Catholic partner to the Catholic faith. In this way the couple could share the rest of their sacramental life. For some this remains a desirable goal, but increasingly couples wish to retain their particular denominations and share in the common Christian life together. As the significance of the sacrament emerges, it will become increasingly clear that its essential character lies in the relationship of the spouses who encounter Christ in their moment-to-moment life. In the domestic church of love this daily effort to be Christ-like can become the basis of their worship in joined prayer. The public worship takes place in their respective churches, and ultimately it is hoped that there will be inter-communion.

The children are raised in a Christian atmosphere and learn about the values and traditions of the denominations of both their parents. Instead of the task of Christian education being left to one parent it becomes a shared responsibility and in this way an ecumenical approach to faith will be fostered in the community. If a denominational school is chosen, the nearest and most efficient will be the appropriate one. Since there are many more Roman Catholic denominational schools, the chances are that it will be one of these that is chosen.

One of the results of a less authoritarian approach to life, which has been a mark of our age, has been the widely held view that children must be left free to choose their religion in adult life. It has been argued therefore that children do not need a Christian education. This is a mistaken liberal view of life. As the child grows there is need to evaluate, to determine values and the purpose of life. Christianity has a clear answer to these questions and children deserve to become acquainted with this view of life. They can reject this conceptualization later on but at least they are not left without a meaningful faith.

Some 60 per cent of weddings still occur in churches. This is however no indication of an active faith by the participants. Thus the major challenge to the Christian community lies not so much with the marriages of two committed Christians but with those notional Christians of the same or mixed denominations. These are men and women who do not go near a church, show no overt sign of Christian practice but who nevertheless wish to have an exclusive and faithful marriage.

If the starting point of the sacrament is the loving relationship between the members of the family, then a domestic church does exist even though it is not understood as such. Marriage lived in love is also lived in the Lord and as such can become the bridge to a return to an active Christian life.

The sacrament

The use of the word 'sacrament' hides the fact that there is a theological difference between the Roman Catholic and Protestant traditions in its use. As already stated, the Council of Trent defined marriage as a sacrament. Luther did not accept this. He was concerned to show that marriage was of the order of creation and not of salvation. This did not mean that it was purely a secular affair, it was God's work and was a holy state worthy of blessing. This however does not amount to the same treatment as is given by Catholic theology. In particular in the Protestant tradition there is opposition to the view that the mutual consent of two baptized persons creates, of itself, an indivisible *vinculum* or bond. This is criticized as being unbiblical and contrary to the tradition of the universal Church.

All these criticisms are contained in the first report of the Church of England's statement on marriage.[1] The report goes on to say, 'If members of the Church of England are to continue to regard marriage as sacramental, it seems likely that they will use the phrase with the overtones of Eph. 5:32 rather than in the Tridentine sense, and in so doing they will be in line with Orthodox theology . . . Marriage is much more than a contractual relationship. It is an "estate" or status of two people, and not only an agreement made between them.'[2] The report notes that the Vatican II Council has substituted the word 'covenant' for 'contract' and in fact refers to a 'conjugal covenant' which arises from the irrevocable personal consent of the partners.

The word 'covenant' is biblical and the statement of the Vatican II focuses on the relational aspect of marriage which is rooted in the covenant between God and his People and between Jesus and the Church, thus bringing the theology of marriage to a point where the possibility of agreement between the Roman Catholic, Anglican and Orthodox traditions has increased.

There remains a good deal of work to be done to reconcile these different theologies but here is one area where ecumenism might progress in a tangible fashion, so that the richness of Christian marriage may be revealed in its full potential.

Orthodox tradition

The Orthodox tradition accepts marriage as a sacrament, one of the seven, but in fact the roots of this interpretation is the mystery of Christ's relation to the Church. Unlike the Roman Catholic approach, in which the ministers of the sacrament are the partners, it is the priest (who incidentally is allowed to marry) who confers the sacrament, and the primary purpose of it is the conjugal love of the partners.

> It is then as a couple that the partners in marriage become helpers of one another throughout life, exercising mutual forbearance, encouraging one another, so as to bring their different characters into harmony, so as to love and serve one another, experiencing together the same joys and sorrows, supporting one another in their weaknesses, giving a helping hand in the time of need, spending themselves wholly for one another, together carrying the burden of life and the responsibility of a family.[3]

This emphasis on conjugal love as the principal reason for marriage and not the children means that the welfare of the spouses remains of primary importance. So much so that the Orthodox church allows the remarriage of the divorced for a second and even a third time. Marital breakdown is seen as tragic and sinful, but the pastoral approach, called 'economy', allows remarriage. By 'economy' is meant 'that pastoral concern which recognizes the fragility of human life and the infinite forgiveness of God, and which also recognizes that what is best in a given situation may not always be what is absolutely best.[4]

This theological approach of 'economy' was considered worthy of attention by the Roman Catholic Church in its synod at Rome in October 1980. The growing pastoral problem of the remarriage of the divorced affects all the Churches and a thoroughly Christian solution is being sought, a solution which the Greek Orthodox approach may provide.

Ecumenical action

From the brief description given above it is possible to see that all the Christian Churches have an abundance of richness which they need to share with each other. In doing so, in accepting the fundamentals of Christian marriage as an exclusive, permanent, faithful relationship in which God lives and proclaims his presence in the life of the couple and their family, all the churches share a fundamental unity which is rooted in the scriptures. Different traditions and practices have emerged over the centuries which both divide and enrich, and present obstacles. Thus the Church of England has accepted artificial birth control whilst the Roman Catholic Church has not. The former retains to this day the strictest discipline against remarriage whilst the latter combines a strict attitude against divorce but has a varied possibility of annulment. Both can learn from the Orthodox richness of the marital liturgy and their concept of 'economy' which permits remarriage. These are all issues which will engage theologians for some time to come.

There is now a convergence of attitude in the realization of marriage as a relationship which engages the deepest layers of the being of men and women. This engagement, with its rapid expansion of expectations, is at the root of marital breakdown. Widespread divorce is a reflection of the gap between the intuitive drive of human beings for a deeper realization of their potential and the training and support offered by the community to achieve this.

An ecumenical approach to marriage which is regarded primarily as a community of love rooted in the biblical notion of covenant will allow the Churches to combine their efforts and raise the level of consciousness about its importance. This importance will be reflected in its appreciation as the 'domestic' or 'little church', in other words treating the family not only as a fundamental unit of society but also as a fundamental unit of the Church.

If this is the case the Churches can pool their resources in the preparation and support of marriage as well as making an investment in the essential research required to acquire the information which will prevent marital breakdown.

There is a strong case to be made that, at the practical level of preparing and supporting marriages, a united, ecumenical approach is the only tenable one. Experiences, new approaches, experiments have all to be shared in a particular area and further afield. Couples of different denominations can come together in groups and learn from each other, as well as to pray as the married people of God. Pooling of resources in every possible pragmatic way must become a priority in the life of the Church. Ecumenism will receive a welcome dynamism if marriage and the family become one of its central interests.

There is no doubt about the evil of marital breakdown, an evil situated in the agony of the partners as their most important human investment is shattered and the agony and impact on the children.

Recent research on the impact of divorce on the children shows how prolonged and serious it is.[5] Here is a human tragedy that Christianity has a profound duty to understand and resist. This is a call from its Lord and there is no doubt that no historical period in the life of Christianity has been more appropriate than the present for investigating and stemming the tide of divorce. Society is mystified by marital breakdown and stands gazing at it in a dazed way. Christianity cannot afford to take this attitude. It has a specific responsibility to use all the modern methods of research, training and support to bring about a fundamental change in society's view of marital breakdown.

The Christian Church is the only body that can achieve this, for it has the unique combination of using the fruits of the latest research findings with a basic commitment to indissolubility. Knowledge without the will to implement indissolubility halves its value, and the will without the knowledge is deprived of the necessary means of achieving its ends.

Christianity has the privilege of knowing through faith what is consistent with human integrity in the case of marriage. God, the author of marriage, has spoken unequivocably. Modern studies give us precious clues why marriages break down. Faith and knowledge have both to be nurtured and applied to the achievement of God's grand design.

Summary

All the Christian churches share now a fundamental unity of vision of the covenant relationship of marriage. There is much they can learn from each other theologically and there is a great deal they can do ecumenically towards the support and preservation of marriage.

References (Chapter 19)

1. *Marriage, Divorce and the Church.* SPCK, 1971.
2. ibid., p.39.

3. Tsembelas, P., *Dogmatique de l'Eglise Orthodoxe Catholique*, vol III, p.351.

4. *Marriage, Divorce and the Church*, p.122.

5. Wallenstein, J. and Kelly, J.B., *Surviving the Break-up*. Grant McIntyre, 1980.

CHAPTER 20

Love

When a couple get married in Western society, they do so, because they are in love. Furthermore they hope that they will remain so for the duration of their lives. Their experience of each other feels good and they wish it to continue. A quick look at their own parents and the marriages of relatives and friends will tell them that marriage is not a bed of roses. Nevertheless the majority still believe that their marriage will be a success and love will continue to flower in their lives. The breakdown of between one in four to one in three marriages is a sombre reminder that love does not persist, and so the nature of loving in contemporary marriage is a crucial phenomenon that needs understanding.

Love in contemporary marriage includes the traditional expectations of the couple for mutual material and social support. As far as material support is concerned, the task of maintaining the family economically is still predominantly a man's job but increasingly women share this responsibility. In the absence of unemployment, a large number of women work before children arrive and return to it when their offspring are older. In some marriages the dual career of the couple makes heavy demands on sharing responsibility for running the home but this is a challenge which most husbands do accept. The money earned by the wife is in some instances a necessity to ward off poverty, in others it adds a dimension of luxury. Whilst women have entered the labour market in large numbers, societies, with a few exceptions, have not adjusted their provisions to facilitate women's work with, for example, working timetables in which husbands work in the morning and wives in the afternoon. In the absence of such changes, women often work and have to carry the burden of running the home and looking after the children. Often such a timetable causes fatigue and a certain disillusionment. Individual husbands help a great deal to ease this burden, but society as a whole has yet to accept an equity of responsibility in the relationship between home, work and children. Nonetheless there is ample room for spouses to create an atmosphere of love by mutually supporting each other when both work.

As far as the social life of the couple is concerned, the subordinate role of the woman is disappearing. Obedience to the husband is no longer considered a social requirement. Spouses adapt to each other's social needs and ensure mutual satisfaction. Sometimes social activities such as visiting, entertaining and being entertained coincide, in other marriages there may be marked differences of interest which are pursued independently. The wife's world is not restricted to the home and the man's whims. A wife has the ability to be a person in her own right in her social life and often she exercises this freedom.

But it is in the world of feelings and emotions that love shows itself in a new way in Western society. As couples free themselves from the traditions and requirements of the extended family, community and society, a powerful need and expression of personal love emerges. This love recapitulates the kind of love experienced in childhood. The growing child learns the meaning of love by being held, stroked and caressed so that there is a strong physical component. Gradually it recognizes the meaning of feeling acknowledged, wanted and appreciated, of being loved for its own sake. The first rudiments of love are steeped in unconditional loving. In the early years the child does not have to earn love by distinguishing itself in work and achievement. The rudiments of love are physical contact and emotional affirmation. The child learns that it matters simply because it exists. There is a mutual trust between parents and child that it is an object of love because it is their offspring.Only later on does love gradually become conditional to being good and to achievement.

The love acquired in the first intimate relationship between child and parents is relived in the intimacy of marriage. Couples, but particularly women, seek a return to the tenderness of physical and emotional acknowledgement. This is realized in sustaining, healing and growth, and in the innumerable ways that these qualities are experienced. The breakdown of marriage is almost invariably an expression of the fact that a minimum of this personal love is not present. Instead of trust there is mistrust. Instead of acceptance there is rejection. Persistent criticism and invalidation replaces affirmation. Commitment and motivation are replaced by withdrawal and indifference. In the past, provided the roles of the spouses continued in material support and care of the house and children, a couple were expected to live in the midst of an emotional impasse. Today this is no longer acceptable. Couples increasingly seek love in personal fulfilment, and the massive rate of breakdown is an expression of the gap between expectations and the training and support necessary for their realization.

Falling in love

Love in modern marriage falls into two phases. The first is that of 'falling in love' and the second is that of 'loving'. The phase of falling in love is experienced as a powerful emotional event. The body plays a prominent part, offering a combination of sexual attraction and a return to parental care. There is a sense of intimate harmony between bodies, and gradually minds and feelings. This harmony is idealized. The beloved acquires unique qualities in the eyes of the beholder. He or she is not only attractive but stunning, not simply good-natured but the embodiment of concern. Their presence elicits a total response of joy and desire. They want to be close and constantly in each other's company. Quarrels are patched up quickly and good will is prevalent. The defects are reduced in size and the talents exaggerated. The tendency is to minimize dissonance and heighten accord. There is a powerful conviction that what is wrong now will be righted in due course. In other words feelings of accord and pleasure prevail. This is romantic love which governs the process of falling in love. The cynics will say that it is not a good basis on which to form a permanent relationship and that the presence of such powerful feelings dismisses common sense and prudence. There is some truth in this comment particularly if the courtship is brief. Nevertheless romantic love has become the commonest way of establishing intimate relationships leading to marriage, and the strength of this approach is that marriage then is based on a mutuality of trust, acceptance and availability. These qualities become the background of the later loving.

Loving

Falling in love is transformed into loving after marriage. The daily contact with each other reveals reality instead of idealization. Time together becomes more limited particularly when children arrive. Disappointments, hurts and limitations reduce each other to size. Gradually the aura of wonder diminishes and so does the thrill and excitement of falling in love. Loving replaces the intoxication and romanticism. In this loving the partners view each other as the most important person in the world, but others such as parents, relatives and friends resume their importance.

Love is not now experienced as an atmosphere but as the daily commitment to sustain, heal and help each other to grow. This involves empathetic communication, recognition of change, patience during periods of stagnation and stalemate, or when one partner needs to catch up with the other. It means recurrent renewal of availability against the pull of withdrawal and self-interest. Conflict, arguments and pain are inevitable and forgiveness, reparation and reconciliation are an intrinsic part of loving. But all the time the couple are seeking to be understood and responded to with all the skill and insight of a mother or father. They really do feel loved when the needs of the inner world are grasped and indeed antici-pated with the minimum of explanation and effort. They are dis-tressed and dismayed when they feel they make no sense to their spouse or the latter makes no sense to them, for loving is the blending of separateness into unity.

This is of course realized in many ways but most powerfully in sexual intercourse. Here, bodies, minds and feelings become one in an experience in which unity and wholeness approaches ecstasy. The physical becomes the medium for total unity just as the physical oneness of mother and baby has no boundaries.

This loving between the couple, which sustains, heals and grows in an environment of continuity, reliability and predictability pro-vides the loving atmosphere for the development of children and indeed is the only secure basis for their growth. In this way the home is indeed the basic unit in society where love is learned.

In the course of this loving several things happen to the members of the family. Each member gradually differentiates himself/herself. The child grows physically, mentally and emotionally in a process of gradual separation from the parents. Spouses continue the development of their bodies, minds and feelings. They learn more and more about themselves and integrate progressively the various parts of their personality. They learn to become a husband/wife, mother/father. They develop their meaning and significance as they gain in confidence regarding their resources and talents. They integrate their will with their emotions and bridge the conscious and unconscious. All this allows a sharpening of their sense of themselves so that whilst they depend on others, they do not live by their kind permission. Differentiation brings the personality to fruition as a unique and distinguished entity, which in the Christian tradition has an eternal destiny. There is no reincarnation into another person. We have one life and one personality to develop fully, and the fuel for this growth is love received principally from parents and spouses.

This differentiation is accompanied by a progressive affirmative possession of ourselves. Men and women emerge from childhood with a variable degree of the sense of possessing themselves and feeling good about each part of themselves. This process of possession and affirmation is completed by the assistance of the spouse whose love reveals and confirms the unfolding richness of each other. Spouses are not of course the only people who do this. Children, friends and relatives contribute but spouses play a prominent part.

The differentiated affirmative self of the spouse lives in a balance between separateness and oneness. The separate spouse develops their own characteristics and blends with their partner to a variable degree, ultimately fusing into the total unity of intercourse. This blending is reflected in a growing mutual awareness of the inner world of each other. Spouses know the habits, outlook, opinions, values, priorities, limitations of each other. There is a correspondence of feelings and action.

Divine love

The love of husband and wife mirrors that of Christ for the Church and that of the Trinity. The Trinity is made up of three distinct and different persons whose nature is one. What unites them is love, the love of absolute equals in relationship with one another. Thus the key to the Trinity is persons in relationships of love. Each person is totally differentiated from the other and possesses themselves fully and affirmatively. The love of spouses is similarly one of complementary relationships in which spouses become gradually differentiated and acquire possession of themselves in an affirmative manner. They become fully available to themselves and thus can donate themselves fully to and for others, their children and ultimately the whole world. Jesus Christ, the differentiated second person of the Trinity, possessed himself fully and affirmatively and could donate himself fully for the whole world until the end of time.

The members of the Trinity do not marry but relate in love. We know from the teaching of Our Lord that marriage ceases in this world; it is not an element of the next. What characterizes the next is relationships of love, and marriage is the commonest way of preparing men and women for relationships of love. The Kingdom of Heaven has indeed started in this world.

Home and love

The above summary of love shows clearly that in marriage, and particularly sacramental marriage, God has placed in our hands one of the principal means of developing relationships of love which prepare us for our eternal state. The home is the cradle of love and thus there is no sacrament, after baptism and the eucharist, which is more important. It is the domestic church which creates the conditions for reaching the full potential of love in its members, a love which reflects and participates in the love of the Trinity, the sharing of which is our ultimate destination.

Index